# First Steps Toward Teaching the Reggio Way

## JOANNE HENDRICK,
**Editor**
*University of Oklahoma, Emerita*

Merrill, an imprint of
Prentice Hall
Upper Saddle River, New Jersey    Columbus, Ohio

AG13 3062

**Library of Congress Cataloging-in-Publication Data**
First steps toward teaching the Reggio way/Joanne Hendrick, editor.
    p. cm.
Includes bibliographical references and index.
ISBN 0-13-437302-2
1. Education, Preschool—Philosophy. 2. Education, Preschool—Italy—Reggio Emilia (Province) 3. Public schools—Italy—Reggio Emilia (Province) 4. Education, Preschool—United States.  I. Hendrick, Joanne
LB1140.3.F57   1997
372.21—dc20                                                            96-3739
                                                                          CIP

Cover art: Ellery Davis
Editor: Ann Castel Davis
Production Editor: Sheryl Glicker Langner
Design Coordinator: Julia Zonneveld Van Hook
Cover Designer: Tom Mack
Text Designer: Anne Flanagan
Production Manager: Laura Messerly
Electronic Text Management: Marilyn Wilson Phelps, Matthew Williams, Karen L. Bretz, Tracey Ward

This book was set in Zapf Calligraphic 801 by Prentice Hall and was printed and bound by Book Press, Inc., a Quebecor America Book Group Company. The cover was printed by Phoenix Color Corp.

© 1997 by Prentice-Hall, Inc.
Simon & Schuster/A Viacom Company
Upper Saddle River, New Jersey 07458

Printed in the United States of America

10 9 8 7 6 5 4 3 2 1

ISBN: 0-13-437302-2

Prentice-Hall International (UK) Limited, *London*
Prentice-Hall of Australia Pty. Limited, *Sydney*
Prentice-Hall of Canada, Inc., *Toronto*
Prentice-Hall Hispanoamericana, S. A., *Mexico*
Prentice-Hall of India Private Limited, *New Delhi*
Prentice-Hall of Japan, Inc., *Tokyo*
Simon & Schuster Asia Pte. Ltd., *Singapore*
Editora Prentice-Hall do Brasil, Ltda., *Rio de Janeiro*

# *About the Cover*

We are indebted to Ellery Davis for the birds that adorn the cover and Part and Chapter openings of *First Steps Toward Teaching the Reggio Way*. Ellery was five years old when she drew them while participating with a group for 3- to 6-year-olds at the College School of Webster Groves, Missouri. Together with *atelierista*, Louise Cadwell, and resource teacher, Nancy Klepper, the children were studying zebra finches that lived in a flight cage in their room. They observed the birds' habits, songs, shapes, colors, and daily life and expressed what they learned by means of words, drawings, writing, sculpture, and constructions.

# Preface

*First Steps Toward Teaching the Reggio Way* is only the third book published in the United States about the municipal preschools of Reggio Emilia, and it is the *first* one written primarily for teachers and soon-to-be teachers who are interested in that approach. It presents the most significant growing edge of early childhood education written in practical terms by leading advocates of that philosophy.

Some of the authors—Lella Gandini, Baji Rankin, Eva Tarini, Lilian Katz, Becky Kantor, Rebecca New, Brenda Fyfe, Louise Cadwell, Pamela Houck, Rosalyn Saltz, and Joanne Hendrick—are already well-known proponents of the Reggio Approach. Others—such as Donna Williams, Cheryl Brieg-Allen, Jan Dillon, Frances Donovan, Barbara Geiger, Karen Haigh, Jeanne Goldhaber, Susan Sortino, Dee Smith, and Mary Jane Moran—will be refreshingly new to the reader.

Because *First Steps Toward Teaching the Reggio Way* is written for practicing and potential teachers and directors, it first describes the most essential features of the Reggio philosophy from the Italian point of view and then concentrates on providing examples and practical advice from people in the United States who have been inspired by that philosophy and who are grappling with how to apply aspects of it in their American settings.

These settings range from descriptions of what it is like for a teacher who has studied at Reggio to return to teaching an American first grade, to a teacher working with 4- and 5-year-olds in a university nursery school, to a director managing a huge children's project in the heart of downtown Chicago, to an education specialist for a children's museum. These are followed by two down-to-earth examples of university professors who are incorporating the Reggio Approach into their own classroom practice. The book concludes with some predictions and encouragement about future trends and possibilities.

The interesting thing about all these authors is that, no matter what the disparity of their backgrounds, all of them have two things in common. For one thing, they all express admiration, humility, and concern when discussing the philosophy because they recognize they have only begun the long journey toward understanding and incorporating this tightly integrated approach into their work with young children. For the other, they all stress they are not attempting to duplicate what transpires in the Reggio Emilia preschools. The Reggio philosophy is a source of inspiration to them that encourages them to think anew about educational approaches and possibilities, not a model to be duplicated.

I am also indebted to the following reviewers for their thoughtful comments and suggestions: Nancy Benz, South Plains College; Anita Brehm, East Carolina University; Jane H. Bugnand, Pace University; Barbara Foulks, Radford University; and Stacie G. Goffin, Ewing Marion Kauffman Foundation.

It has been an unparalleled opportunity to serve as the editor of this volume, and I thank the authors of the chapters with all my heart for their contributions and forbearance. Summing up years of work in such brief chapters is a difficult and challenging task, and I want to express my admiration and thanks to everyone who has contributed to this effort. I also owe a special vote of thanks to my editor, Ann Davis, and to Jeff Johnston, vice president of Merrill/Prentice Hall, who were willing to step onto new ground themselves by publishing this handbook. If *First Steps* enlightens and encourages our readers to do the same—to take that first step—our work and faith will be well rewarded and the children well served.

Joanne Hendrick

# Contents

**9    The Challenge of Reggio Emilia's Research:
     One Teacher's Reflections                                    112**

*Donna Carloss Williams & Rebecca Kantor*

**10    Implementing the Process of Change
      in a Public School Setting                                  126**

*Cheryl Breig-Allen & Janis Ullrich Dillon*

# I

## *Introduction to Reggio Emilia*

Part I is intended to serve as an introduction and/or a reminder for readers who want to know more about the municipally sponsored early childhood schools in Reggio Emilia. It begins with two classic chapters by Lella Gandini, who was a *pedagogista* there for many years. She explains how the schools came into being, how they operate, and then describes the basic philosophy that forms the educational foundation for what children, families, and teachers do there together.

This is followed by the chapter by Pam Houck, curator for "The Hundred Languages of Children" exhibit that is touring the United States. She takes us beyond the impressions an ordinary visitor might glean from the exhibit and clears up some common misunderstandings about the Reggio Approach. Then she takes us even further behind the scenes and tells us about some aspects of the Approach the exhibit does not reveal.

Finally, in the chapter comparing Reggio Emilia and American schools, Joanne Hendrick helps readers identify some of the most interesting points of agreement and disagreement between the two philosophies.

# 1

# The Reggio Emilia Story
## History and Organization

*Lella Gandini*
Adjunct Professor, School of Education, University of
Massachusetts, Amherst, and Liaison for Reggio Children in the
United States

*A simple, liberating thought came to our aid, namely that things
about children and for children are only learned from children. We
knew how this was true and at the same time not true. But we
needed that assertion and guiding principle; it gave us strength
and turned out to be an essential part of our collective wisdom.*
                                    (Loris Malaguzzi, 1993b, p. 44)

# BEGINNINGS

What were the first steps that led toward what we now know in the States as the "Reggio Emilia Approach"? This is a question frequently asked by the many people who visit the schools in Reggio Emilia, or who view the exhibit entitled "The Hundred Languages of Children," or who watch a slide or video presentation about the program. As they marvel at either the real thing or the images that show the extraordinary level of work by teachers and the impressive quality of representation by children, set in such beautiful yet diverse environments, they cannot but wonder, How did this come about?

It all started at a particular place and time, namely Reggio Emilia in 1945, just at the end of the Fascist dictatorship and the Second World War. It was a moment when the desire to bring change and create a new, more just world, free from oppression, was urging women and men to gather their strength and build with their own hands schools for their children. Some of these schools continued until 1967 (when they were handed on to the city government), thanks to the strength, initiative and imagination of workers, farmers, and a famous group of the time, the Union of Italian Women (UDI).

One of these women told me recently how they would go around from home to home with a wheelbarrow to gather dry food for the children at the schools and how everybody would contribute, knowing full well that the children, like all of them, were hungry. This woman, who has many lively episodes to narrate, is the mother of the current superintendent of education for the city of Reggio Emilia; she proudly showed me a group photograph of the children from the school in her neighborhood (actually a village in the plains outside the city), pointing out her daughter as well as one of her daughter's schoolmates who currently serves as the city's mayor. How proud this woman remains of the schools of those heroic times.

Each of the schools of Reggio Emilia has particular histories of these early years that are kept very much alive. For example, the story of one particular school in Reggio, la Villetta, goes back to 1970. The women of a working-class neighborhood on the outskirts of town were growing increasingly upset because their forceful protests and requests to obtain a school for their young children were being ignored. There was an empty house in their neighborhood. It was still elegant, though it was surrounded by an overgrown garden. One day the women moved into the house, pronounced it *the* school for their children, and stood fast in occupying the building. In the following days they organized their resistance, looked for a teacher, and cleaned and repaired the dusty rooms.

One warm, late afternoon while they were working, a large, beautiful butterfly entered the house and flew from room to room. The women were elated by this visit; they took it as a sign, a message of good fortune for themselves, their children, and their new school. Since that day the butterfly has become a symbol of the history of la Villetta. The children designed a colorful butterfly canopy for the entryway, and the butterfly now turns up time and again in children's paintings, drawings, and collages. It reminds us all of the strong involvement of the community in that school (Gandini, 1991).

Loris Malaguzzi always remembered the legacy of those committed citizens who started the schools. In one of his interviews, speaking of the first school, Villa Cella, he said:

> [Those] events granted us something . . . to which we have always tried to remain faithful. This something came out of requests made by mothers and fathers, whose lives and concerns were focused upon their children. They asked for nothing less than that these schools which they had built with their own hands, be different kind of schools, schools that could educate their children in a way different from before. . . . These were parents' thoughts, expressing a universal aspiration, a declaration against the betrayal of children's potentials, and a warning that children first of all had to be taken seriously and believed in. (Malaguzzi, 1993b, p. 51)

In the region of Emilia Romagna, where Reggio Emilia is located, there is a long history and tradition of cooperative work done in all areas of the economy and organization: agriculture, food processing, unions, entrepreneurship, solution of crises, and so forth. Therefore, for people to get together and start the schools, and for teachers and parents to work together to run the schools now, is in line with established tradition, with a traditional and successful way of life, which, although occasionally disrupted under adverse conditions, such as the Fascist regime, is then revived as soon as feasible.

In the 1950s and early 1960s, a teachers' movement was active in Italy around the goal of innovation in education. With strong motivation and commitment, these teachers hoped to develop new ways of teaching in tune with the new democratic society, with the new realities of the modern world, and with greater relevance to the life of children. In this way they hoped also that the public schools would become nonselective and nondiscriminatory. Some of their ideas found inspiration and encouragement in the works of John Dewey, and they were also influenced by theory and practice coming from France. Furthermore, the work of Jean Piaget and others, such as Lev Vygotsky, proved stimulating and supported the teachers' observations and discoveries about children and their development. These and several other important foreign works and experiences in psychology and educational philosophy had a particularly powerful impact after the Liberation because they had just not been available during the Fascist era.

In this time of ferment, Loris Malaguzzi took time off from teaching to specialize in psychology at the Center for National Research in Rome. He was aware of the tremendous potential value of all these sources of energy and of combining these with his own energy and ideas. He soon became a leader, first along with others better known in Italy and then by becoming a point of reference for teachers wanting to bring innovation to schools for young children. It was Malaguzzi who was ready and able to support the schools started by common people in Reggio in 1945 and who carried the battle to get the city government to take upon itself the running of the people's schools and open the first municipal school in 1963.

## THE ESTABLISHMENT OF THE MUNICIPALLY SUPPORTED SCHOOLS

The sixties in Italy were marked by the tremendous economic development known as "the boom." This era consisted principally of a basic transformation from a mostly agricultural economy (with limited industrial development in the north) to a well-developed and diversified economy with modern industries. Along with this there took place notable development in the areas of social services and workers' benefits, in part due to the bargaining power of a strong union system. Women entered the workforce and demanded support from the government for child care. The same period indeed saw the emergence of the women's movement, which in a way transcended the age-old party division between the right and centrist conservative Catholic forces (which preferred that women stay at home in their traditional roles) and the more progressive, socialist left. Furthermore, in the late sixties and early seventies, a strong student movement shook up the university system and the traditional values of a still highly stratified society.

Through all those years of upheaval, many different groups kept the pressure on elected representatives to bring innovation in all spheres of life for Italian citizens. Among the results was a series of national laws passed between 1968 and 1971 that were true landmarks, including those that made possible the development of the comprehensive program we are discussing here. They included the establishment of free schools for children 3 to 6 years of age, infant-toddler centers for children 3 months to 3 years old, maternity leave (in part with full pay), a new family law more favorable to women, and equal pay for equal work between men and women.

The new law passed about government schools for children 3 to 6 years old rewarded citizens and city governments, such as the one in Reggio Emilia, that had been working hard to support the grassroots demands for establishing public schools and who moved more quickly at the local level than the central government had done. By the end of the seventies, the schools for young children in Reggio Emilia had grown to 19 in number (and have remained so to the present), and the building of new infant-toddler centers was in full swing (there are now 13 of them).

## FURTHER DEVELOPMENT AND INFLUENCE OF THE PROGRAM IN OTHER SETTINGS: 1980s AND EARLY 1990s

Loris Malaguzzi was able to gather around him a group of devoted and competent educators who, along with parents and other citizens who felt strong ownership of the schools, supported his work toward creating and maintaining a very high quality in the programs, continuously updating the preparation of teachers and exploring new avenues of innovation in teaching young children. In some of the interviews that Malaguzzi granted late in his life, he presented a long list of scientists, philosophers, scholars, artists, and writers who had influenced his thought and therefore the work of educators in the schools that he did so much to shape. His complex system of education, which takes into account the human desire to "do nothing without joy" and which pays close attention to individual as well as group interests and potentials, is a form of socioconstructivism. This term is defined and its connection with Reggio made by George Forman in the following way:

> The basic premise [of socioconstructivism] is that knowledge is constructed as a system of relations, so that the simple association between two stimuli, or between a stimulus and a response, is insufficient for defining the knowledge-building process. It is only through a process of re-reading, reflection and revisiting that children are able to organize what they have learned from a single experience within a broader system of relations. These processes are individually and socially constructed, and herein lies the image of the child as an active constructor of his or her own knowledge, which is one of the fundamental premises of the philosophy and practice that has come to be known as the "Reggio Approach." (Forman, 1995, p. 6)

During the 1980s, the accomplishments achieved so far in Reggio Emilia became known elsewhere in Italy and on the international scene as well. Upon the initiative of Loris Malaguzzi and leaders in other city systems of early childhood education, along with some university experts in the field, an association for the support of research and development concerning the education of young children, the National Preschool Research Group, took shape and began its work. In 1981, the educators of Reggio Emilia prepared the first exhibit about their work, and it opened in Sweden at the Modern Museet in Stockholm. This was just the beginning of a way to carry through images their extraordinary message of hope about early childhood education throughout the world.

To respond to Loris Malaguzzi's dissemination effort and in appreciation of the great interest developing in the United States about the work done in the schools of Reggio Emilia, in 1992 Eli Saltz of The Merrill-Palmer Institute and Wayne State University launched *Innovations in Early Educa-*

*tion: The International Reggio Exchange*, a quarterly publication that carries articles by Reggio and U.S. educators who are reflecting on the adaptation of ideas from Reggio Emilia.[1]

The interest in the Reggio Emilia schools continues to grow as delegations visit in increasing numbers and a worldwide concern for supporting and protecting these extraordinary programs intensifies. Shortly before his death in 1994, Loris Malaguzzi had proposed the establishment of two organizations developed for that purpose. In the spring of 1994, the *Reggio Children* organization was formed in Reggio Emilia to support the early childhood program. One of the goals of Reggio Children is to disseminate the accumulated knowledge in theory and practice. This goal is achieved through publication and distribution of books, articles, videos, and slides that document the Reggio Approach. Reggio Children also responds to the increasingly numerous requests for information and cooperative exchanges that arrive from all over the world. Reggio Children is a private, for-profit company governed by a board of directors and supported by shareholders—corporate, private (parents, teachers, and other citizens of Reggio Emilia), and the municipality of Reggio Emilia, which holds the majority of shares. Until now this organization has not been open to individuals outside Italy.

In the fall of 1994 *Friends of Reggio Children* was also formed, a nonprofit, international organization open to all.[2] One of the goals of Friends of Reggio Children is to create an endowment that would establish a library for collecting documents about the Reggio Approach and to provide funds for student research on the Reggio philosophy and principles.

## THE ENCOUNTER OF THE REGGIO EMILIA APPROACH WITH THE UNITED STATES

In the mid-1970s, as I was working on my master's degree in education, I became aware of the difference between theory and practice in the United States. In particular, it became clear to me that while theoretical studies were

---

[1] To subscribe to *Innovations*, write to The Merrill-Palmer Institute, Wayne State University, 71-A Ferry Ave., Detroit, MI 48202.

---

[2] A one-time, $40 donation will entitle people to become members of an international group of educators who believe in the educational principles that the Reggio program exemplifies and in the right of children to obtain the best care and education possible. To become a member of Friends of Reggio Children, request a form from Friends of Reggio Children, c/o Innovations, The Merrill-Palmer Institute, 71-A E. Ferry Ave., Detroit, MI 48202. A membership card will be sent to you.

carried on at an impressively high level, what was being done in terms of public funding and investment in early childhood education and toward building high-quality programs lagged far behind—in particular, far behind Italy. Therefore, I started to do a two-way information job. I would bring to various municipalities in Italy who had invited me to work on teachers' training the information and publications about the latest research on child development and education in the States, while in the reverse direction I would bring back to the States information and pictures about the beautiful environments from choice programs in Italy.

Starting in the early 1980s, a number of educators and academics started to take a strong interest in the program, visit the schools, and support enthusiastically the dissemination of knowledge about Reggio. Among them were Carolyn Edwards, George Forman, Becky New, Baji Rankin, and Rosalyn and Eli Saltz.

The first article about the Reggio Emilia schools was published by me in 1984 in the magazine *Beginnings*. Other articles appeared in the following years, for example, a notably comprehensive and informative one by Becky New published in *Young Children* in 1990. At that time also, Lilian Katz became involved in studying and supporting the Reggio schools.

After lengthy negotiations, the exhibit "The Hundred Languages of Children" arrived in the United States in 1987. Its powerful message has now reached viewers at 20 different sites in the United States. The exhibit includes a video, *The Portrait of a Lion*, which shows the children actively engaged in a project from its inception to its completion.

Many conferences, seminars, and visits to the Reggio Emilia schools by Americans have made known many aspects of the approach of Reggio Emilia. But there was a frequently asked question that could only be answered when a teacher from Reggio Emilia, Amelia Gambetti, came to work in the States: Can the Reggio way of working with children be transplanted to a school in the United States?

## A Teacher from Reggio Emilia Comes to Study and Work in the United States

After working for 25 years in the schools of Reggio Emilia, Amelia Gambetti arrived at the laboratory school of the University of Massachusetts in 1992. Invited by George Forman, she immediately found great support in Mary Beth Radke, who became her coteacher. The situation differed greatly from a classroom in Reggio Emilia. Here the schedule for the children was of three mornings a week, on a university calendar, and as many as eight student teachers might be assigned to the classroom for each semester. Amelia and Mary Beth started first to work on the environment of the school, involving the student teachers, the children, and, at first a little hesitantly, the parents, who came from many different nationalities and backgrounds. Next they gradually developed work on documentation. This approach proved to be a powerful means of involving the parents, helping the children feel a sense of belonging and derive pleasure from learning and forming friendships.

At the end of that year, I asked these two teachers with such different cultural backgrounds, What suggestions do you have for educators in the United States who are struggling to use the ideas they are learning from Reggio Emilia?

> Mary Beth said: Start with respect for children. Question what it means to you and how your actions reflect your image of the child. How can you improve consistency about respect for the child through what you do every day? Look at collaboration among all adults in the school in a new and different way—try to learn to question things together, to exchange ideas, and trust each other.
>
> Amelia said: People here want quick results. We should help teachers to understand that they have to look for and find answers in themselves. One has to accept the idea that the way to work with children is something that one discovers observing day by day the process of children and teachers. In Reggio with the long experience we have we continue to ask questions, to have doubts, and to work things out together. I know it is not easy, but working here with Mary Beth we realized that sharing responsibility in a true sense gives a great sense of joy. (Gandini, 1994b, pp. 65–66)

In 1993, Amelia was employed by Ann Lewin, then director of the Model Early Learning Center, as master teacher consultant. The Model Early Learning Center is a preschool and kindergarten for 3- to 6-year-olds. The children are Head Start eligible. Amelia's job was to work with the teachers, and once again she had to deal with a completely different cultural situation. Here the question Amelia had in mind was, Is it possible to adapt ideas from Reggio Emilia to an inner-city school for young children?

The first steps she took were to observe the situation and build a sense of trust with and among the teachers in order to develop a spirit of cooperation. In an interview in the spring of 1995, the teachers said:

> We believed in the most important elements of the Reggio Emilia approach, and it is important to know that we did not face the many issues one by one but we faced them at the same time as one element supported the other. However, we proceeded in small steps. Considering the child and the child's potentiality brought us closer to establishing a new style of communication with the families. We began to communicate our projects and experiences through documentation which became more detailed every day. Documentation was not just seen as a product but always an evolution. Everything that we did needed time and organization. The importance of working in a team became clearer through the evolution of projects and the quality of our observations. Our deeper level of observing contributed to our relationship to children, and a

new kind of awareness blossomed that did not exist before our new-found skills.

With regard to parents we realized that before we did not let parents know enough about their children's experiences and what was happening in the program. In order to build a relationship of esteem and collaboration it took us more than 40 different meetings. This means that parents had many different opportunities to be involved and to participate in the life of the school according to their different levels of availability and needs. The quality of participation of parents in the life of the school grew, as well as the number of people at our meetings and the variety of initiatives on their part. Of course we need to continue this process; we do not take anything for granted. Every year children and parents change and we have to be available to meet their problems. The work of the team of teachers has been and continues to be very hard. The school is a remarkable place of learning with pleasure; where the presence and the voice of the children are evident all around in a beautiful way. The teachers realize now that when children give time to listen to each other, to use each other's ideas, to respect different opinions and to work collaboratively on a project, then is when they know that the hard work has paid off.[3] (Sheldon-Harsh & Gandini, 1995b, p. 3)

## ORGANIZATION AND STRUCTURE OF THE PROGRAM FOR CHILDREN 0 TO 6 YEARS OF AGE

In the information booklet published by the Department of Education of the Municipality of Reggio Emilia, under the heading "In Praise of Organization," we read this remarkable statement: "Organization, discounted or undervalued by educational theories—but not by other components of our social and working life—returns as a necessary, dynamic, and constructive element" (Municipality of Reggio Emilia, 1994, p. 13). The entire department, under the leadership of the superintendent who is an elected official, consists of 1 director, 1 pedagogical coordinator, 7 *pedagogisti* (of whom one is an expert in special education), and a 400-member staff. All of these people cooperate in such a way that together they constitute a pedagogical–didactic coordinating team. Next to this system and strictly connected with it is a Community Advisory Council for each of the 19 schools and 13 infant-toddler centers, composed of elected parents' representatives, teachers, staff members of the school, and citizens from the community. Representatives from each of the 32 Community Advisory Councils along with representa-

---

[3] From "The Model Early Learning Center: An Interview with Teachers Inspired by the Reggio Approach," by L. Sheldon-Harsh with L. Gandini, 1995, *Innovations in Early Childhood Education: The International Reggio Exchange*, 3(1), p. 3. Copyright 1995 by Innovations. Used with permission.

tives of the pedagogical coordinating team and of the administration of the Department of Education form an Advisory Council Board that deals directly with the city government about questions concerning the schools (see Figure 1–1). This complex system ensures proper representation of all the people connected with the schools and a shared responsibility in running them.

Schools do not have a director on the premises. They are run by the team of teachers and staff members with the support of one of the *pedagogisti*. The *pedagogisti* are an essential part of the system and have a complex role. Each one of them has a degree in education or psychology and helps guide and sustain the workings of a mix of three or four schools and infant centers. It is their responsibility to help teachers with the interpretation of the philosophy, to mediate the connections with parents and administrators, to organize training sessions, to follow the development of projects and activities, and much more.

The parents are also an essential component of the system, besides being part, through their representatives, of the Community Advisory Council. They participate in the life of the school through a variety of meetings at the individual level, at the level of the classroom group, or at all-school meetings. Parents also participate in work done through small committees on specific tasks and projects. These are not assigned by teachers or the administration, but they are instead discussed in advance in meetings where all the components of the system and of each school are represented. In this way, when the task is planned, it represents a mutual choice, and it will be carried out with a strong engagement and motivation.

## *Specific Organization and Schedules*

Infant-toddler centers (for children 4 months to 3 years of age) usually have a total of 69 children divided into four groups by age (the first, up to 9 months; the second, from 10 to 18 months; the third, from 19 to 24 months; and the fourth, over 24 months). There are 11 teachers, 1 cook, and 3 full-time and 3 part-time auxiliary staff—a total of 18 adults in each center. The schools (for children 3 to 6 years of age) usually consist of three classrooms, one for the 3-, one for the 4-, and one for the 5-year-old children, for a total of 75 children. There are, however, a few larger or smaller schools that also have mixed-age groupings. Each classroom has 25 children and 2 coteachers. In each of the schools of this size, besides the six teachers there are an *atelierista* (or studio teacher), one cook, two full-time, and three part-time auxiliary staff members. Every one of these people belongs to and fully participates in the team that runs the school.

The schedule of the schools and infant-toddler centers is from 8:00 A.M. to 4:00 P.M., Monday through Friday; in addition, there exist alternatives

**FIGURE 1-1**
The network of educational services of the Reggio Emilia Municipal Administration

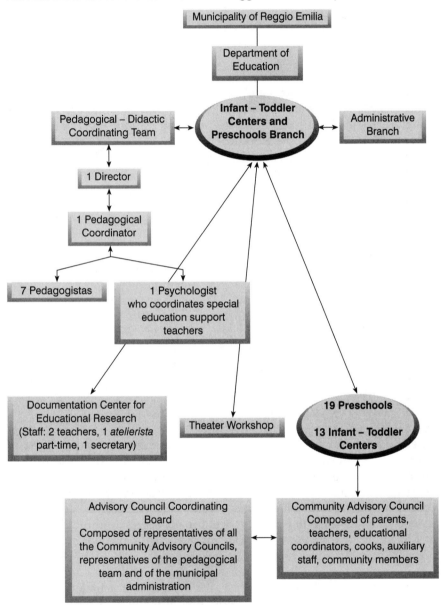

for an early arrival at 7:30 A.M. and an extended day until 6:20 P.M., for families able to demonstrate that they have this need. Teachers and staff members work 36 hours per week, of which 31 are in contact with children and 5 are used for planning, meeting with parents, working on documentation, participating in professional development, working on community management, or attending to school matters such as correspondence, archives, and the like. The work schedule is planned with great care in rotating shifts in order to maximize the efficiency of work and the supportive, flexible presence for the benefit of the children. The personnel calendar runs from about August 22 to July 10 of each year. The schools and centers are open for children from September 1 to June 30. In July, one school and one infant-toddler center remain open for families that make a special request for this service.

The teachers' salaries are lower but comparable to those of elementary school teachers in Italy. Such salaries are not high when compared to public school standards in the United States, but the benefits—in terms of job security, health insurance, retirement plans, and paid vacations—are equal to all public employment standards in Italy and, although they are under scrutiny now and have been reduced, are considerably better then those in the States.

## CONCLUSION

In telling this story of the schools for young children in Reggio Emilia, I touched only some of the many facets of that complex history. One source of this complexity is the fact that the system touches the lives of so many people who have been participants in the construction of its success. Furthermore, this dynamic educational approach, which is constantly questioning itself, changing, and inventing new ways of understanding and supporting high-quality children's learning, teachers' development, and parents' participation, cannot easily be captured and presented with only one language.

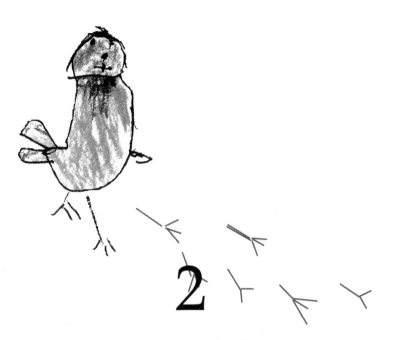

# 2

# Foundations of the Reggio Emilia Approach[1]

### Lella Gandini

Adjunct Professor, School of Education, University of
Massachusetts, Amherst, and Liaison for Reggio Children in the
United States

---

[1] Earlier versions of this chapter appeared in L. Gandini (1993), Fundamentals of the Reggio Emilia Approach to Early Childhood Education, *Young Children*, *49*(1), 4–8, and L. Gandini (1994), Not Just Anywhere: Making Child Care Centers into "Particular" Places, *Childcare Information Exchange*, *96*, 50.

As we saw in the previous chapter, publicly funded, municipal, and national programs for young children have been in place in Italy for about 30 years. During that time, women have been especially active and effective advocates of the legislation that established infant-toddler centers for children 3 months to 3 years and schools for children 3 to 6 years of age. Of special note is that in these programs, both education and care are considered necessary to provide a high-quality, full-day program. Therefore, the schools combine the concept of social services with education, an approach that is widely accepted in Italy.

What, then, is so unusual or special about Reggio Emilia, a town of 130,000 inhabitants in northern Italy? It is that in Reggio Emilia the city-run educational system for young children originated in schools started by parents, literally built with their own hands, at the end of World War II. The first school was built with proceeds from the sale of a tank, some trucks, and a few horses. Moreover, right from the start Loris Malaguzzi, then a young educator, guided and directed the energies of those parents and teachers.

In Italy, about 90% of the children 3 to 6 years old attend some kind of school, whether municipal, national, or private; in Reggio, 93% of preschool-age children are enrolled in a variety of such schools. Among these are 19 schools run by the municipality for children aged 3 to 6 years and 13 infant-toddler centers for children aged 4 months to 3 years. Children from all socioeconomic and educational backgrounds attend the programs: 41% and 31% of the two age groups, respectively, are served. Children with disabilities are given first priority for enrollment in the centers and schools.

Through many years of strong commitment and cooperation, parents and educators in Reggio have developed the present excellent program, which, in turn, has become a point of reference and a guide for many educators elsewhere in Italy, various European countries, Australia and East Asia, and, in the last 10 years, the United States as well. Thirty years of successful experience with schools for about half of the children in a city of 130,000 inhabitants have generated much interest. Such interest is evidenced by the number of international visitors, the number of articles and conference presentations describing the work, and the large number of people viewing the Reggio Emilia exhibit, entitled "The Hundred Languages of Children," which has been touring Europe since 1980 and North America since 1987.

## THE AIMS OF EARLY CHILDHOOD EDUCATION IN REGGIO EMILIA

The Reggio Emilia Approach, developed by the late Loris Malaguzzi and the group of committed, competent educators around him who now continue to develop theory and practice, is built on a solid foundation of philosophical principles and extensive experience.

Educators in Reggio Emilia have no intention of suggesting that their program should be looked at as a model to be copied in other countries; rather, their work should be considered as an educational experience that consists of reflection, practice, and further careful reflection in a program that is continuously renewed and readjusted. However, the Reggio Emilia schools and their approach to early childhood education are not considered "experimental." These schools are part of a public system that strives to serve both the child's welfare and the social needs of families, while also supporting the child's fundamental rights to grow and learn in a favorable environment, in the company of peers and with caring, professional adults.

Bearing these facts in mind, the educators in Reggio Emilia are pleased to share their experience with other educators in the hope that knowledge of the Reggio Emilia schools' experience will stimulate reflections on teaching, helpful exchanges of ideas, and novel initiatives in other schools, for the benefit of children and families and teachers.

## BASIC PRINCIPLES OF THE REGGIO EMILIA APPROACH

An examination of some of the principles that have inspired the experience in Reggio Emilia immediately reveals that these concepts are not new to American audiences. Indeed, many of the basic ideas that informed the work of educators in Reggio Emilia originated in the United States and are, in a sense, returning to their point of origin. From the beginning of their work in building their program, the educators in Reggio Emilia have been avid readers of Dewey, and over the years, in addition to studying Piaget, Vygotsky, and other European scientists, they have continued to keep abreast of the latest research in child development and education in the United States. However, their approach, based on continuous research and analyses of their practice, has caused them also to formulate new theoretical interpretations, new hypotheses and ideas about learning and teaching.

The following principles, or fundamental ideas, are presented one by one for the sake of clarity, but *they must be considered as a tightly connected, coherent philosophy, in which each point influences and is influenced by all the others.*

### The Image of the Child

The educators in Reggio Emilia first and foremost always speak about the image they have of the child. All children have preparedness, potential, curiosity, and interest in engaging in social interaction, establishing relationships, constructing their learning, and negotiating with everything the environment brings to them. Teachers are deeply aware of children's potentials and construct all their work and the environment of the children's experience to respond appropriately.

## Children's Relationships and Interactions Within a System

Education has to focus on each child, not considered in isolation but in relation with the family, other children, the teachers, the environment of the school, the community, and the wider society. Each school is viewed as a system in which all these relationships, which are all interconnected and reciprocal, are activated and supported.

## The Three Subjects of Education: Children, Parents, and Teachers

For children to learn, their well-being has to be guaranteed; such well-being is connected with the well-being of parents and teachers. Children's rights should be recognized, not only their needs. Children have a right to high-quality care and education that support the development of their potentials. It is by recognizing that children have rights to the best that a society can offer that parents' rights to be involved in the life of the school and teachers' rights to grow professionally will be recognized.

## The Role of Parents

Parents are considered to be an essential component of the program, and many among them are part of the advisory committee running each school. The parents' participation is expected and supported and takes many forms: day-to-day interaction, work in the schools, discussions of educational and psychological issues, special events, excursions, and celebrations. Parents are an active part of their children's learning experience and, at the same time, help ensure the welfare of all children in the school.

## The Role of Space: An Amiable School

The infant-toddler centers and schools are, of course, the most visible aspect of the work done by teachers and parents in Reggio Emilia. They convey many messages, of which the most immediate is that this is a place where adults have thought about the quality and the instructive power of space.

The layout of physical space, in addition to welcoming whoever enters the schools, fosters encounters, communication, and relationships. The arrangement of structures, objects, and activities encourages choices, problem solving, and discoveries in the process of learning.

It is also true that the centers and schools of Reggio are simply beautiful. However, their beauty does not come from expensive furnishings but rather from the message the whole school conveys about children and teachers engaged together in the pleasure of learning. There is attention to detail everywhere: in the color of the walls, the shape of the furniture, the arrangement of simple objects on shelves and tables. Light from the windows and doors shines through transparent collages and weaving made by children. Healthy, green plants are everywhere. Behind the shelves displaying shells or other found or made objects are mirrors that reflect the patterns that children and teachers have created.

But the environment is not just beautiful—it is highly personal. For example, in one of the halls, a series of small boxes made of white cardboard creates a grid on the wall. On each box the name of a child or a teacher is printed with rubber stamp letters. These boxes are used for leaving little surprises or messages for one another. Communication is valued and favored at all levels, and it is regarded not as a small matter. For a child to engage in communication by preparing messages deepens human relations and also helps that child appreciate and become interested in the value of reading and writing before they are formally presented in the elementary school curriculum.

The space in the centers and schools of Reggio Emilia is personal in still another way: it is full of children's own work. Everywhere there are paintings, drawings, paper sculptures, wire constructions, transparent collages coloring the light, and mobiles moving gently overhead. It turns up even in unexpected spaces like stairways and bathrooms. The reflection of the teachers, the photographs of the children, and their dialogues are part of the displays to help the viewer understand the process of children's thought and explorations. The results of so much work, thoughtfully selected by the teachers and the *atelierista*, literally surround the people in the school.

## The Value of Relationships and Interaction of Children in Small Groups

In preparing the space, teachers offer the possibility for children to be with the teachers and many of the other children, or with just a few of them, or even alone when they need a little niche to stay by themselves.

Teachers are always aware, however, that children learn a great deal in exchanges with their peers, especially when they can interact in small groups. Such small groups of two, three, four, or five children provide possibilities for paying attention, hearing and listening to each other, developing curiosity and interest, asking questions, and responding to them. It provides opportunities for negotiation and dynamic communication. Loris Malaguzzi suggested that it is desirable that adults initiate the settings of such situations because a more homogeneous age group helps the communication among children in planning and decision making. This type of small group also favors the emergence of cognitive conflicts that can initiate a process in which children construct together new learning and development.

## The Role of Time and the Importance of Continuity

Time is not set by a clock, and continuity is not interrupted by the calendar. Children's own sense of time and their personal rhythm are considered in planning and carrying out activities and projects. The particular, leisurely pace that an observer notices is enhanced by the full-day schedule. Such a schedule, rather than overwhelming the participant, seems instead to provide sufficient time for being together among friends in a good environment and for getting things done with satisfaction.

Teachers get to know the personal time of the children and each child's particular characteristics because children stay with the same teachers and the same peer group for 3-year cycles (infancy to 3 and 3 to 6). Each year the group changes environments because their developmental needs and interests change, but the relationships with teachers and peers remain constant and intact.

## Teachers as Partners

To know how to plan or proceed with their work, teachers observe and listen to the children closely. Teachers use the understanding they gain in this way to act as a resource for them. They ask questions and discover the children's ideas, hypotheses, and theories. Then the adults discuss together what they have recorded through their own notes, or audio or visual recordings, and make flexible plans and preparations. Then they are ready to enter again into dialogues with the children and offer them occasions for discovering and also revisiting experiences since they consider learning not as a linear process but as a spiral progression. In fact, teachers consider themselves to be partners in this process of learning, which might proceed with pauses and setbacks but which is an experience constructed and enjoyed together with the children. The role of teachers, therefore, is considered to be one of continual research and learning process, taking place with the children and embedded in team cooperation. Doing this research, reflecting, and listening to children together with other colleagues, and with the support of the pedagogical coordinator (the *pedagogista*), contributes to a situation of continuous individual and group professional growth.

## Cooperation and Collaboration as the Backbone of the System

Cooperation at all levels in the schools is the powerful mode of working that makes possible the achievement of the complex goals that Reggio educators have set for themselves. Teachers work in pairs in each classroom, not as head teacher and assistant but at the same level; they see themselves as researchers gathering information about their work with children by means of continual documentation. The strong collegial relationships that are maintained with all other teachers and staff relies on this information to engage in collaborative discussion and interpretation of both teachers' and children's work. These exchanges provide on-going training and theoretical enrichment. This cooperative system is further supported by a team of pedagogical coordinators, called *pedagogisti*, who also support the relationships among all teachers, parents, community members, and city administrators.

The team of *pedagogisti* meets once a week with the director of the whole system to discuss policy and problems related to the whole network of schools and infant-toddler centers. Each *pedagogista* is assigned to support three or four schools and centers, helping the teachers to sustain and implement the philosophy of the system. The support of each school includes work with the teachers to identify new themes and experiences for continuous professional development and in-service training. In each particular school, the *pedagogista* helps the teachers deal with educational issues concerning children and parents. However, the goal is to support teachers by promoting their autonomy rather than by solving problems for them. The complex task of the *pedagogisti* is to collaborate with the various parts of this complex system and maintain the necessary connections, while at the same time analyzing and interpreting the rights and needs of each child, family, and group of teachers.

## The Interdependence of Cooperation and Organization

The high degree of cooperation requires much support, which is supplied by a careful and well-developed structure or organization. From the details of each teacher's schedule, to the planning of meetings with families, to the children's diet, *everything* is discussed and organized with precision and care. In fact, the high level of cooperation is made possible precisely because of such thoughtful organization. Likewise, the organization is achieved because of the conviction by all concerned that only by working together so closely will they be able to offer the best experience to the children. No fewer than 6 hours in the weekly schedule are set aside for meetings among teachers, preparations, meetings with parents, and in-service training.

## The Many Languages of Children: Atelierista and Atelier

A teacher who is trained in the visual arts works closely with the other teachers and the children in every preprimary school (and visits the infant-toddler centers). This teacher is called an *atelierista*, and a special workshop or studio, called an *atelier*, is set aside and used by all the children and teachers as well by the *atelierista*. The *atelier* contains a great variety of tools and resource materials, along with records of past projects and experiences.

The activities and projects, however, do not take place only in the *atelier*. Through the years the roles of the *atelier* and the *atelierista* have expanded and become part of the whole school. Smaller spaces called *mini-ateliers* have been set up in each classroom; furthermore, teachers and *atelieristi* have been working more and more together transferring to one another the reciprocal skills. What is done with materials and media is not regarded as art per se, because in the view of Reggio educators, the children's use of many media is not a separate part of the curriculum but an inseparable, integral part of the whole cognitive/symbolic expression involved in the process of learning.

## The Power of Documentation

Transcriptions of children's remarks and discussions, photographs of their activity, and representations of their thinking and learning using many media are carefully arranged by the *atelierista*, along with the other teachers, to document the work (and the process of learning) done in the schools. This documentation has several functions. Among these are to make parents aware of their children's experience and maintain their involvement; to allow teachers to understand children better and to evaluate the teachers' own work, thus promoting their professional growth; to facilitate communication and exchange of ideas among educators; to make children aware that their effort is valued; and to create an archive that traces the history of the school and the pleasure of learning by many children and their teachers.

## The Emergent Curriculum

The curriculum is not established in advance. Teachers express general goals and make hypotheses about what direction activities and projects might take; consequently, they make appropriate preparations. Then, after observing children in action, they compare, discuss, and interpret together their observations and make choices that they share with the children about what to offer and how to sustain the children in their exploration and learning. In fact, the curriculum emerges in the process of each activity or project and is flexibly adjusted accordingly through this continuous dialogue among teachers and with children.

## Projects

Projects provide the backbone of the children's and teachers' learning experiences. They are based on the strong conviction that learning by doing is of great importance and that to discuss in group and to revisit ideas and experiences is the premier way of gaining better understanding and learning.

Ideas for projects originate in the continuum of the experience of children and teachers as they construct knowledge together. Projects can last from a few days to several months. They may start either from a chance event, an idea or a problem posed by one or more children, or an experience initiated directly by teachers. For example, a study of crowds originated when a child told the class about a summer vacation experience. Whereas teachers had expected the children to tell about their discoveries on the beach or in the countryside, a child commented that "crowd" was all that she remembered.

Another project on fountains developed when children decided to build an amusement park for birds. This project originated from a request by George Forman and me to observe and document on tape, along with the teachers involved, the process of a project as it developed.[2] The Reggio educators met, discussed, and thought about the fact that during the previous year the 5-year-olds had been very interested in the birds visiting the schoolyard. As a result of this interest, they had built a small lake, birdhouses, and an observatory.

The teachers surmised that a good way to probe what might interest the incoming group of 5-year-olds was to ask them what they remembered about what their classmates had done the previous year. Teachers, including the *atelierista* and *pedagogista*, prepared the questions to ask, made hypotheses about what topics the children would be interested in, discussed the selection of the initial group of 11 children, where the first meeting would

---

[2] The narrative of the whole project and several significant episodes are presented in depth in Forman and Gandini (1994), *An Amusement Park for Birds*. This 90-minute video is available from Perfomanetics, 19 The Hollow, Amherst, MA 01002; fax (413) 253-0898.

take place, and how, by whom, and with what tools the documentation would be organized.

Then they had the first meeting with the children. The children's conversation was full of ideas and surprises as, in the course of it, they became more and more involved. First, they explored the idea of repairing what had been constructed the previous year, and then they thought of improving the area by adding several amenities for the birds to make them feel welcome in their playground. Finally, they became very enthusiastic about the idea expressed by one child of constructing an amusement park for the birds on the playground of the school. (It should be noted that an amusement park is set up each spring at the outskirts of the town.)

After the initial conversation, eight children were interested in drawing what they thought would be useful and nice to include in the amusement park for birds. That very evening the teachers transcribed the first conversation by the children (which they had recorded), discussed it, and, with the *pedagogista*, prepared more questions on the topic because it was clear that the goal of constructing an amusement park for birds was of great interest to the children and also offered many promising opportunities for combining learning experiences with pleasure.

Figure 2–1 illustrates the initial steps that transpired as the amusement park idea began to take shape. It presents the hypotheses (possibilities) formed by the adults before the children's first meeting and also the hypotheses (possibilities) suggested by the children extracted from the transcription of their first conversation and the study of their first drawings. Note that this particular flowchart depicts only one of many ways projects may begin. As the rich images and words in "The Hundred Languages of Children" exhibit reveal, there are many additional ways in which such projects may begin.

# CONCLUSION

In one of his last writings, Malaguzzi (1993c) invited us to reflect on a bill of three rights. He invited us to reflect on the rights of children to realize and expand all their potentials while receiving support by adults who value the children's capacity to socialize, to receive and give affection and trust, and who are ready to help them by sustaining the children's own constructive strategies of thought and action rather than by simply transmitting knowledge and skills.

He invited us to reflect on the rights of parents to participate actively and of free will in the experience of growth, care, and learning of their own children—participation that is so vital to the sense of security for children

# FIGURE 2–1

An illustration of process: An amusement park for birds

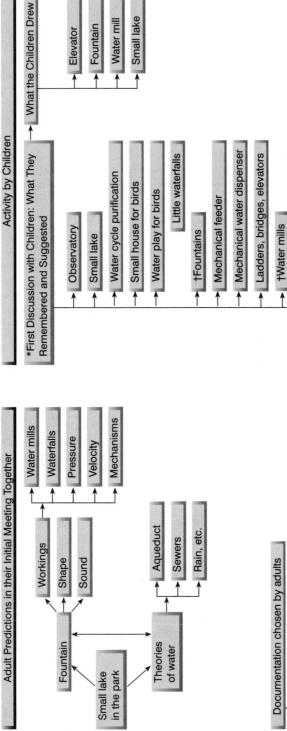

**Adult Predictions in their Initial Meeting Together**

- Small lake in the park
  - Fountain
    - Workings → Water mills, Waterfalls, Pressure, Velocity, Mechanisms
    - Shape
    - Sound
  - Theories of water
    - Aqueduct
    - Sewers
    - Rain, etc.

**Documentation chosen by adults**
- Video
- Slides
- Diary
- Tape recording
- Written notes

**Activity by Children**

*First Discussion with Children: What They Remembered and Suggested
- Observatory
- Small lake
- Water cycle purification
- Small house for birds
- Water play for birds
  - Little waterfalls
- †Fountains
- Mechanical feeder
- Mechanical water dispenser
- Ladders, bridges, elevators
- †Water mills
- Feelings of birds, children

What the Children Drew
- Elevator
- Fountain
- Water mill
- Small lake

*The transcription of the dialogue after the first meeting revealed these interests by the children.

†After examining the dialogue and discussing it together, the teachers found the interest in the water mill and the fountains offered the most promising opportunities to develop for projects.

Source: Adapted from *Amusement Park for the Birds*, by L. Gandini, 1993, unpublished manuscript.

and parents, participation that is an essential part of working together, sharing values, modalities, and content of education.

And, finally, he invited us to reflect on the right of teachers to contribute to the definition of the contents, objectives, and practice of education accomplished through a network of collaboration, supported by the ideas and competencies of everyone, and that always remains open to professional growth and research.

Loris Malaguzzi reminded us that it is respect for these rights that will bring mutual and shared benefits for children, parents, and teachers. It is respect for these rights that makes it possible for them to construct their learning together. And, finally, it is respect for these rights that will render the school an amiable place that is welcoming, alive, and authentic.

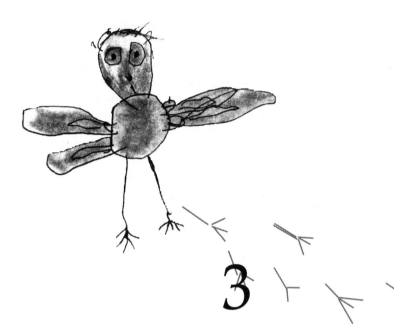

# 3

# Lessons from an Exhibition
## Reflections of an Art Educator

*Pamela Houck*
Experiencenter Curator and Educational Exhibits Consultant, the
Dayton Art Institute

*This exhibit is a statement*
*against any clairvoyant pedagogy*
*that claims to know all things*
*before they happen;*
*that teaches young children*
*that all days are the same*
*and that there are no surprises;*
*and teaches adults that they need only to repeat*
*that which they themselves*
*were never able to learn.*

(Loris Malaguzzi, 1990)[1]

---

[1] This poem was written as an introduction to a European edition of the exhibition "The Hundred Languages of Children." Used with permission.

"The Hundred Languages of Children" is a large and compelling exhibition that documents an approach to early childhood education developed in Reggio Emilia, a prosperous town in northern Italy. The 210 large panels and 16 cases, assembled under the direction of Loris Malaguzzi and a team of Reggio Emilia educators, easily fill several galleries. A version of the exhibit has been touring the United States since 1987; other editions of the exhibition have circulated in Europe, Asia, and Australia since 1984. While the eloquent photographs taken by teachers and the remarkable images created by children immediately capture everyone's attention, it is the literally translated words that tell a story that pictures can only suggest (see Figures 3–1 and 3–2).

Since 1992, I have had the privilege of managing the North American tour of this vivid collection of words, work, and wisdom of a pioneering group of educators and children. It is a rewarding job. The coordinating curator has not only constant access to this exhibition but also the unique opportunity to observe the reactions of visitors as they interpret its messages. For a former art teacher and veteran museum educator for 20 years, this role has been a fascinating experience.

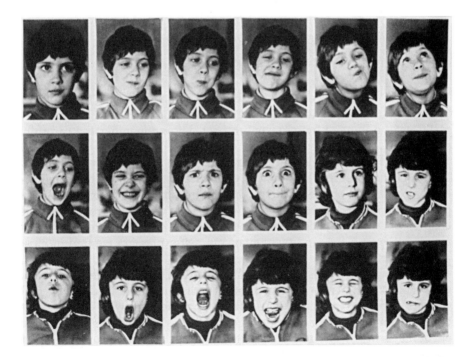

**FIGURE 3–1**
Two children studying the "Language of Faces" in a mirror

**FIGURE 3–2**
A self-portrait made after observing changing faces in the mirror

Most Americans get their first glimpse of Reggio Emilia's schools for young children when they see "The Hundred Languages of Children." Few walk away unmoved by its visual impact. They remember the carefully selected photographs, most often grouped in sequences, that are vibrant records of children's experiences and explorations as they investigate various aspects of a particular theme. Even more beguiling are the extraordinary pictures and objects made by the children themselves—usually interpreted by viewers as children's artwork. However, as the reader of this chapter will discover, these images represented in so many different materials are more than the kind of spontaneous self-expression we find in most preschool art areas in the United States.

Accompanying this exciting visual material is much interesting text. One is quickly drawn to the words of the children, transcribed from actual conversations as they shared observations and questions with each other. It is clear, from the spirit of these peer group discussions, that the children are encouraged to engage in the kind of healthy debate that promotes closer observation and critical thinking skills.

# THE ELUSIVE MESSAGE: COMMON MISUNDERSTANDINGS ABOUT THE REGGIO APPROACH

Why, then, with this abundance of stimulating information, do so many of the exhibit's fundamental messages so often escape the viewer? A closer look at some reasons may begin to unlock doors and reveal unexpected meanings.

The most common misinterpretation among visitors to the exhibition is that it is a collection of children's art. In fact, many become convinced that they are viewing the products of art schools for young children. They see the impressive variety of materials to which students are exposed: paint, markers, pencils, wire, clay, weaving materials, things found in nature, all kinds of paper, and limitless recycled materials. In addition, they recognize that the children have learned how to use tools rarely given to preschoolers.

If not the products of art activities, what do these images really mean? The main clue lies in the title of the exhibition, "The Hundred Languages of Children." Reggio educators have long recognized that children have a far greater capacity than has been assumed to articulate their ideas through visual representation such as drawing. By giving young children the materials, tools, and skills to illustrate what they are thinking and observing at any stage of knowing, the teachers are empowering them to communicate with visual language before they can read and write. This insight has come toe-to-toe with long-held theories about developmentally appropriate practice in art education.

The second pitfall for viewers is how easily and effectively pictures can deceive. This is especially true when an image seems so close to our own experience that it triggers associations that persuade us we understand exactly what we *think* we see. There is much that is familiar in this exhibit, such as providing materials like paint, markers, and clay; learning by doing (isn't John Dewey one of our most cherished gurus?); and involving children in project work.

What is the real story behind the deceptive picture? Much of the answer can be found in the text. And this, ironically, is the third reason why the messages are so elusive. There is a lot to read in the exhibition—more that most people can digest in one visit. Perhaps our inclination to look at the pictures and skim over the words is because our fast-paced, high-tech age has made us increasingly dependent on the visual information available from television, magazines, photographs, and films.

Although a visitor's guide focuses on the exhibit's most important educational issues, viewers who take time to go beyond the guide and absorb the exhibit's own written messages begin to hear a chorus of harmonious voices describing a complex and dynamic approach to early education that is causing many educators to rethink long-held assumptions. Still, some messages remain hidden only because of the inescapable limitations of exhibits.

## *WHAT THE EXHIBIT DOES NOT REVEAL*

As we have seen, the exhibition demonstrates how children use symbolic representation to communicate what they understand about their world at various stages of understanding. It also gives us some notion of the ways that the Reggio educators use children's work to enhance the learning process. But some aspects of their methods require further discussion, including these:

❑ Reggio educators encourage children to describe their hypotheses about phenomena that have aroused their curiosity.

❑ Children's representations are used as memories of their experiences and as visual aides that help them revisit their initial observations and proposals in order to reflect further and revise their perceptions and theories. In his article "Helping Children Ask Good Questions," Forman (1992a) has selected a child's drawing from the exhibition to show how this works in the context of constructivist curriculum. The drawing, representing a 5-year-old boy's theory about where rain comes from, is used as a device to help the child think about his thinking.

❑ Children's work is also used as assessment, to indicate a child's developing understanding in the course of an investigation. In one section of the exhibit, "Summer Fresco," two separate drawings by Carlotta, age 5, show a marked change in her perception of poppies before and after a visit to the fields where they grow (Figures 3–3 and 3–4). (It should be noted that Carlotta, like everyone else in Reggio Emilia's schools for young children, had been exposed to many kinds of drawing tools and experiences before the field trip.)

What is not so obvious in this exhibit are real situation factors, such as the actual dynamics between the protagonists (i.e., the participants—children, teachers, and parents) and the impact that the school environment has on the children—both critically important in the system of social relationships that underlies the Reggio Approach (Gandini, 1993b).

**FIGURE 3–3**
Carlotta's first drawing of poppies

**FIGURE 3–4**
A later drawing of the poppies by Carlotta

These and other issues that the exhibition does not examine are more effectively addressed in books, articles, and conference presentations about the Reggio Emilia Approach. Following are some of the other key aspects of the approach that are difficult to identify when viewing the exhibition:

(1) The rigorous visual training children receive from a very early age is not shown. For example, we do not see that the physical environments of the youngest children are full of visual stimulation and that the

children in Reggio Emilia's infant-toddler centers begin investigating tools and materials when they are only a few months old. This early exposure accounts in large part for the impressive quality of the children's work by the time they are 5 years old.

(2)   We do not immediately catch on to the fact that projects and shorter-term explorations emerge from children's natural curiosity about the fascinating aspects of the world around them—shadows, rain, puddles, plants, animals, computers, found objects, and themselves. Only gradually do we realize that these investigations follow the lead of the child, rather than a structure established by an adult.

(3)   Because the focus is on the children, most viewers are not aware of the many different hats worn by the teachers, a subject that has been thoughtfully explored by Rebecca New and Carolyn Edwards (Edwards, 1993; New, 1993). Teachers see their many roles as necessary to promoting intellectual development among groups of children and often operate on several levels simultaneously:

> as a partner with the child in the learning process;
>
> as the facilitator of a constructivist curriculum;
>
> as a provocateur who challenges children to solve problems;
>
> as the "memory" for the group as documenter of their discussions and activities;
>
> as a nurturer and validator of a child's sense of purpose and belonging;
>
> as a mediator who encourages children to settle their own disputes; and
>
> as learner and researcher, who shares observations and reflections with colleagues on a frequent and regular basis.

(4)   One cannot observe teaching practice and how teachers actually go about working with children—"catching the children's ball and throwing it back," as this process has been described (Edwards, 1993, p. 153).

(5)   The exhibition cannot convey how space is used as a "third teacher." Although it is clear that teachers make all kinds of materials available to children, just how the physical environment of the school affects learning cannot be communicated within the limitations of a traveling exhibit with an ambitious set of goals and objectives. As we have seen in Chapter 2, Lella Gandini has described how space is considered by the Reggio educators as an essential part of their approach. The environment has the capacity to influence how the community feels and functions within it, to serve as a stimulant to exploration, and to communicate what happens inside its walls.

## *FINDING THE MESSAGE: FOR ALL EARLY CHILDHOOD EDUCATORS, AND ART TEACHERS IN PARTICULAR*

Among the many messages that begin to emerge from the exhibit and moti-vate audiences to learn more about Reggio Emilia's schools for young children, several are of special interest to art educators, as well as to the rest of us.

First, this is an approach that puts great emphasis on listening to chil-dren. Their words are everywhere. In sections of the exhibit, the sequences of children's works and words suggest that they have been encouraged to revisit and rethink a particular observation or idea. My favorite example is a series of self-portraits by a 5-year-old, who has represented himself in a series of pencil drawings, small clay busts, and verbal descriptions. As this child was challenged by his teachers and peers to go back to the mirror and take another look, his self-image changed dramatically in the short span of 3 weeks! (see Figures 3–5 and 3–6).

Second, Reggio educators grasp the importance of giving children opportunities to communicate what they are thinking at any stage of know-ing. Before they can read and write, children are encouraged to express

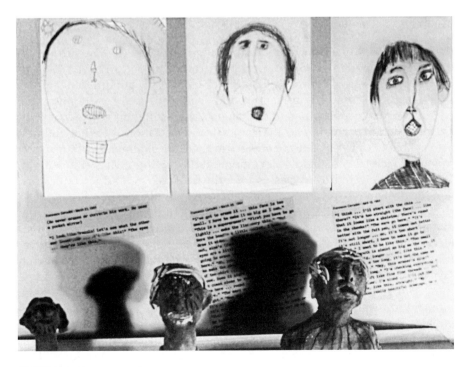

**FIGURE 3–5**
A progression of one child's self-portraits over 3 weeks

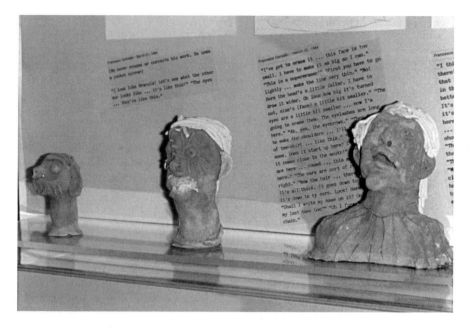

**FIGURE 3–6**
A progression of one child's self-portraits over 3 weeks (continued)

their understandings in symbolic languages that they *can* use—drawing, painting, clay modeling, collage, performance, and so on.

Third, Reggio's approach to "art" for children is a definite departure from what many teachers are taught, and challenges many assumptions we have taken as gospel. Inherent in Reggio's very different way of viewing image making by children is the contrast in expectations of what children are capable of doing at different stages in their development. One has only to study Victor Lowenfeld's developmental drawing charts (Lowenfeld, 1975), often referred to in classes for primary teachers and art educators, and the drawings by average children in Reggio Emilia.

Fourth, the exhibit inspires many who see it to greatly expand the inventory of materials they make available to children and also challenges teachers to use their own equipment and creative potential more resourcefully. Of special interest is the use of the photocopier to help children explore several related ideas without having to laboriously redraw the same thing. For example, in one panel, a group of children's drawings of the human form were copied and reused in another context, to show a group's individual theories of how blood circulates through the body (Figure 3–7). In another panel, a drawing of the school building is duplicated several times so that a child can superimpose a series of representations of an approaching rain storm (Figure 3–8).

**FIGURE 3–7**
Photocopies of children's figure drawings used by them to represent theories about "Our Insides"

Fifth, the exhibition is an example of the kind of documentation that teachers in Reggio conduct as an ongoing way of working. That is not to imply that all the photographs, transcribed dialogues, and work by children that they gather are constantly being arranged as finished exhibitions. Yet, even from the beginning of a project, words and images are put together in well-designed temporary displays (documentation) throughout the schools. These are presented in engaging ways that inform parents and provoke children to ask more questions, participate in more discussion, and pursue further explorations.

Methods of documentation found in the exhibition include photographs, transcribed tape recordings, videotapes, and, of course, the children's own work. These kinds of materials are used in a variety of ways before they are returned to the children, filed, or end up in displays of completed projects.

Sixth, the impact of visual training on a child's intellectual and creative growth is among the most innovative and challenging proposals in the exhi-

**FIGURE 3–8**
Photocopies of the child's drawing of the school used to show an approaching storm

bition and is worth examining in some detail. Considering that children use their eyes as well as other senses to help identify, investigate, sort out, and think, Loris Malaguzzi proposed that visual training through active learning strategies is important from a very early age. He suggested that this instruction should be included as part of every educational project and saw a wealth of benefits from giving children tools that empower children to think for themselves in both creative and rational ways; help them develop emotional maturity and sensitivity to the world around them; and free them from the limitations of passive perception, encouraged by television, that is so common in today's youngsters.

In two of the most pedagogically significant panels, Malaguzzi presents a rationale for providing the children with a visual education from an early age. He recognized that a child's developmental level determines what kinds of information he or she is ready to absorb and the kinds of the perceptual investigations that the child is likely to enter into. In this series of panels, Malaguzzi emphasizes that the quality of these perceptual investigations greatly influences cognitive development and places responsibility on the educator for creating opportunities for high-quality perceptual experiences that invite exploration.

In a charming series of photographs, a 10-month-old child begins making connections between a real watch and the image of a watch (Figures 3–9 through 3–12). Malaguzzi makes the point that the naturally curious child is looking for ways to sort out relationships and connections that help him or her make sense of the world. From an early age, the young child begins to ponder such questions as what is it that changes? How does it change? What remains the same?

The text in another panel describes perception itself as a set of relationships. It points out that once one has the ability to retain the image of an object, one has already grasped certain relationships: the identity of the object (apple); equivalence (these things, among other things, are apples); classification (this is an apple, not an orange); and other factors such as order, cause, and symmetry.

This example shows that relations are really problems themselves to be tested. Is this apple the same on both sides? How is this apple different from the orange? Is this a real apple?

When things are different than they appear, this creates a dilemma to contend with and sort out. Artists and scientists grapple with these dilemmas all the time, but so does the child. The message for the teacher: The child needs to develop the tools to investigate and make sense of an object about which he or she is curious.

Reggio teachers recognize that this need requires opportunities to try things out. Continuing with the apple example: being able to substitute something else that is round and red for the apple; being able to make inferences from the apple (It is red? therefore, it is ripe?); and "violations," or challenges, to a child's first ideas about the apple (all apples are sweet, all apples are red, etc.).

Finally, the last point mentioned here, and perhaps the most mysterious, is the issue of *time*. It is a concern that sparks dozens of related questions from thoughtful visitors. Where do Reggio educators find it? How do they use it so effectively without seeming rushed?

Although the exhibition does not provide specific answers, it does reflect two related characteristics of the schools: (a) Children are given enough time to explore at their own pace, and (b) teachers obviously have made the time to take care of educational priorities. Could we learn a thing or two from the Reggio educators about using our own time with children to better advantage?

## LASTING LESSONS

It is helpful to see this exhibit as a complex situation that, like many others, requires careful consideration and accurate interpretation—abilities educators need to understand student behavior. When visitors practice this skill

**FIGURE 3–9**
Documentation of a child developing her theory about watches

**FIGURE 3–10**

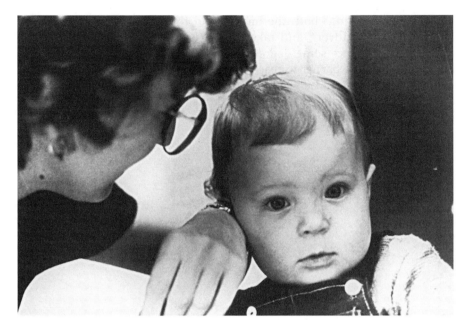

**FIGURE 3–11**

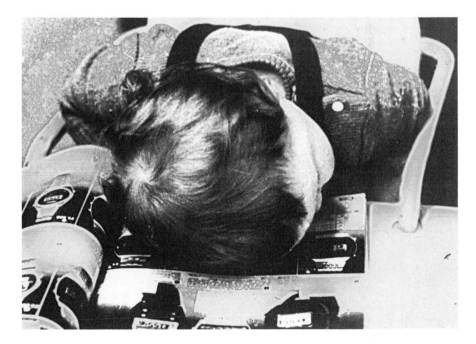

**FIGURE 3–12**

by carefully "reading" both the images and the words in "The Hundred Languages of Children" and take time to contemplate its lessons, they invariably experience some degree of the "Aha! phenomenon"—a sense of breaking through a barrier to reach new understanding. Among the exhibition's greatest gifts to adults is its invitation to slow down, listen to children, and reflect on what they are telling us about what they perceive and what we have yet to understand.

# 4

# Reggio Emilia and American Schools

## Telling Them Apart and Putting Them Together—Can We Do It?

*Joanne Hendrick*
Professor, Emerita, University of Oklahoma

Having given a number of talks about Reggio Emilia and sensed the frustration in myself and my audience as I attempted to explain Reggio's virtues and glories, I was really helped one day by a plaintive question from a member of the audience who asked, "Well, I can see the schools look beautiful and all that, but what I don't understand is why you think they're so different. Just tell me—what's so different about what they do there from what I'm doing right now in my own classroom?"

This chapter attempts to answer that question by discussing some, but by no means all, of the differences and similarities between the Reggian and American approaches to early childhood education particularly as it relates to intellectual development.

Of course, the risk in drawing such comparisons is that it is so easy to make one approach, in this case the schools in Reggio Emilia, seem like the "good guys" and the other, in this case the American preschools, seem like the "bad guys." Having helped educate several generations of young American teachers, I would certainly hate to think of us as being the bad guys—I believe that American "best practice" is very good—but I also believe that we can make it even better, and one way to improve what we do is to learn as much as we can from other very good approaches. Reggio Emilia is an outstanding example of such an approach.

Another peril in writing this chapter is the possibility that after reading it, everyone, both Reggians and Americans, will be irritated, feeling that I have not fully represented their point of view or what happens in their particular school. Therefore, it is important to emphasize that the following comparisons and generalizations are based on my own American point of view having visited, observed, and studied the municipally supported preschools in Reggio. *It does not necessarily reflect the Reggio philosophy from the Italian perspective.* Also, my comments about preschools in the United States are based on 35 years of teaching, observing, and writing about those schools. The comparisons I draw are based on those schools that would be accepted as representing what is currently defined as good practice while remaining in the mainstream of American preschool education.

## *SIMILARITIES BETWEEN THE APPROACHES*

As Baji Rankin explains in her chapter, Reggians and Americans have many values and philosophical roots in common that stem from Dewey, Piaget, and, more recently, Vygotsky. Among the virtues espoused by these philosophers are the value of inquiry learning and talking together with children as effective ways to foster collaborative learning.

In addition to those roots, both educational cultures believe learning should be based on real, concrete experience; they favor learning by doing; they believe a child-centered curriculum is desirable, that individualizing the curriculum to suit particular children is worthwhile, and that including parents is a significant good. Both approaches support the value of creativity and favor teaching that encourages problem solving and fosters inquiry learning.

With so much in common, why, then, is the Reggio Approach so newly admired by many American preschool teachers? What do the teachers in that Italian city do that is so inspiring and different from Americans' approach?

To answer this question fully would require more space than is available here. However, it is possible to consider three aspects of pedagogy and use them to compare and contrast the Reggian and American approaches to early childhood cognitive education. These are attitudes about children, creativity, and what constitutes effective teaching strategies.

## *ATTITUDES ABOUT CHILDREN*

The teachers from Reggio invariably emphasize that they view children as being rich, strong, and powerful. They see the children as possessing great potential—potential it is the privilege of the teacher to perceive and empower. They see children *not* as having needs but, rather, as having rights—as being entitled to good care and sound teaching because of who they are, not because of what they need.

How does this differ from the American point of view? On the surface, at least, we would certainly agree with it. But underneath, do we really see children this way? It seems to me we view them from a much more protective and possibly restricted vantage. For example, we often discuss "meeting children's needs" and "strengthening their weaknesses."

Many American preschool teachers, while no longer seeing their role as "doing to children," still cast themselves in the role of doing *for* them. They interpret care as being the sort of mothering that actually robs youngsters of their independence—for example, handing them something when they could reach it themselves, buttoning their sweaters, and answering for children instead of giving them time to respond on their own.

Some of us who have gone beyond that and who try mightily to enable children to do things for themselves may still limit our expectations unduly because of our awareness of developmental stages and timetables. Although these standards are of undoubted value as protection against inappropriate academic approaches sometimes favored by administrators, parents, or inexperienced teachers who push children beyond their abilities, we might ask ourselves what is the flip side of honoring those standards? Perhaps we have carried our respect for them too far, and this devotion to the concept has led us actually to underexpect what children can do, thereby, as Eli Saltz maintains, infantalizing our youngsters. Certainly the accomplishments of the young children in Reggio Emilia offer many interesting examples of realizing potentials we have not dreamed possible in the United States.

## *ATTITUDES ABOUT CREATIVITY*

The most obvious differences between the Reggian and American ways of fostering creativity are the multitude and variety of materials the Italians make available for the children to use combined with the special work areas, typically separate rooms, they call *ateliers* where children come to construct their ideas. Moreover, a special staff person (an *atelierista*) is provided along with the room to facilitate that process. Although the majority of schools in the United States would not find it difficult to extend the range of creative materials they make available to children, it is a rare school, indeed, which could find the wherewithal to support the salary of an *atelierista* much less provide a permanent space in which that person could hold forth. Nevertheless, as visitors behold the results made possible by this support, it leaves us hungering to provide similar opportunities for our children, and some of us, as the chapter by Karen Haigh demonstrates, are actually finding ways to make this support possible.

But this admiration for the color, beauty, and quality of the Italian children's products often blinds the visitor to another real difference between American and Italian purposes in providing artistic materials. In the United States, a frequently cited benefit of using such self-expressive materials is that they permit children to express their feelings and come to terms with them.

On the other hand, it appears to me that the purpose of providing graphic materials in the Italian schools leans more toward enabling children to express their ideas—to explain, for example, how the water actually gets to the fountain or what causes rain to fall (see Figure 4–1).

Coming from the school of thought that prizes originality and fears stifling it by providing models or, worse yet, urging children to make something just like the teacher has made, I believe I understand the source of our hesitancy about fostering any sort of activity that smacks of copying a model or painting what the teacher suggests. But as Williams found out in her water project, asking children to draw what they have been working on or thinking about certainly does not result in identical products—far from it!

**FIGURE 4-1**
Here some of the children from Reggio illustrate their theories of where rain comes from.

Whereas the teachers in Reggio Emilia *do* foster the children's powers of close observation by providing opportunities for them to "draw from life," this is not intended to be copying, per se. Children are often asked to first draw their ideas—of a poppy, for instance—and then taken to visit real poppies in the field. There they are encouraged to observe the flowers closely, draw them on the spot, and compare the previsit drawings with those results. This process greatly enhances the children's powers of observation and possibly their appreciation of the beauty of the world as well.

The final difference in approaches to creativity I will discuss here is the kind of support and teaching the Italian and American preschool teachers provide for the children when they are using creative materials. Here, again, Americans are hesitant to intervene in any way lest we cause the bird of creativity to fly out the window. Therefore, children are typically provided with clay or easel paints or carpentry materials and, provided they use them safely, are scrupulously left to discover on their own how to use them effectively.

The Italians, on the other hand, think nothing of showing a child how to wipe the brush on the edge of the cup to avoid dripping or how to wet the edges of clay so it will stick (see Figure 4-2). For me, this was one of the

more troubling aspects of watching that staff work until I understood their reasoning.

They maintain that lending adult assistance when needed, whether it be bending a recalcitrant piece of wire or hammering in a reluctant nail, empowers youngsters to move ahead with their creations in a satisfying way. The way I have come to think about this is that there is a vast difference between showing a child how to use a brace and bit to make a hole and telling him where to put the hole or what to do with it once drilled. Although the Reggio teachers unhesitatingly teach skills and lend a helping hand when needed, they would never tell the child where to put the hole (though they well might ask her why she is putting it in a particular place).

## ATTITUDES ABOUT TEACHING STRATEGIES

One of the clearest ways of telling the teaching strategies of the two approaches apart is to focus on the differing teacher and child roles in the two approaches. (For the purposes of this discussion, we will focus only on some cognitive aspects of curriculum.)

In the American approach, the teacher may use the children's interests as the source for selecting a theme around which to build the curriculum— or she may dredge something out of a box she has saved from last year and the year before that! Having selected a theme, she then plans ahead and thinks up activities and experiences to present to the children that provide some interesting facts and, possibly, opportunities to practice specific mental ability skills such as seeing similarities and differences, practicing elementary classification skills, and so forth. In short, her responsibility is to be the instigator and leader for whatever preplanned learning transpires.

Of course, it would be unfair not to admit that many American preschool teachers also welcome the spontaneous interests of the children and weave these into the curriculum. Even when this occurs, however, it is generally the teacher who takes the lead in determining what will happen as a result of that interest.

The children's role is to participate in the learning activities provided by the teacher, reply to questions, soak up information, use these teacher-planned activities to acquire some mental ability concepts and reasoning skills, and practice them with the materials the teacher has provided.

Rather than seeing the teacher's role as that of leader and developer of curriculum, the Reggio teachers prefer the role of collaborator—working together with children, parents, and other staff members to generate interest, uncover what the children already know and think about that interest, and foster the emergence of projects based on that interest and the children's degrees of knowledge about it. In this approach everyone has ideas and contributes them to a mutual "pot." The result is a fluid, generative, dynamic curriculum that emerges as the interests and concerns of children and adults develop together.

The children's role is to toss the ball of ideas back and forth with the teacher as the project develops. They are provoked into thinking up ways to express their ideas and solutions to problems and expected to try those out and to show other people what they have concluded by means of language, graphics, and child-constructed models. As they say in Reggio, "You don't know it until you can explain it to someone else."

Unfortunately, this mutuality of roles and consequent honoring of the children's ideas as the curriculum emerges has led to a misconception of the teacher's responsibilities that it is important to clear up here. Sometimes students of the Reggio Approach have been left with the impression that teachers always wait for the children's interests and simply follow along with these, but that is a mistaken interpretation of their responsibilities.

In actuality, while it is true that curriculum projects often stem from the children's concerns, once a potential interest has been identified, the next step is for the teachers to brainstorm a number of possible avenues to investigate. As the diagram in Gandini's chapter illustrates, they meticulously analyze these possibilities—examining them for problems and questions they might pose to the children in order to provoke them into thinking about causes, possible problems and solutions, and/or additional interests to pursue. Then various possibilities are proposed to the children, discussed, discarded, modified or replaced, and then pursued. How different this is from the American approach.

I never discuss how emergent curriculum develops without recalling a member of my American audience who asked, most earnestly and sincerely, "But what if the children don't have any ideas—what then?" This query illustrates to perfection another significant difference between the American and Reggian approaches. It is the amount of genuine attention devoted to what the children have to say. Certainly, we Americans *think* we pay attention and that we will remember how conversations went and what the purport was, but it is a rare school indeed that relies on anything more than the teacher's memory to accomplish this. But when these teacher recollections are compared with actual recordings, as the student's comment reveals in the Goldhaber, Smith, and Sortino chapter, these memories turn out to be partial at best.

In the Reggio classroom, the teacher not only listens closely when the children have discussions but also tapes the conversations and transcribes them for later discussion and analysis by the staff and *pedagogista*. Granted, making these transcriptions and taking time to consider them together is a laborious and time-consuming process, but the data it provides about the children's concerns are well worth the effort. As projects eventuate, additional discussions are recorded and their transcriptions are included along with pictures and other evidence of what is happening on the documentation boards that are placed about the building for all to appreciate. As we shall see in other chapters, creation of these boards is a highly valued cornerstone of the Reggio Approach because they enable everyone to revisit and reflect on what they are accomplishing or have accomplished. Perhaps if we used this way of remembering what the children have said we would not have to worry about what to do if the children have no ideas!

I cannot conclude this chapter without singling out one more fascinating intellectual task with which the Reggio teachers challenge the children. We have already witnessed the way children are asked to use any one of a hundred languages to express their ideas. Thus, one child may draw a picture of how the water gets into the fountain, whereas another youngster might make a model of her idea using clay or a series of pipes.

The intriguing challenge is that the children are sometimes expected to translate their ideas from one language (one symbolic system) into another one. They might draw a picture first, for instance, and then use that picture as a reference for transforming that same idea into another language or medium. Thus, having drawn a diagram of a proposed maze, they were then challenged to actually mark that maze out on the school playground, keeping all the proportions in the same relationships as existed in the original diagram (see Figures 4–3 and 4–4).

**FIGURE 4–3**
After the children decided which diagram of a maze to use, they next had the challenge of figuring out how to move from one symbolic system to another, thereby translating the diagram into reality.

**FIGURE 4–4**

Or they were asked what they could use to represent the sounds of a musical scale so that they could see the differences as well as hear them. Or, to use still another example, having composed a musical accompaniment to go with a story, they had to decide how they could "write it" so the 3-year-old class could understand it and play the same music (see Figure 4–5). In short, the children are often expected to shift from using one symbolic system to using another—this is intellectual functioning of a very high order.

## SOME ADDITIONAL COMPARISONS

I have selected only a handful of the most prominent differences between the American and Reggian approaches to early childhood education to discuss here, but so many more insights and possibilities should be discussed if space permitted that I cannot resist singling out a few additional items for comparison. Hopefully, the reader will understand this list cannot do justice

**FIGURE 4–5**
The teacher is pointing out the symbols the 5-year-olds decided to use that they thought the 3's could "read," understand what was intended, and play the same music.

to the intricacies and values of either system, but it *does* provide some additional food for thought (see Table 4–1).

## Special Strengths of the American Approach

After such a lengthy review of the sterling qualities of Reggio Emilia schools, it is only fair to balance the discussion by singling out a few of the many strengths where I feel American preschools may have an edge over our Italian counterparts.

**TABLE 4–1**
A sampling of some additional comparisons of American and Reggian schools

| American | Reggian |
|---|---|
| "Projects" or themes are short-lived, extending a day or a week. | "Projects" may be brief but often continue for weeks or months. |
| "Topics" are used to provide information and (possibly) practice in midlevel thinking skills. | "Topics" are used to pose problems and provoke thought. |
| Children acquire a shallow smattering of information on many subjects. | Children acquire in-depth knowledge about fewer subjects (i.e., "know more about less"). |
| Inquiry learning focuses on science tables; some problem solving encouraged. | Pronounced emphasis on "provoking" children to propose reasons why things happen and possible ways to solve problems. |
| Children may show what they know by talking to teacher about it. | Children show what they know by talking about it but also by using many different media: models, graphics, bent wire, dance, and so forth to explain their ideas: "You don't know it until you can explain it to someone else." |
| The individual is emphasized; autonomy, self-responsibility, independence are valued. | Existence within the group is emphasized; sense of community and interdependence are valued. |
| Children select whatever they wish to participate in each day. | Children select what they want to do but are also encouraged to work in consistent small groups based on their continuing interests. |

**TABLE 4–1,** *continued*

| American | Reggian |
|---|---|
| Time is highly regulated and scheduled. | Time flows easily in an unhurried way. |
| Record keeping is typically limited to results rather than work in progress— shows what children have learned (checklists, portfolios, observations) or do not know. | Record keeping—Documentation boards record what children "know" at beginning and during, as well as end of project; boards used for everyone to *re*-visit and *re*-cognize their work as it progresses. |
| Teacher changes at least once a year. | Teachers remain with children for 3 years. |
| Staffing is teacher, or teacher plus aide. | Staffing is two teachers of equal rank plus services of a *pedagogista* and *atelierista*. |
| Hierarchy of staff positions (i.e., director, teacher, aide). | There are no directors; everyone accepts various responsibilities. |
| Confrontation is avoided. | Debate and "confrontation" with different points of view between adults and with children are favored methods of learning for everyone. |
| Teachers tend to be isolated; policy about and regularity of staff meetings varies. | Close collaboration between *all* teachers occurs regularly and frequently. |

For one thing, our devotion to developmentally appropriate practice provides us with a valuable framework of reasonable expectations for young children and of appropriate ways to teach them. In our zeal to help children realize their full potential à la Reggio, we must be careful to retain our hard-won sensitivity to the dangers of overstressing and/or hothousing children right out of their childhood. It would be easy to misinterpret how teachers teach in Reggio and to press the children beyond what is good for them unless we retain that sensitivity.

I also hope we will retain the wealth of fine picture books and the plenitude of block building that I see in American schools and that we will continue to emphasize the excellent large-muscle outdoor equipment prevalent in our play yards. Our emphasis on midlevel cognitive skills and appropriate integration of emergent literacy strategies are additional aspects we should continue to encourage while sustaining our concern for the emotional well-being and stability of the children in our care.

The most valuable strength of all for us to retain is our ability to perse-vere despite hardship and adversity. To our credit, we have not allowed low salaries, sometimes inadequate facilities, and an uninformed public to daunt our spirits. Not only do many of us provide good quality care, but we also, as the interest in Reggio schools so amply demonstrates, have kept our insa-tiable appetite for doing even better.

No matter what differences exist between us, let us agree that the trea-sure we Americans and Italians hold in common *is* this mutual desire to do the very best we can for the young children in our care. It is this desire, our real concern for young children, and our devotion to fostering their well-being that cause us to so admire our Italian counterparts as we continue to learn from their example.

# II

# *Applying Key Concepts of the Reggio Approach*

In Chapter 5, Eva Tarini, an American teacher who spent a year in Reggio, singles out three important concepts—collaboration, inclusion of parents, and documentation—for emphasis. She then describes the delights and difficulties she encountered when attempting to incorporate these ideas into her teaching upon her return to the United States.

The next two chapters discuss collaboration in greater detail. Baji Rankin illustrates how the concept of collaboration has its philosophical roots in the theories of Dewey, Vygotsky, and Piaget and then demonstrates how collaboration was practiced during her study of the dinosaur project while at Reggio.

Part II concludes with a practical chapter by Brenda Fyfe and Louise Cadwell demonstrating how to have a truly genuine conversation with children. The chapter includes practical advice about how to carry on open-ended discussions that uncover what they know and encourage children to put their ideas into words. It then adds an example of such a discussion by teacher and children and concludes with a discussion by four teachers analyzing in Reggio style what was said in the teacher-child discussion and formulating ideas of potential projects that might emerge from it.

# 5

# *Reflections on a Year in Reggio Emilia*

## Key Concepts in Rethinking and Learning the Reggio Way

*Eva Tarini*

Teacher, Crow Island School, Winnetka, Illinois

I am a first grade teacher at the Crow Island School outside Chicago, teaching there since 1989. Previously I taught kindergarten at the Beacon Hill Nursery School in Boston, after receiving my master's in early childhood education from Wheelock College in Boston in 1985. During the 1992–1993 school year, I was an intern in the Municipal Schools of Reggio Emilia, Italy. Most of my time was spent at the Pablo Neruda School and the Diana School.

## THE ROAD OF KNOWLEDGE: ACQUIRING FUNDAMENTAL CONCEPTS

My year spent in the Reggio Emilia municipal preschools was the most important event of my professional life. It unearthed in me a kind of intellectual revolution in which I had the opportunity to examine—indeed, was forced to examine—my beliefs about the education of young children, about working with colleagues, about the nature of an educational context, and about the importance of thinking about and rethinking my work with young children. I believe that the nature of my thinking changed during the year I was there. I learned to think more precisely, more questioningly, and more calmly, taking time to understand new concepts, listen to children, and make interpretations about their words and ideas.

I say that I had the *opportunity* to examine my beliefs because simply by being in a different educational context, one very different from the American, upper-middle-class, elementary school in which I work, I was put in the position to make critical comparisons about the differences and similarities of these very different settings (e.g., cultural differences, political differences, differences in age group). I say I was *forced* to examine my beliefs for two reasons. First, I believe it is nearly impossible to come into contact with Reggio in any sort of depth and *not* find yourself automatically thinking about what you do with children and about what Reggio educators do with children, and then begin to ask yourself hundreds of questions relating to the differences and similarities. Second, as a visitor and guest of the educators in Reggio, I wanted to remain as open as possible to learning about their system and trying to understand it in as much detail as possible.

When I first arrived in Reggio, I was inundated with images, thoughts, feelings, doubts, and words. So many words! My Italian was basic, and although it improved drastically that year, at the beginning I spent a great deal of my time concentrating on everything that was said and just trying to comprehend it. It took me a long time, several months, to feel like I had even the most basic understanding of the Reggio system. While I did have a fundamental sense that the system was very elaborate, it was not until late

November before I felt as though I had anything more than the most tenu-
ous grasp on the complexity of Reggio. At that time, two things happened.
First, I was to have a meeting with the four people with whom I was working most closely: Carlina Rinaldi, the *pedagogista* of the Pablo Neruda
Preschool; Roberta Vecchi and Gino Ferri, the teachers of the 5-year-old
group; and Mara Davoli, the *atelierista* of that school. For this meeting I had
to prepare an outline describing my understandings of my experience thus
far. The second event that pushed my understanding was a request by *Innovations* to write an article about my first impressions of my internship in
Reggio. Both of these assignments stirred up some doubts in me about what
I actually understood, yet they required me to do some writing. The process
of writing, from that point on, became a tool for me to explore my understandings, refine my thinking, and identify ideas and concepts that required
further clarification. Essentially, writing became a tool for constructing my
own knowledge about the principles of the Reggio schools.

## THREE KEY CONCEPTS

### The Role of Collaboration

One of the first aspects of the organization of the Reggio schools that I
began to grasp was collaboration. Although Reggio educators stress this
concept in every workshop they give in the United States, it is virtually
impossible to get a mental image of what collaboration looks like or how it
works until you have experienced it over a long archway of time. The
longer you study Reggio, the wider the circles of collaboration become.
Actually, the circles are already there. It simply requires a great deal of time
to see how far-reaching and intertwined they are. For my article in *Innovations* (Tarini, 1993), I wrote:

> As my circles of contact widen, I begin to see how collaboration is a spiral of
> interaction between people who work here. Maybe it's more than one spiral,
> something similar to those figures of DNA strands, spiraling around each
> other. Only it's not even just two strands that power this living entity, but
> many strands which cross paths in more ways than I know. It must have been
> last week sometime that I realized how interconnected the work/lives of peo-
> ple are here, and how this contact fuels the entire project. I think I was sort of
> stunned to realize the depth of this phenomenon. And simultaneously it made
> so much sense to me. Instead of setting up shop in a myriad of separate class-
> rooms, where individual teachers are doing their own thing, working hard
> and sharing a little bit, instead of all that, the teachers here use all the power
> and energy and inspiration that MUST come from people cooperating to cre-
> ate a system that truly works. I don't think that the teachers here necessarily

work any harder than we do at home, it's that they work differently, that they work together. (p. 4)

Collaboration is fairly easy to see at the level of the individual school. The primary unit of collaboration is the pair of teachers who run each classroom throughout the schools in Reggio. Clearly, each pair of teachers will have their own style of working together based on personality, length of time they have worked together, individual styles of communication, and interests and strengths. Each pair of teachers (usually there are three pairs per school) works closely with the *atelierista*. Depending on the school, the three pairs of teachers coordinate their work and research with the children and with one another. It is not uncommon for the teachers and children in one classroom to begin a project and then have it spill over to the teachers and children of another classroom. This might occur because the children become curious about the work of other children (this happened at La Villetta school when the 3- and 4-year-olds wanted to be involved in the Amusement Park for Birds Project). Or it may be that one class begins a project/research and the teachers become interested in the themes and information emerging about what the children are understanding. Teachers in the other classrooms may begin to explore the same theme with their group as a way of expanding the research base and extending their fundamental understanding of childhood and what/how children think. This kind of "spillover" can only take place when there is a great deal of communication among colleagues, interest in all of the activities and projects that occur throughout the entire school (not just one's own classroom), and an absence of competition and possessive feelings of ownership about good ideas.

Collaboration expands when the *pedagogista* enters the picture to be informed about the various projects and research at a school and also to explore with the teachers what can be interpreted about what the children are doing and what might be some possible paths to take.

Collaboration also occurs *among* schools, as is true of the City and the Rain Project (documentation of this project can be seen in "The Hundred Languages of Children" exhibit). This was an exploration undertaken by at least six schools, all working on investigating different aspects of rain as it pertained to life in their city. (This project had special significance since Italians, as Mara Davoli explained to me, do not like the rain.)

And, of course, collaboration occurs between the schools and the parents. In addition to being essential members of each school's advisory board, parents of each class meet collectively with teachers about four times a year to discuss various projects, developmental issues, and parental concerns or simply to plan for a celebration. I attended meetings with the parents of the incoming 3-year-olds at the Pablo Neruda School where the basis of the teacher presentation was the transition the children were making to the new school. Teachers informed parents of the routine of the day, highlighting some of the more important moments (including separating from parents in the morning, adapting to new activities, toileting routines, lunchtime, and nap time). Parents listened attentively and then asked questions, some about specifics of the program, but some related to issues at home, asking not just the teachers for input but also other parents.

I was particularly struck by the openness at these meetings, and this was a characteristic I noted repeatedly throughout the year. In a meeting at the Diana School, parents were asked to come and discuss discipline issues. Apparently, many parents had been bringing this topic up with teachers as an area of difficulty. All the teachers decided to have meetings with their respective classes and to take notes in order to compare information later. I attended the meeting of the 4-year-old class, where parents talked frankly about personal philosophies concerning discipline, difficulties, and possible strategies. I remember in particular one mother discussing the decisions she and her husband had made to have a family and also continue working full-time. Although they were initially convinced that they could maintain their lifestyle and be good parents simultaneously, she was beginning to reevaluate their assumption. She was beginning to feel that her two sons were not getting enough attention, and she attributed the difficult nature of her oldest precisely to that fact. Clearly, this openness has a great deal to do with the nature of Italian society and culture. But I think, too, that the continuity afforded these parents when their children remain together with the same two teachers for 3 years (coupled with the tradition of meeting in whole groups) increases the opportunities for trust, for sharing with one another and seeing one other as a resource to rely on and share with.

Had I not spent an entire year in Reggio, the image I currently have of collaboration would not be so broad. Likewise, it is entirely possible that had I stayed in Reggio for 2 or 3 years, I would have an even richer idea of the ways educators in Reggio work closely together.

## The Role of Documentation

Another fundamental aspect of the Reggio Emilia municipal schools is documentation. As with collaboration, it took a long time for me to understand the depth and breadth of the meaning of documentation. It was fairly easy to link the word *documentation* with the panels that cover the walls of all the schools and to equate it with the word *display*. One could say that at their most superficial level, the panels *are* a display. But since the panels include not just examples of work done by children but also photographs of them working, transcriptions of conversations they had while working, and, possibly, observations and interpretations made by adults, the panels quickly become a far more communicative tool than is typical of a simple display. The panels inform the viewer of the *process* the children went through in a project. That is, by means of the panels, many of the steps within a project are made visible to an outsider who did not participate. In a simple display, where only the final product is shown, the viewer is left to infer what steps the child may have gone through to arrive at the final product. The panels in Reggio Emilia immediately communicate at least part of the process the children underwent during a project.

I ultimately learned that a definition of documentation cannot be limited to a discussion about the panels and the purposes they serve. Beyond the panels, documentation also involves the process of gathering information that can be used later to construct panels, create documentaries, or communicate with colleagues about an ongoing project to decide where to go next.

I recall that in the spring of my stay in Reggio, I was busy working with some children in a play store, observing the way they dealt with play money. I was to take notes on various aspects of their play, including what they chose to buy, how much it cost, how the storekeeper wrote the receipt and added up the total, how the buyer chose to pay for the items, and whether there was an expectation of receiving change, regardless of the amount of the payment. This experience helped me understand something that I now believe is relatively simple: *documentation is a tool that an observer uses to record information.*

It took me a long time to determine what the most efficient way was to record the information I was gathering. I needed to create a form that would allow me to take notes with a minimum of distraction from my actual observing. Further, I had to be able to read my notes easily. But even more than that, my colleagues had to be able to read my notes easily so that we could discuss what the children were doing, what they seemed to understand, and what seemed to confuse them. I finally created a form divided into three sections side by side—one each for the buyer, seller, and teacher. The buyer and seller sections were subdivided into columns appropriate to the actions of each role. For example, in the buyer's section, I included a column to note the price and another to record the exact way a child paid. In the seller's section, I added columns for noting how the seller wrote out the receipt and what change, if any, had been given.

My colleagues in Italy would probably say that the processes I went through to heighten my ability to observe the children were an important teacher-training device. They forced me to be clear about what information I wanted to gather and helped me realize the necessity of communicating clearly with my colleagues and the importance of reliable reporting tools for collecting the most accurate data (knowing that, in the end, everything is subjective).

## The Role of Projects in the Curriculum

A third key concept that figured prominently in my understanding of the fundamental aspects of the Reggio Emilia schools is "the project." In most American preschools, a project usually refers to an activity—an activity, in fact, that can be easily completed in one day. It is not uncommon, for example, to have a different art project available to preschoolers every day. I did exactly that when I taught kindergarten and also during the first several years that I taught in elementary school.

In Reggio, *project* cannot be defined at all as an activity, since it involves so much more than that. A project in Reggio, first of all, unfolds over time. It is not something that will be available on a certain table for just one day. A key characteristic of a Reggio project is that most of it is *not* predetermined. It is unclear, at the beginning of a project, how long it will last, in what direction it will actually go, what activities will be involved. What *is* determined, or known, at the beginning of a project is that it will be a process undertaken by children and adults in a collaborative manner. It will involve investigation, expression, reinvestigation, and more expression by means of various symbolic languages. A project can be short, just a few days long. But, in my experience, most projects took longer, continuing for weeks or even months. (This does not necessarily mean that children involved in a project are working on only that project every day for months on end. While children did easily work for very long periods of time in a very focused manner, they did not always work on the project day after day. The parts of a project took place more infrequently, perhaps once or twice a week, although in some cases children might work for several days on end.)

The word *project* came to have a much broader meaning, beyond the definition of the way work unfolds with children. In Reggio, *project* was also used as a verb, "to *pro*ject" (with the accent on the first syllable). The way that Reggio educators approach all aspects of their work mirrors the way a project emerges when working with children. Reggio educators collaborate to "*pro*ject" all aspects of the system. Decisions are not made unilaterally, for example. Instead, issues are discussed and explored collaboratively, opinions are expressed, and decisions are made in the most democratic of ways by means of discussion, conciliation, and, ultimately, consensus.

## BACK IN WINNETKA

### The First Step

When I returned to the States in July 1993, I was excited about making some changes in my first grade classroom based on my year-long experience in

Reggio. It was hard to know where to start, so the first thing I did was look at my room arrangement and reorganize it trying to keep images of the classrooms in Reggio in my mind. I wanted the room to feel more open than it had seemed before and easily "readable" by young children. I wanted them to feel that they could find things easily (and clean up easily). I wanted the room to look appealing to anyone who walked in, not too cluttered or messy, but definitely lived in by young children.

One-third of my classroom space is devoted to a meeting area and a block area that are separated by a couch. The carpeted meeting area is also used by children during Choice Time for reading books, listening to books on tape, and playing card games. The remaining two-thirds of my classroom is set up with four large tables, seating four to six children comfortably. Each child has a special work spot assigned to him or her for work times, but during Choice Time, the tables are identified by the activities that take place at each one: games and puzzles, messages, drawing table, and math table. The work area and the meeting/block area are separated by four free-standing shelf units, holding materials for the various choices.

This room arrangement is more open than my previous ones. In earlier years, I tried to put shelving near each table so that materials were always very close by. Now materials are a bit farther away, but traffic patterns are clearer; I ultimately have more space to work with; and the room seems easily manageable, in terms of both children navigating their way around and finding and putting away materials. Our social worker has told me that she finds my room to be very organizing for children. It does not look like the classrooms in Reggio, which is OK. I suppose I would like to have more counter space to place appealing, engaging materials, perhaps a big mirror in the block area and another one in the science area, and maybe a larger studio art space, but I am very happy with what I do have. I am lucky because I have more space than most schools, and I have a lot of windows that make a bright, sunny room and also great wall space, which is perfect for putting up documentation.

## *The Next Steps: Dealing with Difficulties*

Once school began, the big challenge for me quickly became "What next steps do I choose to take?" I had a lot of information and enthusiasm, as well as encouragement from my administration and colleagues. But I lacked the organizational structure around me that in Reggio acts as a crucial piece of the puzzle. I quickly became aware of how important this piece really is. I believe that it is difficult for American teachers to truly grasp the nature and the different feeling of a fundamentally collaborative system. I would never have fully understood had I not gone to Reggio for a year and then come back to the States to try to implement some of the things I learned. When I was in Reggio, it took a long time for me to feel comfortable in the daily back and forth that is characteristic of teachers there. They express doubts and concern more readily than we do. I often felt that I had to present polished, interpreted information to them, just so they could see what I had done, but it turned out that what I had to do was present organized (but not polished) information to them and then go over it with my colleagues, to interpret and question and wonder about *together*. Back here in the States, it became clear to me that such a concept did not really exist, certainly not with the depth one sees in Reggio. Although I had colleagues who would readily listen to me if I asked for help or serve as a sounding board, there was not an *expectation* of collaboration, of group decision making. It was then that something Malaguzzi said made a lot more sense:

> Co-teaching, and in a more general sense, collegial work, represents for us a deliberate break from the traditional professional and cultural solitude and isolation of teachers. *This isolation has been rationalized in the name of academic freedom, yet wrongly understood. Its results, certainly, have been to impoverish and desiccate teachers' potential and resources and make it difficult or impossible for them to achieve quality.* . . . I remember, however, that the archetype, one teacher per classroom, was so strongly rooted when we began our work, that our proposal of co-teaching pairs, which *should* have been seen as a welcome liberation from excessive stress, did not at first find ready acceptance among teachers. [Eventually] the work in pairs, and then among pairs, produced tremendous advantages, both educationally and psychologically, for adults as well as for children. (italics added; Edwards, Gandini, & Forman, 1993, p. 64)

In answering the question "What next steps do I choose to take?" I realized that *I* had to make those decisions completely on my own. They had to be based in part on my relationships and interaction with the children but also on what I felt that I could accomplish as a single teacher acting alone. This problem of isolation continues to be a major struggle for me.

## *Introducing Message Boxes*

I started the year by setting up message boxes, a common feature of many of the Reggio classrooms. I attached one box for each child and both teachers to the wall and put their names on them, but not alphabetically. I let the children "invent" the use of these boxes. They quickly began to send pictures to one another, and I encouraged this practice. (Had they begun to use the boxes as personal storage spaces, I would have discussed with them other possible uses and guided them to the idea of message boxes.) I tape-recorded and transcribed a discussion with the children about the word *communication*. I took photographs of them communicating in various ways and made my first panel, a very simple one, with a transcript of their communication conversation together with six large photographs of some of the children involved in activities that commonly took place in my room.

In the meantime, every once in a while we would sit in front of the message boxes, and individual children would have the opportunity to show some of their messages to the group. These meetings were sometimes long, but they served several important purposes. First, by holding them, the children automatically knew that I thought the pictures and notes they sent to one another were an important part of their lives. Second, it gave me the opportunity to stress some basic requirements in sending messages: that the message had to say for whom the message was intended so the receiver knew it was especially for him or her and that the sender had to write his or her own name on it so the receiver could tell who had taken the time to make the message.

These group moments also accomplished some other goals. Children saw a wide range of types of messages, which broadened the possibilities for each individual of *how* one could make a message. They were particularly captured by some of the more beautiful designs, and in these cases I always highlighted the care the sender had taken in making the design. Whenever a child actually *wrote* a message to another child, I made sure that I pointed it out to the group. Since my first graders were learning to read and write, I wanted to showcase any message that used writing as a communication tool. I wanted the children to see the message boxes as an avenue for communication, but I did not want to be too authoritarian by restricting messages to only written messages because I wanted them to know we can communicate in many different ways, so I followed their lead on the types of messages they were most comfortable sending.

Another issue that came up in the group message meetings had to do with children who had not yet received messages. Inevitably, someone would lament their lack of messages. I did not avoid this situation since I anticipated it would come up, nor did I try to "protect" the child who had no messages. I would point out to the class that so-and-so was sad because she or he had not yet received anything. The other children contributed to my observations by pointing out that if you do not send messages, you might not get any. One child explained, "If you give messages, you can get more, and that's how I got that one from Alex and Nick and Michael because I was sending 'em messages from the beginning of the year." Those who had not received messages quickly responded in various ways, announcing, "I want to write a message, 'cause then someone will write me back," or "I'll take a message from anyone in this class." Later, I had another discussion with the children. I reminded them of our earlier conversation about communication and asked them whether giving and getting messages was a way of communicating:

> "Yes, because you're communicating with someone who sent it."
> "You're communicating by talking if you write something."

"Like when Lucy got hurt and Ami sent her a note, she said that she felt sorry and she asked if Lucy felt better."

"You could communicate anytime: if you're at messages, if you're at drawing, if you're playing a game and someone tells you how to play it or helps you. You could communicate at meeting, in sign language, or maybe just talking to each other in the middle of a game."

Then I asked the children what they liked better, sending messages or getting messages?

"Getting them, because I feel happy and thankful."

"Giving, because when you give messages, you get messages."

"I like sending messages because when I give then people will like it and then they'll send some to me and I'll feel good and then I'll meet new friends and I'll have more friends." [This comment was from a child who was new to the school and who had left a group of special friends at his old school.]

"I like both. (1) For having, because that means that they like me and I *know* that they like me. And (2) for giving, so the other people that I sended to, so they know that *I* like *them*."

Once again, I made a panel using this discussion (which was edited for the sake of space). This time I used photographs of one child making a message for another child. A third panel was eventually made onto which I attached various examples of messages children were sending.

## Another Step: The Butterfly Project

I think that one of the major changes in my teaching is a primarily internal one. Although I believe that I was a child-centered teacher before I went to Reggio and that I listened closely to children, upon my return, I found myself automatically hearing so much more of what they said, and I was also so much more interested in pursuing what they said. In fact, I quickly found that I was following up on too many things. This forced me to spread myself too thin and inevitably minimized the depth with which I could pursue a topic. I realize that I must choose very carefully because I cannot do everything at once. I have to approach my own development as a teacher slowly and think of taking baby steps so I will be able to incorporate aspects of Reggio gradually into my first grade classroom.

An example of a baby step that I took with my first group of post-Reggio children involved challenging not just the children in new ways but myself and my teaching style in new ways as well.

One of my students came up to me during Choice Time one day and asked whether she could draw a butterfly. I happened to have a book of beautiful photographs of butterflies, so I gave it to her to look through, to find one she wanted to draw. (Previously, I would have given her a piece of paper and a pencil and pretty much left it at that.) I want to emphasize that I gave her the book *not* because I wanted her to *copy* the butterfly *exactly* but because I wanted her to have a realistic point of reference from which to start her drawing. I wanted to challenge the image of a butterfly that most young children have in their heads, an image that is typically anthropomorphic, having a face with eyes and a smiling mouth, in addition to wings and antennae. She promptly chose one she liked and sat down to draw but not copy it. This child happened to be a keen observer, and she drew a breathtaking butterfly.

Her work attracted the attention of some other children in the group who also became interested in drawing butterflies. However, with all of these children who then asked to "do a butterfly," I gained the courage to push them in their observations, point out the angle of a line of a wing, tell them that they had made a good first try, and support them closely as they made second and third tries, slowly constructing a butterfly that in all cases looked far more sophisticated than what most children had produced in my classes in the past. This was not because I had an unusually gifted group of children that year but rather because I knew a little bit more about how to help them look and see, and I was better able to help them calmly draw and redraw until the product was finished.

The project continued when the child took his or her drawing and traced it onto a transparency and then used an overhead projector to project the image onto the wall. Now many times bigger than the original, the child traced her own work one more time, making a poster-sized butterfly that was easy to paint. This entire process took as much time as each child desired. Some children, once they reached the painting stage, painted for several days in a row until they were finished. Others worked in spurts, often asking, "Can I take a break from my butterfly today?" I found that it was important to respect and follow the rhythms of each child, because in doing so, they seemed to produce their best work. In some cases, I sometimes had to push certain children to work for longer periods of time, but, in general, the children monitored themselves nicely without much input from me.

Sometimes, when I talk with colleagues about how Reggio educators guide children in their work much in the way I have described, I am asked whether we should not just let children explore and be free when they draw and paint. One thing I learned when I was in Reggio is that children *like* to show what they know. Drawing a butterfly, for example, is a graphic representation of something they know, something they have contact with. But children *most* like to show what they know when they can do it well, and they often become frustrated when they feel less than capable. They want to have skill with a pencil or a paintbrush, just as they want to have skill with the alphabet and numbers. (It should be noted that children in

Reggio have a long experience in exploring materials with the guided support of adults and other children.) And just as we adults guide them in acquiring skills in reading and math, I am finding that giving them skills in other areas can be just as rewarding for both them and me. And I think that when children feel comfortable enough and supported enough to spend a good portion of time (several hours over several days) drawing a butterfly, they learn a great many things. They learn to be better observers; they learn some things about the way butterflies look that they never knew before; they learn that to persevere has its rewards; they learn that finishing something faster than everyone does not always mean better or smarter.

As a teacher, I have learned that to guide children more closely is OK; I have learned that to expect more from them is OK; and I have also learned that the product *is* important, because it is *part* of the process, and it tells us something about the process.

I saved all the children's first, second, and third tries, I kept the transparency, and I tried to photograph each child as they traced from the overhead and also as they painted. Each butterfly was eventually cut out and placed high up on the wall outside the classroom. Included were the small original drawing, the transparency, and one or two photographs. This documentation highlighted the process for those who were not present, as well as serving as a memory for those who were.

## FINAL REFLECTIONS

I cannot say that the butterfly work is a pure example of a Reggio project. It involved some principles of the Reggio philosophy in terms of expecting more from children, learning to support children, finding creative outlets for children to express knowledge, and including some documentation in the display. The paintings were *not* part of a larger study of butterflies or insects. I did not engage children in conversations about butterflies, nor did I record their spontaneous comments while they were working. I did not have children represent butterflies in more than one medium (e.g., with wire or clay). I wish that I had, but that would have included too many pieces for me to juggle at that time. And this is what I mean when I refer to taking baby steps. Having carried out this butterfly project, I can now reflect on what I did and how I might expand it or alter it in the future in order to provide more opportunities for children to express what they know, come into contact with some of their own faulty notions perhaps, and create situations where children can construct knowledge for themselves.

The next step for me is to embed an experience such as the butterfly painting within a larger exploration of a topic. I believe that this will provide all of us, children and teachers, with a richer experience. Another challenge for me will be to let a project emerge and unfold, based on what I determine to be some issues the children need to grapple with. Carlina Rinaldi always pointed out to me that this can be hard to do because it involves living side by side with uncertainty. When a project is not preplanned because we are letting the curriculum emerge *with* the children and based on our observations of their understandings, misunderstandings, curiosities, doubts, and puzzlements, it, by definition, involves a level of uncertainty on the part of the teacher. But I am sure that what *can* come from this uncertainty is a richness of experience that we could never plan or predict ahead of time and that can infuse the classroom with a special excitement and focus and sense of purpose.

# 6

# *Education as Collaboration*
## Learning from and Building on
## Dewey, Vygotsky, and Piaget

*Baji Rankin*
Teacher, Trudy's Community School, Taos, New Mexico

In 1989–90 I conducted a 9-month study investigating the principles that lie behind curriculum development in the city-run schools for young children in Reggio Emilia. I wanted to find out, if I could, what were the central operating principles, the core aspects, of the Reggio philosophy that make possible such an integrated approach to education that so effectively engages the creativity of young children. To accomplish this, I hoped to collaborate with the Reggio educators and follow one project all the way through in order to understand how a project begins, develops, and concludes.

The project I was invited to observe and participate in was the Dinosaur Project at the Anna Frank School. This was a 4-month adventure with thirteen 5- and 6-year-old children; the *atelierista* of the Anna Frank School, Roberta Badodi; the *pedagogista* for the school, Carlina Rinaldi; and me. The choice to study dinosaurs— tentative and exploratory at the beginning—was made by Roberta, Carlina, and the two coteachers of the 5-year-old classroom after observing children's intense interest in the topic.

I was present at the school every day during those 4 months with the children as we studied dinosaurs in a variety of ways. In the first several days we investigated—using drawing, discussion, and clay sculpture—what children knew, did not know, and wanted to know about dinosaurs. By reading the transcripts of the first discussions, the teachers discovered that the children were curious about four major areas about dinosaurs: their origin and disappearance, their size and shape, their physical and moral characteristics, and their lifestyles and habits. The major interest of the children centered around the size and shape of dinosaurs; therefore, the project evolved in this direction.

Although space does not permit a comprehensive discussion of that project here (see Rankin, 1992, 1993, & 1995 for more information and details on this project), I have included several examples within this chapter to illustrate how collaboration was the underlying principle of this project and how Roberta used it to facilitate and stimulate learning.

During that same period, besides observing and analyzing the children's learning, I also worked with Roberta and Carlina discussing, evaluating, and planning the project as we participated together in a process of reflecting on the children's learning and deciding what to do next. I observed and investigated the adults' behavior to understand how the educators worked with each other. During these conversations, I shared my ongoing and developing thoughts and insights with Carlina and Roberta as I also listened and searched out the meaning these two adults gave to their own behavior and the children's behavior. It was an amazing opportunity to learn firsthand how the Reggio philosophy is actually put into practice.

I kept a record of these encounters, and after analyzing my observations, conversations, and interviews—looking at the social relationships among educators, between them and children, and among children—I ultimately concluded that collaboration was the central operating principle, the core category of the Dinosaur Project around which all other aspects were integrated. It was not only the glue that bound together everything that happened in the Dinosaur Project; it is also the glue that binds together the philosophy of the Reggio Emilia schools.

It is important to note that parent participation, central to the Reggio experience, was also a major aspect of this project. However, since it was outside the scope of my study, I do not focus on it here.

This chapter is intended to illuminate the educational theory of Reggio Emilia—bringing to light some of the principles and details that characterize the vital collaborative process between educators and children—and also to show how collaboration as defined here is related, in turn, to certain ideas set forth by three educational philosophers: John Dewey, Lev Vygotsky, and Jean Piaget.

## WHAT IS COLLABORATION?

Collaboration in the context of curriculum development is a particular type of social interaction. It is defined as the mutual guiding of the educational process by participants. This mutuality includes a sense of reciprocity and community among participants in which different partners take the lead at different times and influence each other in a reciprocal process. All participants do their best to remain open to something new that might happen as the work progresses. Simultaneously all participants also influence the direction and timing of the investigation. Collaboration is seen as a system of social relationships whereby children and adults, including both educators and parents, coordinate their action and restructure their thinking and resources in relation to each other. It includes the sharing of power and resources of children and educators, and it places all participants together in a joint planning process (Kagan, 1991). As a result, people become interdependent, social relations deepen, and new structures emerge.

## PHILOSOPHICAL FOUNDATIONS SUPPORTING THE CONCEPT OF EDUCATION THROUGH COLLABORATION

The idea of education based on collaboration has roots in the works of three renowned theorists: John Dewey, Lev Vygotsky, and Jean Piaget. Each of these theorists has greatly influenced early childhood education in both the United States and Reggio Emilia, yet in my experience and observations, Reggio educators have taken the concept of collaboration further than any of these theorists did by themselves. The focus of this chapter is twofold: (a) to examine the impact of these theorists on theory and practice in Reggio Emilia and (b) to investigate how Reggio educators have extended the thinking of these three theorists.

## Philosophical Contributions of John Dewey: Points of Agreement

Dewey views learning as "a continuing reconstruction of experience" (1959b, p. 27). Education is a process of "continual reorganizing, reconstructing, transforming" (1966, p. 50). Distinct from traditional education, in which teaching is conceived as a "pouring in" (1966, p. 38) and learning as "passive absorption" (1966, p. 38), Dewey sees education as being active and constructive. This kind of education has a social direction through "a joint activity" (1966, p. 39) within which people consciously refer to each other's use of materials, tools, ideas, capacities, and applications.

Dewey's view of education as continual growth in a social direction is similar to the view held by Reggio educators. Loris Malaguzzi, founder of the Reggio schools and their director for 25 years, lists the basic values of the approach in Reggio as including "interactive and constructivist aspects, the intensity of relationships, the spirit of cooperation, and individual and collective effort in doing research" (1993b, p. 59). He writes about children's learning:

> In my view, relationships and learning coincide within an active process of education. They come together through the expectations and skills of children, the professional competence of adults, and more generally, the educational process.
>
> We must embody in our practice, therefore, reflections on a delicate and decisive point: *What children learn does not follow as an automatic result from what is taught. Rather, it is in large part due to the children's own doing, as a consequence of their activities and our resources.* (1993b, p. 59)

Similar to Dewey, Reggio educators see learning as active and constructive. Children and adults participate in a two-way collaborative process among and between themselves.

> Active exploration and creative production by educators and children proceed without complete certainty but with a shared representation of the point of destination, the ultimate goal. What is most appreciated all along is the shared sense of satisfaction and accomplishment as individuals and as a group. (Malaguzzi, 1993a, p. 9)

Dewey values uncertainty and the unknown. "All thinking is research" (1966, p. 148); a thought is creative because it leaves the known and ventures into the unknown. It is "an incursion into the novel" (1966, p. 158). Similarly, Rinaldi clarifies that "the process of acquiring knowledge is the same process as that of creativity" (1992, p. 11). Knowledge is *created* through active inquiry.

Growth for both the child and the adult is important to Dewey and Reggio educators. As children investigate and reflect on their experiences, they are growing toward a more expanded and organized view of these experiences as well as gaining understanding of how their investigations relate to diverse subject matter (Dewey, 1959a). Adults are growing in other ways—in openness of mind, curiosity, and responsiveness (Dewey, 1966).

In Reggio during the Dinosaur Project, for example, Roberta continually listened to and observed the children, adapting and modifying her tentative plans on the basis of the children's thoughts, ideas, and behaviors. When the project started, Roberta did not know how—or whether—it would unfold. Before she suggested specific ideas to the children, she worked with them three days, listening to their ideas and discussing various possibilities with the children and her colleagues. Even when she did introduce ideas, she did this tentatively, searching for ideas of the children to guide the activity. Roberta observed herself; she reflected on her behavior with other people; she was open to learning about herself as a teacher.

Learning is a reciprocal and collaborative process for both Dewey and Reggio educators. During a project, no one person knows exactly how things will turn out or where they will go. Collaborative exploration in a social setting takes place where all participants influence the direction, timing, and outcome of the investigation. In such a setting, "doubt and amazement are welcome factors in a deductive method similar to the one used by a detective, . . . where the probable and the possible are assigned a place" (Rinaldi, 1992, p. 5).

Reggio educators particularly emphasize the mutuality of learning. The adult educates the child and the child educates the adult as well.

> "To educate" means additionally and above all "to be educated" through relationships with children in the same way one is educated through relationships with adults. . . .
> Children thus become sources of enrichment, discovery, the future, and openness to different points of view that will all contribute to our understanding. This is because, in our view, there is no possibility to acquire knowledge, understanding, and growth without openness to others. It is usually said that the adult educates the child, but it is necessary to add that also the child educates the adult. In fact, there is no true educational act where there is no reciprocal exchange. (Rinaldi, 1992, pp. 6–7)

This does not mean that children and educators learn the same things from each other. Similar to Dewey's thinking, the educator in Reggio Emilia has a specific role that is informed by his or her prior experience and knowledge. For instance, in Reggio Emilia, the educator has responsibility for tasks that are beyond the capacities of young children. These include conducting research, sustaining the ongoing social and cognitive processes among children, and calling attention to the ideas of particular children.

When educators in Reggio Emilia speak about education as self- and social construction, they refer to adults as well as to children. Malaguzzi (1992) discusses the importance of teachers being open to change and reconstruction of themselves as teachers. Rinaldi (1992) clarifies that the qualities inherent in their image of the child apply to adults as well: "Therefore, reflecting on the identity and rights of children means to reflect on the identity and the rights of men and women, regardless of age" (p. 4). Rinaldi states that in discussing the transcripts of children's work, educators come to question themselves, internally, and question each other in the group. This is similar to how children question themselves and each other. This disposition on the part of Reggio educators to question themselves and then to change their interactions with children based on their reflections is behavior that is valued and encouraged (Rinaldi, 1992, 1993a) and central to their concept of emergent curriculum.

An example of this reflective and flexible disposition among educators took place during the "measuring and drawing phase" of the Dinosaur Project when six children wanted to draw a life-size dinosaur. Roberta and I did not know how to present a particular problematic situation to the children and were discussing it among ourselves. Federico, a child who was deeply engaged in the process, walked the length of the school, insisting on finding out when the project would start. Roberta turned him away two times, sending him back to the classroom so that we as educators could continue talking. At his third request, Roberta changed tactics and invited him in to help solve the problem. It was Federico's thinking that led to the solution of the problem. While collaboration among educators at first blocked the participation of Federico, it was Roberta's openness to his participation that ultimately resolved the situation.

Dewey advocated teachers' learning about themselves as well:

> The teacher is not in the school to impose certain ideas or form certain habits in the child, but is there as a member of the community to select influences which shall affect the child and to assist him in properly responding to these influences. (1959b, p. 24)

This statement indicates the value Dewey places on teachers being responsive and observant. He also argues against focusing conscious attention on drawing rigid distinctions between seeing the teacher as only a teacher and the student as only a learner:

In such shared activity, the teacher is a learner, and the learner is, without knowing it, a teacher—and upon the whole, the less consciousness there is on either side, of either giving or receiving instruction, the better. (1966, p. 160)

What is important to both Dewey and Reggio educators is that children and adults learn from each other. The educators in Reggio Emilia, as documented in the Dinosaur Project, work explicitly on being aware of this process of mutual exchange and how they can learn from children.

## Further Development of Deweyan Ideas in Reggio Emilia

Although there seems to be basic philosophical agreement between Dewey and Reggio educators on the importance of collaboration among educators, I believe Reggio educators have extended Dewey's framework in developing the organizational structures that sustain the implementation of these principles. In Reggio, teaching in a team of coteachers is seen as fundamental. It is "the foundation for any form of collegiality" (Rinaldi, 1992, p. 9). This team in each classroom is the starting point for collaboration on all levels between and among educators, children, and parents. Each school is managed by the group of staff that works at the school. There is no director; each staffperson takes particular responsibility for some of the specific tasks that need to be done. This organizational structure in Reggio promotes collaborative exchange among participants in which educators reflect, rethink, restructure, and even transform their experiences. "When colleagues work closely together and share common problems, this facilitates the alignment of behaviors and a modification of personal theories. We have always tried to encourage this" (Malaguzzi, 1993b, p. 82).

The Dewey School, though promoting widespread discussion among all participants (Mayhew & Edwards, 1936), distinguished between assistants and teachers. "Younger and less experienced teachers" served as assistants (p. 370). Once the school reached a certain size, it had "heads" of departments who were primarily responsible for certain aspects of the work.

Although both Dewey and Reggio educators give attention to education as a two-way collaborative process among and between children and adults, Reggio educators have developed an organizational structure that gives more emphasis and direct attention to adult learning and growth than Dewey did. In Reggio, this structure provides their practice of coteaching with the necessary supports to make that successful. This includes, for example, time and space to work together and the resources of a *pedagogista* who can support communication processes.

The use of audio- and videotape recorders, tools that were not available to Dewey 100 years ago, has become a common, greatly valued practice in Reggio Emilia. Transcripts of the recorded dialogues give the teachers the opportunity to study not only the children's tentative hypotheses but also their own—and their colleagues'—interactions with the children. This process among the adults is considered as valuable as the discussions among the children. "The teachers' reflections then modify, at times radically, their thoughts and hypotheses about the children, and, even more importantly, their interactions with the children" (Rinaldi, 1993a, p. 106).

While Dewey promotes the idea of collaboration where all participants grow and change, Reggio educators have taken this concept further in both theory and practice. Reggio educators promote an explicit, conscious investigation of how children and teachers learn from each other.

Presently, Dewey's work and influence in contemporary U.S. programs are associated with the concept of cooperative exchange that helps the teacher facilitate social interaction among the children (Bredekamp, 1987; Weber, 1970, pp. 8, 9). This corresponds to cooperation in which interaction is grounded in personal relationships (Kagan, 1991). Different from this cooperative social interaction, in Reggio Emilia collaborative learning between adults and children is a central principle in the philosophy of the schools and the practice I observed. In collaboration there is intense joint planning and sharing of power and authority (Kagan, 1991). While in the United States it is more likely that the teacher facilitates cooperative social interaction among the children, in Reggio Emilia the teacher more often participates in a collaborative learning process in which cognitive conflict is central to the learning.

## Philosophical Contributions of Lev Vygotsky

Vygotsky's ideas (1978, 1987) are also important to Reggio educators in the area of collaboration. Both approaches recognize the importance of learning taking place in the social realm and emphasize the active role of adults (and children) in the learning process of others. "For our part in Reggio, Vygotsky's approach is in tune with the way we see the dilemma of teaching and learning and the ecological way one can reach knowledge" (Malaguzzi, 1993b, p. 80).

To Reggio educators (Filippini, 1990; Malaguzzi, 1993b), Vygotsky's concept of the zone of proximal development—the area that lies between the actual and the potential level of development—is important in opening up many rich possibilities for interactions and collaboration among adults and children. While pointing out that this is a delicate situation because it could cause teachers to regress to old ideas of teaching that are adult centered and instruction oriented, Malaguzzi (1993b) maintains that where there is a very small gap between what the child and adult see and where the child shows an "expectation and readiness to make the jump" (p. 80), the adult has an important role:

In such a situation, the adult can and must loan to the children his judgment and knowledge. But it is a loan with a condition, namely, that the child will repay. . . . Vygotsky's suggestion maintains its value and legitimates broad interventions by teachers. (p. 80)

Rinaldi (1993b) adds to this by pointing out that the role of adults,

then, is to create contexts which stimulate research and thus learning, to encourage the ability to learn that children already possess, both individually and in groups. Only when the children's resources become weak or when they need extra support can adults legitimately offer their "loan of knowledge" to children. And these loans will be promptly repaid, enriched and made more precious by the experience that the children go through. (p. 3)

Both Vygotsky and educators from Reggio Emilia view the social realm and social interaction as a place for the coconstruction of understanding among participants. Both give great value to learning in a social setting; both see a correspondence between cognitive and social processes.

In Vygotsky's (1978) view, learning in a social setting takes place when a partner more skilled interacts with a partner less skilled. For Vygotsky, social guidance and modeling are needed from the more skilled partner, but Reggio educators have developed a different view. Incorporating Piaget's insights, as well, they believe that even a child with less skills than his or her partner or with "incorrect models" (Rinaldi, 1992, p. 13) has the power to promote learning in a social setting. This takes place by provoking a second child—or even causing the first child—to question his or her thinking or examine his or her errors.

In the Dinosaur Project, Roberta took full advantage of Vygotsky's view of teaching and learning in a social situation. She interacted with the children in a way that neither provided solutions nor simply left them to their own resources. Rather, at times she made "loans," helping children do what they could not quite do by themselves. She had the belief and the confidence that children, with her "loans," would come up with their own ways to define, set up, and solve the problems.

For example, Tommi got stuck in reproducing on paper, in small scale, the 27 × 9-meter rectangle the group had constructed in the sports field a few days before. He made two 27-dot lines and was very surprised to see they were of unequal length. He did not know how to proceed. Roberta made a few suggestions to help him keep going: "You could turn your paper over" and, later, "You could get a new piece of paper." While this advice helped sustain him during a difficult period, what was more effective was interaction with Federico, Tommi's peer working alongside him. Federico had solved the problem for himself and was able to give Tommi some information that enabled him to resolve the problem.

*Federico:*    Because, I think, here you made them closer together—
yeah, here you made them too close because, look here,
they are all messed up here. And look how they are here
[comparing the top and bottom lines].

Roberta's role was to give information to Tommi and provide the opportunity for Federico and Tommi to interact.

Roberta had the skills to support the children within their own ways of thinking. Examples include listening attentively; waiting, searching for ideas of individual children that could be a focal point for group discussion; helping the children remember what they did, thought, and decided; offering ideas and information to the children; and intervening enough to keep the social and cognitive processes going without stepping outside of the children's way of thinking. In their role as group members, teachers contribute to the learning process, as do children. They help shape it and influence it by valuing certain questions and focusing attention.

For example, in the Dinosaur Project when a group of 12 children were discussing how to construct a large dinosaur, they began by talking about different kinds of materials they could use. Several minutes into the discussion, one child said, "Well, the thing to think about the most is what dinosaur to make—which dinosaur." Roberta responded by calling attention to Francesco's idea. She said, "It's true. We know many dinosaurs, and maybe the first thing to do is to understand which one we want to make. Why is that important to you, Francesco?" In this exchange, Roberta reinforced Francesco's idea and invited him to talk more about it, which he did. Roberta thought that this idea was important and that it could lead to further cognitive and social processes.

## *Philosophical Contributions of Jean Piaget*

Educators in Reggio Emilia have had a complex relationship with the research and theories of Piaget: they have benefited from his work and have also tried to "overturn" his theories (Malaguzzi, 1993b).

*Points of Disagreement.*    Malaguzzi (1993b) summarizes some of the major differences between Piaget's work and Reggio Emilia's:[*]

---

[*] From "History, Ideas, and Basic Philosophy," by Loris Malaguzzi, 1993, in *The Hundred Languages of Children: The Reggio Emilia Approach to Early Childhood Education,* ed. C. P. Edwards, L. Gandini, and G. Forman (pp. 76–77), Norwood, NJ: Ablex. Copyright 1993 by Ablex. Reprinted by permission.

Now we can see clearly how Piaget's constructivism isolates the child. As a result we look critically at these aspects: the undervaluation of the adult's role in promoting cognitive development; the marginal attention to social interaction and to memory (as opposed to inference); the distance interposed between thought and language (Vygotsky criticized this, and Piaget, 1962, responded); the lock-step linearity of development in constructivism; the way that cognitive, affective, and moral development are treated as separate, parallel tracks; the over-emphasis on structured stages, egocentrism, and classificatory skills; the lack of recognition for partial competencies; the overwhelming importance given to logico-mathematical thought; and the overuse of paradigms from the biological and physical sciences. After making all of these criticisms, however, we must go on to note that many constructivists today have turned their attention to the role of social interaction in cognitive development. (pp. 76–77)

Within the perspective used in Reggio Emilia that the school is a system of social relationships where all participants interact as "inseparable and integrated subjects of education" (Rinaldi, 1992, p. 8), Malaguzzi's view of Piaget's constructivism—that it isolates the child—makes sense. However, it is important to remember that Piaget was a psychologist looking at the cognitive development of individuals. He was not looking at a system of education. When Reggio educators understood that Piaget's "main goal was to trace the genesis of universal invariant structures" (Malaguzzi, 1993b, p. 76), they became more interested in him.

*Points of Agreement.*    Although these points of disagreement between the philosophy of Reggio educators and that of Piaget exist, there are also many insights contributed by him concerning the role of collaboration that are valued in Reggio Emilia. Reggio educators have retained the necessary elements of constructivism—endogenous reconstruction and reflective abstraction—while simultaneously using Vygotsky's perspective on the importance of learning in a social setting (Forman, 1992a).

In small-group work, for example, like Piaget, Reggio educators value ideational conflicts and exchanges of different points of view. They maintain that the cognitive conflict such disagreements provoke not only pushes children to build a higher order of thought but also provides the basis for learning within the social setting.

The concept of error plays a crucial and central role in the theory and practice of Reggio in a way that is close to the views of Piaget and later constructivist educators. Here error and conflict are seen as a way of moving forward. Error takes on a very different meaning than it does in traditional education.

Error, for example, can generate important conflicts. We should keep in mind that conflict seems essential in order for a situation to produce structure, as it is not necessary that an answer be correct. Reasoning can also be corrected through a comparison of incorrect models and through the examination of one's own errors as well as those of one's peers. (Rinaldi, 1992, pp. 12–13)

In Reggio, collaboration in small groups of children provides an essential forum for examining different and conflicting views, including mistakes. The Dinosaur Project illustrates using Piaget's thinking during the measuring and drawing phase. Roberta had worked with the girls and then, on a separate occasion, the boys. The two groups developed different tactics. The three girls had constructed and drawn the 27 × 9-unit rectangle focusing on the three horizontal lines that were in the original drawing, marking the height of the dinosaur at 3, 6, and 9 meters (see Figure 6–1). The boys, on the other hand, had focused on the length of the body parts, constructing vertical lines that measured the length of the head, neck, body, and tail (see Figure 6–2). Roberta then brought both groups together and asked the children to tell each other what they had done, thus provoking exchange of conflicting points of view. Roberta's role was to bring out and clarify the children's different hypotheses and to encourage them to discuss their ideas. This activity exemplifies Piaget's concept of cognitive conflict within individual children, as well as Vygotsky's concept of the zone of proximal development where children learn from each other—and from adults—in a social setting.

**FIGURE 6–1**
The three girls focused their attention on the horizontal lines that were in the original drawing. They reproduced these lines on graph paper, marking the height of the dinosaur.

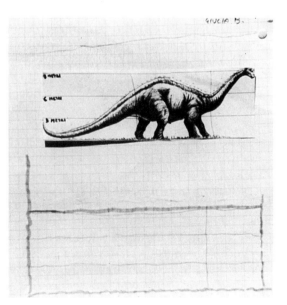

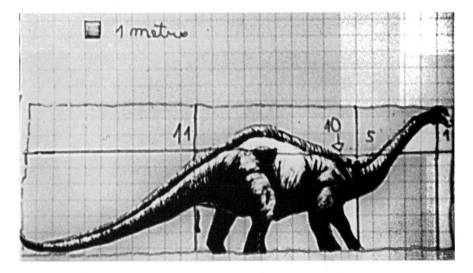

**FIGURE 6–2**
The boys were most interested in the length of the body parts. They drew vertical lines to figure out the length of the tail, body, neck, and head.

## SUMMARY

For more than 30 years, the educators in Reggio Emilia have viewed learning as a collaborative, reciprocal process best experienced through socialization in small groups. In these groups, everyone, both children and adults, expresses themselves and exchanges experiences with others. Growth occurs through mutual guidance, support, conflict, error, and an exchange of different points of view.

This collaborative approach honors Dewey's idea that learning is a two-way reciprocal process. It is also influenced by Vygotsky's perspective emphasizing the use of guidance and modeling in a social setting and by Piaget's concepts concerning the value of argument and error as a means of constructing knowledge. It has been strengthened by ongoing reflections Reggio educators continually make on their own experiences (see Malaguzzi, 1993b).

In Reggio, where teachers are open to the unexpected, power and resources are shared between children and adults as they tell each other what they think and know. Reggio educators have taken collaborative learning, a concept that Dewey wrote about, and expanded it by establishing and promoting reciprocal relationships between adults and children. This strong commitment to collaboration—to mutual learning—has made possible a system of education in which the educators:

❑ have a clear image of the child as resourceful, competent, and active;

❑ have constructed a working concept of emergent curriculum that is based on their image of the competent, resourceful child and their view of collaborative learning;

❑ promote learning as a two-way collaborative process in which children and teachers learn from each other and share resources as the system evolves and grows;

❑ have retained the tenets of constructivism—cognitive conflict, reflective abstraction, and endogenous reconstruction—while simultaneously incorporating Vygotsky's perspective on the importance of learning in a social setting;

❑ perceive and use mistakes of children and adults as a challenge and opportunity for new growth;

❑ have developed a continuity between theory and practice in which theory and practice are interactive and in constant creation and in which theory serves to improve practice;

❑ promote learning as an individual process and a social process;

❑ have developed an organizational structure and use educational tools that support child and adult learning; and

❑ have developed the concept of self- and social constructivism to define their reflective practice.

This chapter has discussed some philosophical foundations set forth by Dewey, Vygotsky, and Piaget that support the idea of collaboration as an important aspect of education and has illustrated how collaboration forms the foundation for the philosophy embraced by the schools for young children in Reggio Emilia.

The contributions of these men are of undoubted value, but what is taking place in the schools of Reggio Emilia is of greater value still. Reggio educators have developed ways to encourage a disposition for collaboration, exploration, and inquiry as these schools have turned theory into practice and practice into theory. As the Reggio experience demonstrates that collaboration is the essential foundation for learning, I hope their success will inspire us to the challenges and joys of collaboration as well.

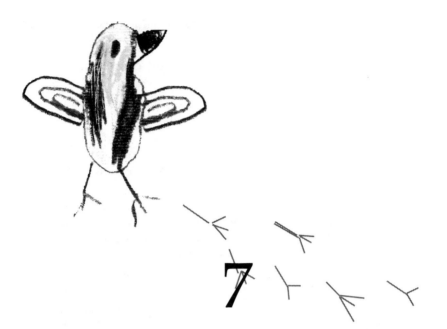

# 7

# *Conversations with Children*

*Louise Boyd Cadwell*
*Atelierista*/Consultant, College School, Webster Groves, Missouri

*Brenda Varel Fyfe*
Professor of Education, Webster University, St. Louis, Missouri

A network of teachers from several schools in St. Louis, Missouri, has been working together for 3 years to study the principles and practices of the Reggio Emilia Approach. The content of this chapter is drawn from our work with these teachers and reflections on our individual and collective experiences. We wish to express our thanks to all of the teachers, parents, and administrators with whom we collaborated in this learning process and especially to Jan Phillips, director of the College School, a private and independent school in Webster Groves, Missouri, who took the administrative lead in codirecting this project with us. And, of course, we are indebted to all of the Italian educators who have been and continue to be our friends, teachers, and colleagues.

We have chosen to focus on one particular area of our learning that has been strongly influenced by the Reggio Emilia Approach—dialogue with children. Louise begins by reflecting on what she learned as an intern for 1 year in Reggio Emilia and then practiced and further developed through her work in St. Louis. She identifies potential barriers and conditions that affect teachers' abilities to facilitate and analyze dialogues with children. This discussion is followed by a set of guidelines for facilitating good conversations.

To illustrate the process of analyzing dialogues and using them to inform emergent curriculum, we have chosen to share a synopsis of a meeting among a team of four educators who came together to study the transcripts of dialogues that had been facilitated by Louise. Brenda describes this meeting and the curriculum planning that emerged from the study of children's words. This is followed by her analysis of the process of planning for emergent curriculum and the professional development benefits for teachers who collaborate in this kind of work.

## CONVERSATIONS WITH CHILDREN

A key component of the work in the Reggio Emilia preschools is dialogue—serious talk with children about their ideas about something of importance. The group of children can be large (the whole class), medium (around 10 to 15), or small (around four to six). Teachers also have conversations with pairs of children or one child at a time. The idea every time is to explore the children's ideas.

The teacher's role is to ask good, open-ended questions that stimulate children's thinking and provoke discussion—to facilitate, orchestrate, and gently guide so that the conversation does not stray too far from the subject, so that every child has a chance to participate, so that children consider the matter at hand with all their critical and creative thinking skills. The teacher should not fish for right answers or impart information. Rather, the teacher's role is to extend and deepen the children's thinking. This approach is a departure from the traditional idea of the teacher's role.

The motivation for placing these conversations at the center of the curriculum is to enable children to develop their critical and creative thinking ability to its fullest capacity; to promote cooperation, interaction, and negotiation among children; and to celebrate children's natural curiosity and wonder about the world and how it works (Fyfe & Cadwell, 1993). It is also a way of taking time together, teacher and child, to focus on important aspects of life and living; to examine an experience, object, or idea closely; to wonder and search together.

Carlina Rinaldi, senior consultant to Reggio Children, said recently:

> Children are searching for the real meaning of life. We believe in their possibilities to grow. That is why we do not hurry to give them answers; instead we invite them to think about where the answers might lie. The challenge is to listen. When your child asks, 'Why is there a moon?', don't reply with a scientific answer. Ask him, 'What do you think?' He will understand that you are telling him, 'You have your own mind and your own interpretation and your ideas are important to me.' Then you and he can look for the answers, sharing the wonder, curiosity, pain—everything. It is not the answers that are important, it is the process—that you and he search together. (McLaughlin, 1995, p. 68)

We have learned from the teachers in Reggio Emilia not only how important it is to listen but also how important it is to schedule time together to carefully read and understand transcribed conversations. When studying the conversations, we need to ask, What knowledge can we say these children have? What examples can we find in this conversation of their use of intuition, conjecture, logical and creative thinking? When have they made analogies and used metaphors to communicate their ideas? How has listening to the ideas of their classmates challenged them, informed them, offered them a new way of viewing the problem? What misconceptions do they have? What can we, as adults, learn from them about the way they look at and think about this subject? What might we do next with these children and perhaps a larger group with whom we could share these initial ideas to support further learning?

In the Reggio meetings, they might also analyze the teacher's participation. Were the questions good ones? Did the teacher do a good job facilitating the conversation? What about the timing of the questions? Was she or he supporting the children enough? Did every child participate? Why? Did the teacher intervene too much or too little? In this way, with the critical support of their colleagues, the teachers become better and better facilitators of this kind of inquiry.

The educators in Reggio Emilia prepare for conversations. They devote enough time and full attention to the children and their ideas in a quiet space, giving children and teachers the respect they need. They then study the transcripts with colleagues to use children's ideas as the core of the curriculum. This is a style of working for them.

## BARRIERS

It has been difficult for teachers here to move into this process. After 3 years of working together in our network, we all have a better understanding of the difficulties we face. We have identified seven barriers to incorporating quality conversations and discussion with children into our curriculum planning and daily practice.

The first barrier is fairness and equity for teachers and children (Fyfe, 1994). Is it fair to give a small group of children this kind of focused attention? What happens to the other children? Do they feel left out? Is it fair for one teacher to have the luxury of focusing on a small group of children for 45 minutes or more? Isn't she or he supposed to be responsible for all the children? If there is no coteacher, how would this ever be possible? If there is, is it fair to leave the coteacher with the majority of the children?

Teachers must agree to differentiate their work so that one can stay with a small group, while the other monitors the rest of the class. When there is no coteacher, parent volunteers or teacher aides might be used to monitor the activity of the larger group while the teacher facilitates a small-group conversation. In some cases, teacher aides or parent volunteers might learn how to facilitate dialogue among children. The fairness issue has come to be reframed. Teachers who have experienced the power of small-group conversations are beginning to ask, Is it fair to deny children the opportunity to participate in small-group conversations? How am I ever going to know what these children are thinking if I do not take the time to really talk with them?

The second barrier is noise. It is impossible to have a quality conversation if children and teachers are distracted by the noise of a busy classroom and constant distractions of other children who interrupt. To think, listen, and discuss, children and teachers need separate, quiet spaces. These are hard to come by in early childhood settings. Some teachers have shared this problem with parents and found that together they were able to develop a fund-raising plan and designs to renovate or build new spaces that support quiet, small-group activity. Others have reorganized rooms or made arrangements to use temporarily unoccupied rooms (e.g., a resource room or lounge) or, in good weather, a secluded place outdoors.

A third barrier is expectation. Traditionally, most teachers do not expect young children to sit in a small group for a reasonable amount of time to discuss ideas and theories about the workings of the world. Teachers might think this is too much to expect of preschool children. Maybe it is even harmful to them to expect them to sit and think when they might rather play with manipulatives, blocks, or dress-ups.

Many of our colleagues have been amazed at what happens when they take the time to listen to children's ideas, seek to understand their points of view, and help children listen to each other. As a result, their former beliefs about the length of a young child's attention span change quickly.

A fourth barrier is rationale. Why do this? What value is there for children? What value for teachers? What do children and teachers learn from this kind of activity? How do you make use of this kind of information? Where do you go with it? How does it fit in with the rest of the curriculum? What happens to the skills and information teachers are supposed to teach if they are spending so much time listening to children's ideas?

Teaching is a complex activity. Emergent curriculum requires teachers to study the ideas expressed in children's conversations and actions. Most conversations are loaded with possibilities for topics or questions for further study. It is often not possible or appropriate to consider following up on every idea. Teachers must make decisions about which of these are most worthy of pursuit. This is a time when the goals and values shared by teachers and parents should be considered. It is a critical juncture for connecting our curriculum goals with children's ideas and interests.

A fifth barrier is lack of skill. It takes skill and practice to be able to lead a productive conversation with young children. It is only human to avoid situations in which one feels inept and prone to failure, but teachers need to risk failures and flops in order to learn. A sympathetic group of coworkers struggling to learn together can provide the support and modeling needed to acquire these skills.

A sixth barrier is recording what the children say. It is possible to take notes, but it is very hard to lead a conversation and take notes at the same time. A tape recorder works well, but that requires time to transcribe the tape. If there are two people, one can record, but that requires two teachers with one small group. Parent volunteers may be willing and able to assist in either taking notes or transcribing tapes.

A seventh barrier relates to the time, energy, and skill necessary for teachers to review and analyze conversations and then plan, based on this study. Finding time for this process of planning for emergent curriculum takes commitment, organization, and skill. Unless it is done, a necessary piece of the curriculum puzzle is not in place. Conversations are left behind without connection or relationship to the life of the children and teachers in the school. They become isolated events rather than critical connectors and resources for children and teachers.

Granted, these seven barriers raise complicated issues, and surmount-
ing them has not been easy or without anxiety. Clearly, what seems a relatively simple, new way to work with young children may turn out to require
teachers to rethink and change their assumptions about and expectations of
children, their way of organizing their time and style of working, their way
of developing curriculum and planning their days and activities (Fyfe, 1994).
It requires them to develop new skills and take risks, give extra time, collaborate, and critique each other. None of these changes are simple. After 3 years,
we are still struggling with some aspects of all of them, even though we have
made progress together and are committed to finding solutions.

## FACILITATING GOOD CONVERSATIONS

What have we learned through our attempts at having conversations with
children?

1. Think about appropriate questions beforehand. Try to brainstorm with colleagues first. Think about what kinds of questions would stimulate children's curiosity, provoke and challenge them to wonder and hypothesize, invent, and
   compare.
2. Arrange to have the conversation in a quiet place where neither you nor the children will be distracted.
3. Choose a group that you feel will benefit from being together
   and that will work well together for any number of reasons.
   Combining interested children with not so interested children, verbal with not so verbal, can work. Pay as careful
   attention to the group composition as the situation allows.
   Some opportunities will be more spontaneous than others. A
   group of five seems to be an ideal small-group number when
   working with 4- and 5-year-olds, but this figure may vary
   depending on the particular children.
4. Plan in advance how you will record. Some people can write
   quickly and keep up with the flow of the conversation,
   though this task is difficult. If you tape-record, be committed
   to listening and transcribing the important parts of the tape
   as soon as you can. If another teacher can be with you, one
   can lead and one can write.
5. Let children know right away that you have no interest in
   quizzing them and that you do not know all the answers,

that instead you want to wonder and search with them, that you are interested in big ideas and you know they are too.

6. Communicate through your tone of voice your wonder, your belief in the children's capabilities to think creatively and critically, your excitement at this opportunity to talk together about important ideas.

7. Use the questions you have prepared as possibilities. Remain open to the flow of the conversation. It may go in interesting directions you had not anticipated. On the other hand, guide the conversation back to the main subject if it strays too far off.

8. Be the children's memory. Every once in a while, summarize for them what has been said, using children's names, if possible. This will help them realize you are listening carefully and that their ideas are going on record. It will also help them look backward to what has been said and move forward with new ideas.

9. When the children begin to talk to each other, debate, ask each other questions, try to stay in the background as much as possible. This way the conversation begins to belong to them, they become more invested, and they begin to learn to discuss among themselves without intervention.

10. Enjoy the conversation! Laugh together. Be amazed at their perspectives. Share some of yours.

11. Use the conversation. Share some of the things that were said that day or the next with the whole group of children. Use it again with the same group or a different group. Ask children to expand on their ideas, critique their ideas, draw their ideas, paint or sculpt their ideas—translate and transform them into different languages. Analyze the children's ideas with your colleagues to decide what to do next—further questions, further exploration, work with drawing or sculptural materials.

12. Children and adults need time and experience with this way of being together. Most children need time to understand what this is all about—that you really are serious about wanting them to think and tell you and the other children what they think and that you have high expectations of them.

13. As adults, be brave enough to critique each other's conversations with children. It will help you gain skill and confidence.

## ANALYZING CONVERSATIONS IN ORDER TO PLAN FOR EMERGENT CURRICULUM

Planning for emergent curriculum is based on the ongoing observations and study of children. The study of group conversations can reveal children's curiosity; their understanding of the dimensions and relations of complex situations; their ability to create analogies, metaphors, anthropomorphic meanings, and realistically logical meanings. Our image of the child is built on this understanding of young children's capacity. If we underestimate it, our curriculum plans will fail to engage and challenge them.

Group conversations can provide a great deal of information about questions, concerns, and ideas that could be the focus of further investigation or exploration. When teachers understand these ideas, they are better able to think of ways to provoke children to dig a little deeper or rethink an idea. They are more likely to be able to connect with what Vygotsky (1978) calls children's zones of proximal development, the distance between the level of capacity that children might be able to exhibit on their own and their levels of potential development, attainable with the help of adults or more advanced peers. By understanding children's current schemas and everyday knowledge, teachers are in a better position to know how to offer children the appropriate kinds and amount of scaffolding to support and challenge them toward new levels of learning.

In the next section, we share what we have learned about the process of using conversations as a basis for curriculum planning. We thought this approach could best be communicated with an example. We do not claim that this is an example of how teachers in Reggio Emilia might plan for emergent curriculum. We have studied the Reggio Approach for several years and give credit to their influence on us, but our work is, and always will be, an interpretation of theirs.

A conversation with a small group of children was analyzed by a team of teachers. The conversation, with a little background on the experiences that preceded it, is presented, followed by a description of the curriculum planning meeting based on it.

The children and their teachers had already begun an investigation of the changes in the natural world that were happening all around them. They had taken walks outside to look, listen, and smell. They had collected leaves and examined them on the light table, then used tempera paint, water colors, oil crayons, markers, and black pens to do observational drawing and painting of the leaves. These experiences ensured that the children had common reference points for a group conversation. The teaching team agreed that it would be a good time for Louise to engage small groups of children in conversation about their observations, ideas, and theories related to this subject, so that we might better understand how to go forward with this project.

## A CONVERSATION ON LEAVES

### The College School, October 21, 1992

Michael—4 years, 11 months    David—4 years, 9 months
Katie—4 years, 8 months    Dan—4 years, 6 months
Meredith—4 years, 10 months    Elysia—4 years, 9 months
Devyn—5 years, 2 months    Louise Cadwell—teacher

*Louise:*    What do you see?

*Michael:*    This part is white and this is red [turning the leaf over]. I wonder why? That must be the skin [pointing to the underside]. This must be the body [pointing to the top]. The sticks, the little things going out in the leaf, must be bones!

*Katie:*    You can see parts of bones on mine, too. See the things pointing out. The red is the body. Those little stubs must be the bones.

*David:*    I found the spine!

*Katie:*    I found the spine, too.

*Meredith:*    I know that. Everybody has a spine.

*David:*    It's straight. [Feeling his spine] I can feel the bumps of it.

*Meredith:*    It's like little hills. It goes up and down.

*David:*    Don't break it [the spine], then you can't move at all.

*Katie:*    This part is like the leg [pointing to the stem].

*Louise:*    Does the leaf walk?

*Michael:*    No, it flies! I guess its flying is its walking.

*Katie:*    And it jumps and skips.

*Louise:*    Why do you think the leaves fall?

*Devyn:*    Because at the end of fall they kind of curl up to sleep, because they are tired.

*David:*    Because they are dead.

*Louise:*    When they fall off the branches, are they dead?

*Devyn:*    They are asleep, when they fall. They curl up so they don't get cold. The leaves fall down because they are asleep. They die. It's too cold for them to live.

*David:*    But the tree doesn't die. Maybe it does, but not for a very long time.

| | |
|---|---|
| *Louise:* | How could the leaves ever turn these colors? |
| *Meredith:* | They turn that way, 'cause I know why. Magic comes when it's fall. It turns the leaves to red and all colors. It gets very, very cold. |
| *Michael:* | It's like Terminator. The bad guy changed to different things, like the leaves, so nobody knows who he is. It's just like putting on Halloween costumes. Maybe somebody has the power to change the leaves. |
| *Elysia:* | The wind has the magic power. It makes the leaves change. |
| *Michael:* | I think the more the wind blows, the more the magic goes into the leaves and changes them. |
| *Dan:* | 'Cause somebody gots magic. |
| *Katie:* | I know who does it; the wind and the rain and the clouds and the sun. God does it. |
| *Michael:* | I knew something was going on. |

## *The Meeting*

Jennifer Strange and Joyce Devlin are coteachers of 4- and 5-year-old children at the College School in Webster Groves, a suburb of St. Louis. Louise Cadwell has been working with the early childhood teachers at the College School as a studio teacher (our version of the *atelierista*). Brenda Fyfe is associate professor at Webster University and has been consulting with the College School teachers in a way that could be compared to the *pedagogista* in Reggio Emilia. This team of four met one day to examine conversations that Louise had facilitated with two small groups of 4- and 5-year-olds from the school. We had 1 hour to focus on this task, and during this discussion, we tape-recorded and took notes as we talked. We have learned never to have a meeting without keeping minutes and distributing these minutes as soon as possible after each meeting. Too often great ideas come from such a meeting of the minds and then are lost or never followed through because time passed and memories are distorted. Amelia Gambetti impressed upon us the importance of approaching teacher meetings as well as parent meetings with this kind of efficiency. An agenda is set in advance, and minutes are kept to help everyone remember what was accomplished, planned, and promised.

We began this meeting by taking parts and reading the conversations out loud. We have discovered that by doing this instead of just reading silently, we can sometimes better capture the feeling, tone, and dynamics of the conversation. After the readings, we asked ourselves, What do these dialogues tell us about what children already know, think, feel, question, or wonder? We reminded ourselves to complete an exhaustive list of the children's thoughts and to be careful not to project ideas into the conversation that were not explicitly stated by the children. Only after this was accomplished would we move on to planning for emergent curriculum.

## Analyzing the Children's Conversation

We began with the question "What do children know, think, hypothesize, feel?" The conversation was lively. At first we just listed single ideas expressed by the children. Then we identified clusters of ideas or themes that connected ideas, such as the fact that both groups related leaf structure or leaf behavior to that of humans. They described leaves as asleep, dying, breathing, having bones and spines, having a body and skin. They said the leaves curl up when they are cold or tired. We noted that this kind of thinking is what Piaget characterizes as the young child's prelogical and egocentric beliefs in animism. We marveled at the intuitive thoughts of these young children.

A second category of ideas related to the falling of leaves. One described the falling as skipping and jumping. Another explained, "Its flying is its walking." One child said they are asleep when they fall. Others commented that the leaves fall down when it is fall; they fall down in the wind.

A third category related to comments about magic and power and change. Magic seemed to be a quickly accepted hypothesis that could explain the unexplainable (e.g., why leaves change color). One attributed the source of change to God. Another child thought about the change in the color of leaves as a kind of disguise. He likened this to Terminator's ability to change so nobody knows who he is. He said that somebody has the power to change the leaves.

We took a little time to reflect on the questions Louise used to provoke the children to think of analogies ("What do you see?") and express hypotheses ("Why do you think leaves fall?"). We noted that children were quite willing and able to think on these levels. We also noted that this was a conversation, unlike some earlier conversations, in which children were really talking to each *other* rather than just to the teacher. We observed that Louise had asked some pivotal questions that helped the children talk to each other. Frequently through the conversations it appears that children piggybacked on each other's ideas or continued a line of thought. This was a good indication that children were listening to each other. Though a few children had little to say, the relevance of their comments indicated that they, too, were listening and involved in the dialogue. We also knew that the prior experience these children had shared in collecting, observing, and drawing the leaves not only contributed to the ideas they expressed but probably gave them a sense of collective ownership of the topic and a respect for their own and each other's ideas.

## *Using Conversations to Inform Emergent Curriculum*

Now we were ready to move on to curriculum planning. We knew that we needed to plan for several possibilities, possibilities that could help to make children's ideas visible and thereby help them revisit, reflect, reconstruct their thinking, and communicate this thinking to others. Although we have adopted a set of curriculum goals from Project Construct, a curriculum and assessment framework from the Missouri Department of Elementary and Secondary Education (1992), that guided our thinking about what is worth learning, we have tried to follow Rinaldi's (1993) advice about allowing curriculum to emerge in response to the children's needs and interests. We did not formulate specific goals for each activity in advance. Rather, we considered the ideas, hypotheses, and choices of the children and then projected possible activities that might help children answer their own questions (Forman, 1992a), test their hypotheses, and explore their ideas. We proposed ways that the project might evolve and then examined how these activities might support and integrate the goals of our curriculum.

We began with the first cluster of children's ideas: the relationship of leaves to humans. We thought that since the children talked about leaves having bones and spines, maybe we should consider helping them examine human or animal bones and spines and compare them to those of leaves. We could invite them to search for ways to look at human bone structures. We could ask whether they had ever seen pictures of their bones. This could lead to the possibility of finding real X-rays. One of the parents is a doctor; it is likely that he could help us in getting access to some X-rays. We could compare human bones with what the children have described as bones in leaves. We could ask children to then draw the "bone" structure of the leaves and the bone structures of people. This could enable us to talk with them about the discoveries or observations they would be making about similarities and differences. We would try to provoke conversation about hypotheses regarding form and function of leaf bones versus human bones. As children's questions emerge, we could encourage them to search for answers and sources for these answers (e.g., family members who know something about human bones or leaf structure; books or videos on the subject; local experts; collections of more leaves to examine firsthand; observations of leaves on trees). We could invite children to use their drawings as plans or designs for making skeletons or bone structures out of wire. This medium would enable us to think about how structures within leaves and bodies help support the rest of the structure (skin, muscle, organs). We might ask, Why do leaves have "bones"? Our goal would be to provoke thinking and a desire to know more about the form and function of leaf structures. We would be promoting a disposition to learn and a beginning understanding of the relationships of parts to the whole, how things work, and insight into the system of relations within and among living things.

The falling of leaves was a subject that stirred a great deal of excitement and a flow of ideas from each of us. We thought that we might remind the children of their ideas about leaves flying, jumping, skipping, falling down in the wind, and curling up. Then we could give them the opportunity to look at slides that were taken when they had observed this falling of the leaves. We could invite the children to dance with us in front of the projected slides to imitate and mime how the leaves fall. We could use scarves or other dress-ups and, with the children, select music that we thought suitable for our dance of the leaves. We might use the shadow screen to play with images of leaves falling behind it. Since we know that in the past year these children have shown great interest in writing and acting out plays, this experience might turn into a performance that children might want to script, practice, and perform for others. We might suggest composing or selecting poetry or songs to go with the dance of the leaves. If leaves are still falling outside, we might go there to observe the many different ways that leaves fall, to study how leaves fall when it is windy and how they fall when the air is still. If possible, we could plan to videotape these observations so that we might revisit this experience at another time or share it with other children. We might suggest that children take sketch pads along with them so that they could draw the path of the leaves as they fall. These sketches might be used later to help us choreograph our own body movements in the dance of the leaves and the flow of our scarves.

Louise remembered that once during her year of internship in Reggio Emilia, she observed Vea Vecchi take a small group of children outside one day and heard her say, "Look at how all those leaves have fallen. Do you see how the wind has created this kind of picture, by the way the leaves are arranged? Now pretend if you were the wind, how would you arrange these things?" The children played outside making patterns and constructions out of leaves. Sometimes they would cover their creations with plastic box tops to preserve them for a while.

The rest of us thought this idea was a great possibility for an experience that both adults and children would enjoy, and it would be a logical extension of the study of the effects of wind on falling leaves. It might lead to observations of other patterns in nature. It could help children think about spatial relationships among elements of a pattern (shape, texture, color). This kind of experience could help children develop stronger awareness of their environment and the beauty and complexity of nature.

So many ideas were pouring forth. As this happened, our own questions emerged. Does the shape of a leaf affect the way it falls? How far from a tree might a leaf fall? One teacher said that the leaves of Ginko trees fall all at once (e.g., overnight) rather than over a period of days or weeks like other trees. She went on to say, "You can go down the street one day and the Ginko leaves are all yellow; the next day they're all on the ground. It looks like it snowed Ginkos." If that is true, we thought, wouldn't it be exciting to study a Ginko tree with the children and try to predict when the leaves would fall? This observation could lead to an investigation of the many different kinds of trees in the school yard. We could try to find out whether different kinds of trees tend to shed leaves at different times, in early or late fall.

Finally, we decided to move on to the third cluster of children's ideas about power, death, and magic in regard to how leaves change color. It occurred to us that these ideas could easily be connected through most, if not all, of the experiences we had already projected. As we engaged in experiences related to the study of falling leaves, we could also discuss and observe color. Sources of information that we seek out in regard to leaf structures might also tell us something about the color of leaves and why the color of leaves changes in the fall. As we observe the Ginko tree to monitor the fall of the leaves, we will surely be noting the change in color that precedes their fall. We might encourage children to paint pictures of their theories about how leaves change color. We might encourage them to mix paints in order to match the many different colors observed. We might take walks to look for examples of leaves that have already changed color and leaves that have not yet changed, leaves that are just beginning to curl up and leaves that are beginning to decompose. We might decide together to represent these different stages through drawing, clay modeling, or other material. This would challenge the children to think about in-between states, thereby focusing more on the process of transformation. These graphic representations should enable the children to converse about their theories and consider each other's ideas.

At this point, our heads were swimming with the many possibilities of this project. We felt a need to reflect on how these experiences related to the goals of our curriculum. We had already discussed the value of several of the activities in regard to their potential for encouraging thinking about form and function, transformations and patterns in nature, and relationships of parts to whole. Though we had not yet talked about it, we could now reflect that, in all cases in which we helped children make their ideas visible (e.g., through various forms of representation such as drawing, construction, dramatic play, and movement—or any of the "hundred languages"), we were enabling them to better communicate and organize their thinking—to revisit, reflect, and re-cognize. The visible representations of children's ideas could enable them to discuss and defend their ideas with peers as well as consider each other's perspectives. We knew that if we supported children in asking and answering their own questions, we would be helping them build dispositions to be curious (e.g., about the physics of falling leaves or the relationships between bone structure of humans and the "bones" and "spines" in leaves), to take initiative (e.g., in seeking information or testing their hypotheses), and to exercise creative and critical thinking (e.g., in developing theories about why leaves change color). Several of the experiences would help children represent ideas and feelings through music and movement, through construction, graphics, and words. Throughout this study, we would be building vocabulary and exercising the skills of discussion, debate, and listening.

We reminded ourselves of the advice that Amelia Gambetti had given us on several of her consultation visits: though we had thought of a wonderful inventory of possible learning activities, we could only go forward with them if we could get the children to agree to pursue them. In other words, we needed to plan ways to use the documentation we had already collected to entice, provoke, invite, and/or negotiate with children in regard to the proposed learning activities. At the same time, we had to keep our ears and eyes open to alternative experiences or directions for the project that might come from the children. We remembered Rinaldi's (1993a) advice in *The Hundred Languages of Children:* that all of the work we had just done to (a) study children's ideas and hypotheses and (b) discuss and record the many possible ways that the project could be anticipated to evolve was "great preparation for the subsequent stages of the project—even should the unexpected occur" (p. 102).

We ended the meeting with a plan to meet again to discuss strategies for presenting one or more of our ideas to the children, to determine the roles each team member would play in regard to facilitating small-group activities, to identify tools (e.g., camera, camcorder, tape recorder, paper and pencil, etc.) and strategies to be used to document our ongoing observations of learning, to find time to analyze documentation, and to involve parents through documentation and other forms of participation or communication. As the project evolved, we would continue to examine ways to use documentation (e.g., photographs; slides; videotape; transcripts of children's dialogues; and children's drawings, writing, paintings, constructions) to sustain children's interests and involvement in the project.

## CONCLUSION

We all agree that planning for emergent curriculum is complex and time-consuming. It requires us not only to know principles of child development but to engage in an ongoing study of the particular children we teach. Children's conversations can be a prime resource for this kind of study.

We have come to learn that serious dialogue and exchange among children, teachers, and parents are critical at all levels. The guidelines offered at the beginning of this chapter focus on our work with children, but we are now realizing that the ability to listen, discuss, debate, question, probe, consider multiple perspectives, and wonder out loud must happen in our work with all members of the learning community. The skills we develop in practicing the kind of team study and planning just described transfer to our work with parents and children. And as we get better at facilitating and participating in dialogue with children, we become better at doing this with adults. Through our efforts to put dialogue at the center of our curriculum, we are beginning to understand how to develop the "network of cooperation and interactions that produces for the adults, but above all for the children, a feeling of belonging in a world that is alive, welcoming, and authentic" (Malaguzzi, 1993b, p. 58).

# III

*American Interpretations of the Reggio Approach*

 Lilian Katz sets the tone for Part III by discussing the difficulties and implications of making changes in an educational system. She questions where we might begin to make such changes in order for our children's lives to become "as rich, interesting, engaging, satisfying, and meaningful" as those we observe in Reggio Emilia. Lilian raises various issues and problems (sometimes called "challenges") related to such changes.

The following chapters provide practical examples of teachers who have been inspired to begin at different places and in different settings to solve some of the problems cited in Lilian's introductory chapter.

Donna Carloss Williams and Rebecca Kantor, the authors of Chapter 9, illustrate how Donna began her initial attempt at generating emergent curriculum by following the 4- to 5-year-olds' lead during an investigation of water. She draws some interesting conclusions about how to tell whether a project is truly emergent or is just another teacher-generated experience.

Next is the chapter by Cheryl Breig-Allen, who teaches very young children, aged 2 to 3 years, and Janis Ullrich Dillon, a kindergarten teacher. Cheryl traces her personal development over 4 years as she moved from a strong behavior modification approach to the Reggio Approach. She includes a chart that makes these various changes plain to the reader. Jan, who teaches in a public school, discusses the problem of "meeting two masters"—that is, satisfying the requirements imposed by the "designated curriculum" while at the same time attempting to honor the more generative approach espoused by Reggio Emilia. She demonstrates how it can be possible to blend and balance these by providing a noteworthy description of the Rat Project.

Still another example of a different kind of problem requiring solution is provided in Chapter 11 by Barbara Geiger, who is the director of Overfield, an independent school serving children aged 3 to 6. She describes how her staff gradually came to terms with balancing child-teacher input as projects emerged. She also explains how they managed to coordinate and continue a long-term project emerging from the children's interests in a milieu where different children attended the school on different days and at different times.

# 8

# The Challenges of the Reggio Emilia Approach[*]

*Lilian G. Katz*

Professor, University of Illinois, and
Director, ERIC Clearinghouse for Early Childhood
and Elementary Education, University of Illinois

[*] A longer version of this chapter was published in L. G. Katz and B. Cesarone (eds.), *Reflections on the Reggio Emilia Approach* (Urbana, IL: ERIC Clearinghouse on Elementary and Early Childhood Education, 1994).

For the last two decades, I have had the good fortune to work with early childhood education colleagues in many countries, on every continent, many times over. I have seen impressive and instructive practices in parts of the United States and many places, including New Zealand, Australia, northern Germany, and the United Kingdom, especially during the so-called Plowden years. But never have I seen provisions for young children as inspiring as those observed during my eight visits to Reggio Emilia. Having now visited eight of their preprimary schools and two infant centers, it seems even more clear to me than ever that in our own collected literature on early childhood practices, we have been right all along:

❏ All young children have active and lively minds from the start, and

❏ children's dispositions to make sense of experience, investigate it, relate to and care about others, and adapt to their environments are inborn and can flourish under the right conditions.

From our colleagues in Reggio Emilia, we can learn a great deal about how such conditions can be achieved. The question is, What steps can we take to bring our own practices closer to those conditions? One of the main goals of this book is to share ideas about how to help interested readers not only learn some of the fundamentals of the Reggio Emilia Approach but also consider possible ways they might be adopted, adapted, and incorporated in our own early childhood practices. With these goals in mind, I want to take up some of the issues they raise. I will then address some of the principles to consider in bringing about desirable changes.

## ISSUES IN ADAPTING AND ADOPTING INNOVATIONS

Doyle and Ponder (1977–78) put forward an interesting analysis of some of the issues of innovation and change under the heading "The Practicality Ethic in Teacher Decision-Making." According to their analysis, the *practicality ethic* has three components. When teachers are faced with pressure to adopt (their term) an innovation, their decisions are based on three criteria, paraphrased here in the form of questions they might ask of themselves and others:

1. *Congruence:*   Is the innovation congruent with my current practices? Does it advance or strengthen what I am now

doing? We might note here that another question a teacher might ask in this situation is, Does this innovation suggest that what I have been doing up to now was all wrong? (Sue Bredekamp [1993] suggested this reaction in her sensitive account of her first visit to Reggio Emilia.)

2. *Resources:*   Will those who urge me to change provide me with the necessary resources (e.g., time, space, materials, woman power, etc.) to make implementation possible, feasible, and practical?

3. *Cost-reward relationship:*   Given the cost in terms of the time and energy required to adopt the proposed innovation, will it provide me with sufficient rewards to make it worthwhile? In particular, will the "psychic" rewards be great enough in terms of children's interest, enthusiasm, and cooperation; parents' support and appreciation; and administrators' approval? The amount of effort is acceptable if the teacher is reasonably certain that the responses of the children and relevant others to the new practices will be clearly positive.

Doyle and Ponder suggest that when the answers to these questions are largely negative, teachers discard the proposed innovation as "impractical." I suggest that we all might consider these three criteria of the practicality ethic before rushing headlong into advocating change. We must be able to answer these questions affirmatively if we are to adapt our way of working with young children to be more like those in the Reggio Emilia preschools.

## Adaptation of the Reggio Emilia Approach in Particular

When thinking about adapting the Reggio Emilia Approach in particular, some additional questions and issues come to mind. First, is the Reggio Emilia Approach adaptable? Can it be made suitable to our context without significant distortions? Can it be adjusted to fit our situations, culture, subcultures, and conditions?

Second, many elements contribute to the Reggio Emilia Approach. Our Reggio Emilia colleagues frequently assert that one must have all the elements of their approach to make it work and to preserve its integrity. This requirement makes the task of adoption so daunting that it may lead to discouragement at the outset. All the elements that constitute the Reggio Emilia Approach took many years to develop and are undergoing continuous refinement. How many years would we need in the United States to get to where they are now? Which elements of the approach are most and least adoptable and adaptable?

*Physical Features.*   The arrangements and kinds of space available in the infant centers and preprimary schools of Reggio Emilia seem to be central elements of their work. How many of the elements of this feature can we realistically expect to adopt? How long would it take? How would the considerable costs be met?

*Parent Involvement.*   American educators have long had serious concern and commitment to meaningful parent involvement. Can we emulate the success of Reggio Emilia along these lines, and how long would it take? Is their outstanding success with parent involvement due to the extraordinary quality of the children's experiences rather than the reverse? Which comes first? Does parent involvement make high-quality experiences for their children possible, or does the quality of the program and the quality of the children's work and involvement they engender entice the parents into enthusiastic, active support?

*Collaboration.*   We have all been impressed with Reggio Emilia's commitment to collaborative relationships among all the adults involved in their work. I am told that in that part of Italy, in particular, there is a long-standing tradition of cooperatives and joint efforts that we in the United States do not share. How can we hope to begin to emulate or adopt such a style of staff relationships? How can sufficient time for such interaction be allocated?

*Documentation.*   The contribution of documentation to the work of our Reggio colleagues is also convincing and very impressive. How much staff time and energy does good documentation require? What kinds of additional resources would be required to yield such a high quality of documentation? How adaptable is this central feature to our situations? How much documentation is enough?

*Atelieristi.*   How many of us can hope to incorporate an *atelierista* into our programs? How could the cost be met? How much of the Reggio Emilia Approach can be adapted without the constant presence and expertise of the *atelieristi*? Or, for that matter, how important to the whole effort is the availability of an atelier?

*Pedagogisti.*   The pedagogical and other kinds of leadership provided by the team of *pedagogisti* seem to me to be a sine qua non of implementing the Reggio Emilia Approach. Indeed, the development of the practices we so much admire seems almost entirely dependent on the quality and frequency of staff development provision in their Approach. Of special note is that the *pedagogisti* are provided in sufficient numbers to make possible their constant availability, sufficient to enable them to know well every teacher and, indeed, every family. How much of such support do we need, and how could the cost of such provision be met?

*Three-Year Grouping.*   One of the features of the Reggio Emilia Approach that provides a variety of benefits is that the children stay with the same teachers throughout the 3 years of preprimary school enrollment. How adaptable is such a practice in our own programs? I would hope that it might be partially accomplished through mixed-age grouping, a practice that would have potential benefits in addition to just having the same teachers for 3 years. For example, children in mixed-age groups exhibit significantly more prosocial behavior and a greater tendency to offer help, instruction, and information and to facilitate the efforts of others in mixed-age than in same-age groups (Katz, Evangelou, & Hartman, 1990). In the United States, interest in mixed-age grouping continues to grow and be implemented in a number of school districts already.

*Project Work.* Involving young children in extended investigations and studies of significant topics is not unique to Reggio Emilia. It was first introduced in the United States early in this century (Isaacs, 1930; Rawcliffe, 1924) and was implemented superbly in Britain during the Plowden years (1960s and 1970s). Sylvia Chard and I have been involved in helping teachers incorporate the project approach all over North America since the late 1980s (Katz & Chard, 1989). I believe that the Reggio Emilia preprimary schools have taken project work with young children further than any other practitioners. In particular, they have succeeded in making the "graphic languages"—as they refer to them—a major aspect of children's project work in fresh and significant ways. Why should we not do more of this as well?

## BRINGING ABOUT CHANGE

The formal and informal literature on educational change continues to grow rapidly. As we contemplate the kinds of changes that adapting the Reggio Emilia Approach might involve, it would be useful to keep in mind that real change is fraught with turmoil, uncertainty, and other uncomfortable processes.

Here the work of the Canadian educator Michael Fullan (Fullan & Miles, 1992) and his insights into the complexities of bringing about *lasting* change are useful. The concerns outlined in the following sections are based largely on Fullan's work.

### Change Is Learning, Loaded with Uncertainty

Fullan reminds us that anxiety, difficulties, and uncertainty are intrinsic to all successful change. All change involves learning, and all learning involves coming to understand and be competent at doing something new and differently. This point is well illustrated in other chapters in this book. We have to recognize explicitly that the ability to tolerate the uncertainty involved in unfolding a curriculum a step at a time instead of depending on detailed advanced planning is not easy to tolerate. Note how Donna Williams and Rebecca Kantor (Chapter 9) question themselves concerning whether their water project is truly emergent or just another teacher-generated "water week," and how Brenda Fyfe's (Chapter 7) teachers struggle with growth as they work at adopting learnings from Reggio Emilia.

## Change Is a Journey, Not a Blueprint

Fullan's message is not the traditional "plan, then do," but "do, then plan, then do, and plan some more, and do some more," and so forth. We can see these processes beautifully exemplified in the Reggio Emilia preprimary schools. As Carlina Rinaldi (1994b) might put it, a plan is a compass and not a train schedule.

## Problems Are Friends

Fullan asserts that improvement is a problem-rich process, and, as such, the problems should be welcomed. Although change threatens existing interests and routines, heightens uncertainty, and increases complexity, Fullan asserts that we cannot develop effective responses to such complex situations unless we actively seek and confront real problems that are difficult to solve. In this sense, he suggests, effective organizations embrace problems rather than avoid them.

## Change Is Resource-Hungry

Fullan agrees with Doyle and Ponder (1977–78) that change demands resources. Among the many resources required for the adoption of the Reggio Emilia Approach, time is probably very high on the list. According to Fullan, time is an important, indispensable, and energy-demanding resource. American visitors to Reggio Emilia frequently express envy at the flexible and comparatively relaxed approach to time in those settings.

## Change Requires the Power to Manage It

Fullan suggests many problems encountered in change can be addressed by openness and interaction among all those concerned with what is to be changed. Openness means that we must all learn a lot about how to respond to complaints, frustrations, disagreements, and conflicts and see them as part of development. Many Americans who know Reggio Emilia practices well have commented on the adults' striking ability to argue, disagree, and criticize each other and yet remain close colleagues and good friends. Similarly, the staff takes serious and appreciative note of arguments among the children and treats them as indications that real growth and learning are in progress.

## Change Is Systemic

Here Fullan agrees with our Reggio colleagues—that all parts of the system must be involved in the desired changes simultaneously. He points out that change must focus not just on structural features, policies, and regulations but also on the deeper issues of what he calls the culture of the system. Such a stipulation presents overwhelming challenges for American early childhood educators.

## All Large-Scale Change Is Implemented Locally

Change cannot be accomplished from the distance but must involve all those who will implement the innovative practices as well as the larger, more distant agencies involved.

## WHERE ARE WE NOW AND WHAT DO WE DO NEXT?

Fullan's last point brings me to my final round of questions. Since all real change must be implemented locally, the responsibility for changes is placed right on our own doorsteps. It pushes us to take stock and ask, Where are we now? As potential implementors of the Reggio Approach, what should we be thinking about now? What should or can each of us do now?

Addressing all the elements of the Reggio Approach is a tall order, to say the least! If we cannot do it all, should we do nothing at all? If we decide that even though we cannot do it all at once but still want to move ahead, where should we start? Should we, and can we, start at different places? Can some start with inservice training? Others with rearrangement of spaces and materials? Can others start with ateliers? Others with long-term projects? Some with documentation? But, of course, there has to be something worthwhile to document!

One idea that continues to haunt me is that perhaps we should be especially careful not to call our efforts "The Reggio Approach." Even if our efforts at change are inspired by Reggio Emilia and what we are learning from it, we must take meticulous care in how we use the term and what we imply about the relationships between what we are doing and practices in Reggio Emilia.

There are several reasons behind this "specter." One is the obvious fact that it would take any of us a very long time to be worthy of that name. Another is that *if we implement the Reggio Emilia Approach insufficiently or inadequately, we might unwittingly and inadvertently give it a bad name, cast doubts about it, and create the impression that it is just a passing fad.*

But if we eschew calling our efforts by the Reggio name, even though inspired by their work, then what should we call them? Why not "developmentally appropriate practices"? Surely the Reggio Emilia Approach exemplifies developmentally appropriate practices at their best.

Finally, I propose an idea that comes from perturbation theory. Imagine, if you will, a cyclist riding along a road without difficulty. Suddenly the front wheel touches a small pebble in the road and is thrown off course. The rider falls, is injured, and her whole life changes forever. In other words, perturbation theory suggests that *even very small items can have huge and lasting consequences.* (If the cyclist is riding very fast, even a very small pebble could create a very large perturbation!)

What we are really asking for in our deliberations together about adopting and implementing the Reggio Emilia Approach are huge and lasting consequences. The question is, Is there a relatively small pebble that we can put in place now that will ultimately have the large and lasting consequences we hope for?

My hypothesis is that if we focus our collective and individual energies on the quality of our day-to-day interactions with children so that those interactions become as rich, interesting, engaging, satisfying, and meaningful as those we observe in Reggio Emilia, we will be casting out a pebble that could ultimately have very large consequences. Consider these points:

❑ It could attract greater parent interest, involvement, and loyalty than all those incantations about parent involvement touted in our commission reports and similar proclamations.

❑ We would all be learning about learning and children's rich and lively minds and their amazing capacities to imagine, hypothesize, investigate, interact, and coconstruct fresh understandings of their worlds.

❑ It would very likely speak more clearly and loudly than many of the other things we say or do.

❑ It would address our children where they are now.

❑ *And we would be doing what is right.*

This is not to say that we should not be striving to change all the other elements of the system and cultures in which we work. But we have to start somewhere, and our children cannot and should not wait until all the elements are in place. We are all deeply indebted to our colleagues in Reggio Emilia for showing us again and again what is possible when a whole community is deeply committed to its children. Though the work ahead of us is formidable, Rinaldi (1994b) reminds us that the possibility of reaching the vision exists. At the same time, however, she urges us to see "the Reggio Emilia experience and practices together as treasures that we have in common, and be careful to look at them with love, respect, and care."

# 9

# The Challenge of Reggio Emilia's Research
## One Teacher's Reflections

*Donna Carloss Williams*
Teacher, Castleton United Methodist Child Care Center and
Laboratory School, Indianapolis

*Rebecca Kantor*
Associate Professor, Family Relations and Human Development,
and Director, A. Sophie Rogers Laboratory School, The Ohio State
University, Columbus

In 1991, we had the privilege of participating in a study tour of the early childhood programs in Reggio Emilia, along with our colleagues from the A. Sophie Rogers Laboratory in Child and Family Studies at the Ohio State University. We went to Reggio with a wide range of emotions: excited to have this group experience as a staff (one more used to the role of host to our own visitors), curious, wishing to be challenged, and, admittedly, a bit skeptical of the amazing products we had seen on display in the traveling exhibit. We left Reggio with even more emotion: inspired yet overwhelmed by what we had seen and learned, and in conflict over how to use what we had seen without losing our own essential character.

What follows is an excerpt from a journal written by Donna Carloss Williams immediately following this excursion. While we have "traveled" even farther from this beginning point in our explorations of the Reggio ideas over the 5 years since our trip, we still recognize the importance and difficulty of the first steps. We share this reflection to encourage others engaged in a similar process and to help others think about their own practices. This above all is what we learned from our visit to Italy: we visit others' programs, and we enter into a dialogue, not for the purpose of imitation but to be provoked to revisit our own understandings, engage in ongoing research and reflection, look forward and outward for resources and inspiration, and remain open to learning.

## CONNECTING HISTORIES

After visiting Reggio Emilia's preschool programs, some elements of the approach there were an instant "easy fit" for us. An "emergent curriculum" (although the term *emergent* was new to us) has been implemented at the A. Sophie Rogers Laboratory School for over a decade. Long ago, the idea of preplanned teacher "themes" had been seen as a less productive means of facilitating children's learning than using their own ideas as the curricular focus. We had been "working from the ideas of children" (in fact, this is our program motto) successfully for so long that this element of the Reggio research felt quite natural to us. However, other elements were new and challenging.

The focus on socially constructed curriculum also characterizes a daily event in the lab school we call "group time," a planned context for working on collaborative projects. Each day, we plan our group time curriculum from an active learning, open-ended materials approach. We would bring materials as a starting point and suggest group projects but always with an eye for capturing the ideas and interests of the children. Thus, we, too, had seen the idea of collaboration as worthwhile. However, while the process was familiar, the time span for our projects was very different from the Italians'. Most materials we prepared were for the day's experience. They were appropriate, developmental, and born of children's input; but they were rarely done over time or in the depth of "study" we saw in Reggio Emilia. The entire project element was an exciting and challenging one to all of us.

Another aspect we saw as challenging was the element of representation across varied media. As part of our experiences, we had typically asked the children whether they were interested in writing narratives about what they perceived to be the experience's salient features. However, we did not consider other media (e.g., art) in this part of the process.

During our week in Reggio Emilia and on the plane trip back to the United States, our entire staff discussed whether our experience would change our practice. We all agreed we wished to use what we had learned in Italy in our classroom—but how? We began not with a blueprint but with the courage just to "try" to construct our own meaning from what we had seen in Italy. This dialogue has been ongoing for 5 years now, but it began with the Water Project described here.

## A TEACHER'S JOURNAL: THE WATER PROJECT

When I returned from Reggio Emilia, it was summer, school was in session, and it was hot. During our outdoor play, the children were making informal observations about water as they played in their small wading pools. Following our typical practice, I decided to bring some of those water experiences inside for our group time. (We have a mixed-age classroom of twenty 3- to 5-year-olds. Each day when we have our planned group time, we divide our classroom into two small groups—10 children in each group for the planned activity. I was the teacher/leader of the group of 4- to 5-year-olds.) Not as typically, I brought my camera determined to watch and listen more attentively to the children's process to see whether any possibilities for extending the experience were suggested by the children in their actions and talk. I wanted to do a project at some point with the children, but I realized I could not just *put* some sort of project technique or method on the children's experience.

## POURING: AN ENTRY POINT FOR A PROJECT

Our beginning experiment was simple. I brought containers of various sizes and one large transparent tub and asked the children whether they would like to fill the tub and see what we discovered about the water.

At first, they were excited only about getting their pictures taken (see Figures 9–1, 9–2, and 9–3). I told them I brought the camera to record what they wanted about their discoveries. After each child had a picture taken, we became involved in pouring the water from the different containers, from varying distances above the tub, and with varying amounts of water. I got so involved myself that I often forgot to take the pictures. (Indeed, the photographs and the other documentation throughout the year were a source of joy, frustration, and validation of my memory loss!) Comments from the children included these:

| | |
|---|---|
| *Steven:* | "Pouring is like spilling." |
| *Audrey:* | "It makes waves." |
| *Allison:* | "Pouring high makes more bubbles, but close makes less bubbles." |
| *Marcus:* | "I got bigger water." |
| *Alexandra:* | "Little tiny containers pour like raindrops." |
| *Thomas:* | "The water makes kind of a hole." |
| *Celia:* | "If it's a small hole, not so many bubbles." |

**FIGURE 9–1**
Marcus drew the water that dripped over the container's edge.

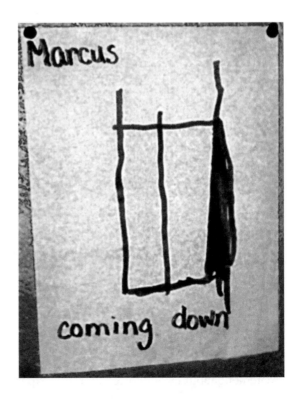

**FIGURE 9-2**
Bubbles made from water
and "pouring into more
water" was also captured in
this drawing.

When the children felt finished, I replayed the group over and over in my mind. Where did they focus? What do I do next? If I bring the experience back, am I just doing it to be *my* first "project," or were *they* really as interested in this as I thought? I decided to go forward.

## BLOWING: A FURTHER AND DEEPER INVESTIGATION

They had seemed most interested in the bubbles and circles made by the pouring. I brought in water, straws, and funnels with the idea of creating circles and bubbles with "wind" (see Figures 9–4 and 9–5). I opened the activity by saying, "Yesterday, we discovered so many interesting things about the bubbles and circles in the water that I wondered if these things could help us discover anything about water too?" I almost held my breath—partly because I was so unsure of myself and partly because I feared I was beginning to "teach about water" rather than experiencing their learning about water. I feared that their interest was not as keen as mine and that I had forced this water exploration on them out of my own excitement about extended collaborative experiences.

**FIGURE 9–3**
Steven was able to represent water entering the container and the motion under the water line.

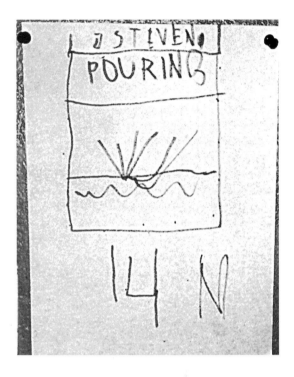

I need not have worried. The children instantly put their *heads* in the water to blow bubbles. (On reflection, we thought this may have come from "blowing" experiences in swimming lessons many children were taking.) They used what I had brought (straws, funnels, etc.) and got other things from around the classroom as well (tubing, paper cylinders, etc.). Although our group typically lasted 15 to 20 minutes, it was 45 minutes later before interest began to subside. Some of their comments were as follows:

*Thomas:*     [With mouth in the water] "It makes little circles and bubbles."

*Marcus:*     [With nose in the water] "Bigger circles."

*Allison:*     [With breath only] "Even little and big circles."

*Thomas:*     [With straws] "Smaller bubbles happen when you bend the straw."

*Audrey:*     [With paper funnels] "Bubbles are there but only wide."

There was more talk about waves and bubbles, but the children's most compelling interest was in what would happen to the water that was spilling out of the tub. Several children recited very accurate, detailed descriptions of the process of evaporation. Two were even "knowledgeable"

**FIGURE 9–4**
In another experiment, we tried blowing ("wind") on the water. With faces in and out of the water, straws, funnels, and a few additional implements (note the water pump in the center bottom picture), we blew!

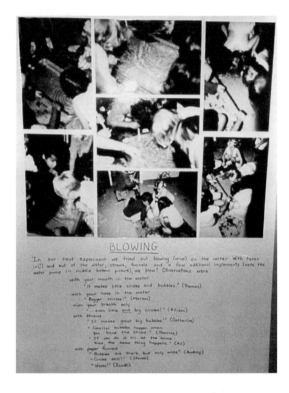

about evaporation and weather. I decided the next experiment might involve these elements.

## *EVAPORATION: THE CHILDREN'S THEORIES ARE REVEALED*

I brought in paper towels and water and asked the children to predict where water would go if we wet the paper towels and left them out for awhile. In spite of their previous "recitations," *not one child* predicted that water will evaporate. In fact, the group agreed that the paper towel would *never* dry, because "paper towels are something that soaks up water" (Alexandra). We wet the towels, children marked their own, and we recorded the day and time. The paper towels, of course, were dry when we returned the next day. The observations from the group were divided: four believed the air was causal in the drying, and four believed the "clothespins and air together did it." Looking back, I am still surprised that I did not go forward with this exploration. I did put a few more wet paper towels up without clothespins for three of the children. These children later decided,

**FIGURE 9–5**
Alexandra worked hard to
document the ripples caused
by blowing into the water.

"Maybe air just does it." However, I never really picked up on their cognitive dissonance with the "clothespin factor" (see Figure 9–6).

## WAVES: WHAT GENERATES THEM?

I did notice that while wetting their paper towels, and for the third time, they were fascinated with waves. So, our next time together, I asked the children for their predictions about what generates waves. Most agreed an *object* was necessary to make this happen. Despite earlier experiences with both pouring and blowing where waves were observed by the children, neither was predicted as a possible wave producer. When questioned about what objects were best for wave making, "boats" were the most popular choice, followed by "hands." After experimenting with both, other predictions and choices were dropping crumbs into the water, blowing, and moving the entire container of water. Blowing was considered mildly successful in making "tiny, little waves" (Allison). Dropping crumbs into the water "just doesn't work" (Alexandra), and moving the whole container "does big ones" (Steven; see Figure 9–7). The summary causal factor was "fastness" (Thomas).

**FIGURE 9–6**
Steven sends the water vapor from the water into the air in this representation of evaporation.

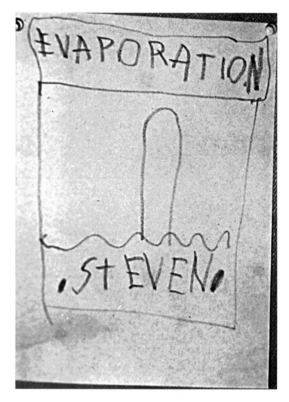

Again, in reflection, the children were showing me many other possibilities with waves that I just did not facilitate. They had decided "fastness" of motion was causal, and I went forward without further experimentation. Part of my decision making was due to my lack of attention to their process and my resistance to the idea of doing a water "theme." As the experiences began to span several days, I was getting excited but also concerned. What was the difference between what I was doing and doing a thematic "water week"? Had I just taken the project idea from Reggio Emilia, or had I taken the understanding that children's process with discovering their own realities of the world could take time and collaboration? I was more and more unsure as I was simultaneously buoyed by how involved the children had become and how collaborative their conversations were. Despite my uncertainties, I went forward.

## *BOAT CONSTRUCTION: ONE PATH TAKEN*

I lost the chance to proceed with wave making, but I did recognize their high interest in the boats they had used as wave producers. I asked whether

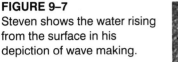

**FIGURE 9–7**
Steven shows the water rising from the surface in his depiction of wave making.

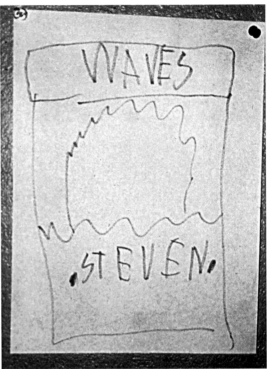

they would be interested in making boats. They were very excited. Before we started, the children decided we would need to have these elements in a good boat: "flat, edges, seats, a point, and it has to float." I brought aluminum foil as the first boat-making material. There was a high level of satisfaction with this foil boat making, though two disappointments came along with the discoveries:

*Steven:*      "It can rip."

*Alexandra:*  "If you put a lot of water in it, it won't work."

The children suggested future boat-making materials should be paper, plastic, and wood.

Following their suggestions, I brought construction paper next. Their only concern about paper boat making was that "even if it works, it will get soaking wet." There was a high level of confidence, because the group was so sure about "making edges" with paper. Marcus discovered the paper could float alone without shape or "edges." This discovery caused a surge of putting flat paper sheets in the water. Disappointment was coupled with frustration when the wet paper began to rip. The children's conclusion was "Foil is a material that can get wet and not be ruined. Paper isn't" (Thomas).

Echoing this conclusion and the sentiment of the group, Alexandra said, "Paper boats always fall apart." Discoveries were made, however, that were to impact future experiments:

*Christine:*    "Paper sticks to another paper."

*Izzati:*    "Putting it under the water gets it wetted easy."

*Allison:*    "If you put a little water on it, it floats still."

Following the children's suggestion of plastic, the next material we tried was plastic-coated paper (used for lining shelves). This material made a superior floater, and the children were quite impressed with the fact that it did not tear when it was wet. They were, however, very frustrated with shaping the material:

*Alexandra:*    "It doesn't bend well. Regular boats look more 'shapey.'"

Using their discovery of paper sticking to paper (the previous experiment) yielded the ultimate solution:

*Celia:*    "Making edges by placing another piece on top. It rolls up and sticks to itself."

They had previously decided that a *little* water in a boat was acceptable. This was the source of much experimentation, and it led to another discovery:

*Catherine:*    "Water can come in any hole in a boat."

Again, I believe there were more paper and plastic substances that would have been possible, but my concern about "how much is too much" was very primary in this first experience. I was, however, tentatively beginning to call this "our Water Project" with the children. I wanted them to begin to have a sense of the cohesive quality of what they had been doing. I was gathering quite a few photos now as well. I continued.

I brought wood next as the children had wanted. This was decidedly the favorite boat-making material. It did cause some questions about their previous conclusions:

*Thomas:*    "They float good, and they don't need *edges.*"

*Alexandra:*    "You can't *fold* it, but it floats!"

These wooden boats were used the longest in play, and the group experimented more with water motion. Perhaps the choice to construct (as a group) a wooden boat would have extended their excitement, but instead I chose to bring in another material: clay.

Clay boats were the source of the richest conversation and problem solving. They were also the source of the greatest frustration and eventually spelled the end of the project. Some conclusions:

Christine:    "It has to be very flat."

Audrey:    "It has to be not heavy."

Alexandra:    "Cracks let water in and out."

Catherine:    "Water makes clay heavy."

Audrey:    "If a boat floats, you know it's not heavy."

After the clay boats, the children clearly were finished with their Water Project. It had been 2 weeks long. Water is such a universally interesting material to children, and it had become a first-step "project" for us. I was elated. I already knew some of the errors in judgment I had made, but I was pretty sure I had not accomplished a water theme and so felt reassured. A theme is an integrated but preplanned experience that does not build on the unfolding inquiry process of the group. Integration and social construction are two different qualities related to curriculum design. Preplanning content feels more like a "monologue"; constructed projects feel more like a "dialogue."

## REPRESENTATION AND DOCUMENTATION: NEW EXTENSIONS FOR THE TEACHER

After our water experiments, I ventured into another unfamiliar experience: to see whether I could facilitate their recording of their own experience. I had many photos now, and I mounted them with a simple, handwritten narrative of the experience (see Figure 9–8). It was unlike the beautifully done graphics on the panels I had seen in Italy, but it was the first such "panel" I had ever attempted or the children had ever seen. When I put it up, they surrounded it. They were amazed at viewing their own discoveries and called friends over to see the Water Project. (At the day's end, they brought their parents to see it as well.) This was as gratifying as much of the process itself. Their sense of accomplishment and mastery was obvious.

While gathered around this panel, I also showed them a handful of unmounted photos. I said, "These all remind me of the things we did during the Water Project. I thought we could use these materials (markers and paper) to record what we remembered about our project." Now, I *really* was

**FIGURE 9–8**
After our water experiments, I ventured into another unfamiliar experience. I mounted pictures of what the children had done together with a simple, handwritten narrative of the experience. When I put it up, the children surrounded it. They were amazed at viewing their own discoveries.

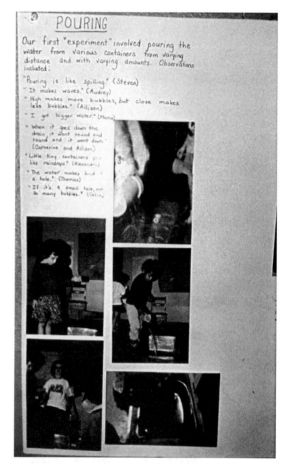

unsure. I had always been taught to allow children to draw/create whatever their imaginations suggested. I had always resisted the idea of a teacher insisting on everyone drawing "the same thing." How close to that line was I now? Had I stepped over it? I decided to venture the risk. The results astounded me: they did not draw the same thing at all. Although their drawings were nowhere near the beauty of the children's art in Reggio Emilia, they were the most revealing drawings I had seen from these children.

## REFLECTION

Looking back, this part of the project felt comfortable and appropriate after all. I was not directing the children's content or limiting their creativity (which I was afraid I was going to do); I was giving them a tool (a "language," in the Italians' terminology) to communicate what they had found out about water. Indeed, they were able to capture on paper what they had discovered: Steven captured pouring; Alexandra chose to draw the effects of flowing the water; Marcus even remembered water coming down beside the tub as well as the bubbles we had often seen; waves were also a subject for Steven, as was the evaporation process. I gave them the opportunity to further the dialogue by means of an additional language and that was the difference.

The evening after the group had drawn their pictures, I mounted them. Then, I sat in front of the bulletin board crying. My tears were from the joy in sharing the children's new experience, the sadness at not having given other children the "rights of their own potential," and the excitement of knowing that at this point in my career, I am beginning something new and exhilarating. In spite of my doubts and resistance, it felt so *right*.

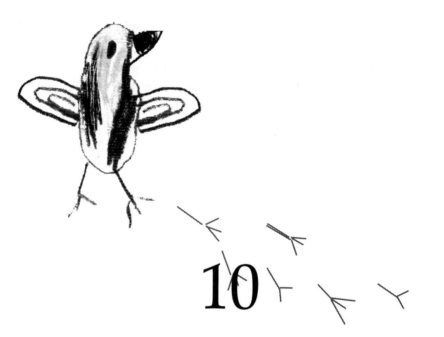

# 10

# Implementing the Process of Change in a Public School Setting

*Cheryl Breig-Allen*
*Janis Ullrich Dillon*
Teachers, Clayton School District, Clayton, Missouri

We both work in the school district of Clayton, a suburb of St. Louis, Missouri. Cheryl teaches at the Family Center, the parent education and early childhood component of the district. Her three-morning parent-child co-op program of developmental play experiences serves children 2 to 3 years old. Janis taught kindergarten and second grade at Glenridge School and currently teaches kindergarten at Meramec Elementary School. In Clayton, teachers are encouraged to study educational research from around the world and use it to meet the needs of the diverse learners in the district. This chapter tells the story of how we have been implementing some of these principles of the Reggio Emilia Approach in our classrooms over the past 4 years.

## CHERYL'S STORY

### Year 1: Learning About Reggio Emilia

In October 1991, I sat in a dark, stuffy, little room at the "Crucial Early Years" conference that is held annually in the St. Louis area. It was an afternoon session, and the crowds had dwindled because it was a gorgeous day outside. Thirteen early childhood educators viewed slides of a child care center in Reggio Emilia, Italy, which was said to practice "excellent" early childhood education, following the principles of constructivism in its purest sense. Both my undergraduate and graduate programs in special education had been heavily influenced by behaviorist theory (educational objectives, reinforcement, and scheduling), which lies at the opposing end of the educational spectrum from constructivism, and I was enthralled with the constructivist ideas being presented. I saw them as a way to improve my work with children, so I began to research everything I could find concerning Reggio Emilia. I examined articles, attended a series of lectures, and visited "The Hundred Languages of Children" exhibit at Webster University.

After hearing the lectures and visiting the exhibit, I left with the feeling "We can do things like this—in fact, we already have!" I knew that our 2- and 3-year-old children were just as intellectually capable of observing what was going on around them and expressing their feelings and understandings as the Reggio children were, if only we would let them have the opportunities. I knew this, but it had never occurred to me to act on it in a focused way and use it to direct my work with children.

I was so determined to learn more about this program that I paid my own way to attend a 1-week seminar in Reggio Emilia. As I was viewing the work done there, the possibilities overwhelmed me to the point that my brain hurt! I was experiencing a classic case of "information overload" as I was trying to make so many connections between things I had done with children in the past and what new things I could offer now that I had seen all this. I immersed myself completely in an exploration of what this all meant to me. I had never put so much of myself into my learning. Despite the uneasiness of this disequilibrium, I felt empowered to take more risks and see what could really be done and try to document it.

## Year 2: The Seasons

During this year I began work with a new team teacher, Janet Hill. I also participated in a Danforth study group, consisting of other early childhood educators also trying to apply the Reggio principles in the St. Louis area.

The Italians refer to the environment as the "third teacher," with the room acting as an open book that tells the story of projects as they emerge. Teachers and children are able to revisit experiences throughout the year. So Janet and I set out to create a similar learning environment and capture that same vitality in our room. The first and easiest aspect of change we addressed was to make our environment more welcoming. We softened and personalized the room with plants, baskets, and other natural materials.

Traditionally, I had made monthly plans, consistently fine-tuning procedures to make them more developmentally appropriate and process oriented. Materials were usually brought out for only one day, with new activities being introduced daily with hopes of keeping the children's interest stimulated. The ideas were teacher generated and carefully planned to avoid problems and keep conflict among the children to a minimum.

Inspired by Reggio, I totally abandoned this carefully worked out curriculum. One of the most important things that we did when making this change was *slow down* and tackle fewer activities on which we could emphasize more in-depth research. We used the seasons to provide a natural laboratory in which the children could explore materials and use their senses to develop physical knowledge. We observed what the children were already noticing, for example, the various natural things around them on the playground (e.g., acorns, twigs, bark, feathers, leaves). Because thinking is so closely tied to action for young children, we encouraged them to continue gathering these things. We augmented the materials, providing numerous opportunities to manipulate them and sufficient time to reflect on their discoveries, to construct new and more elaborate understanding. Children who were not initially interested in certain materials were allowed a chance to explore them on another day.

We had kept all the children's work and photos to help document the learning process. As a result, our room began to feel more comfortable, and, as the year progressed, it became quite beautiful and awe-inspiring. The "whole" was ever so much more than the bits and pieces hanging from the ceiling and on the wall. Our classroom reflected such dramatic changes in the children's explorations and self-expression that I actually had fears of anticlimactic denouement, that we would never be able to do this again. To ward off these feelings and because I was aware that I had much farther to go, I sketched out professional goals for the coming year concentrating on closer observation of children's activities and providing scaffolding to facilitate their thinking.

My own growth was reflected in the fact that for 9 years before my introduction to Reggio, I felt I had been doing terrific, traditional work with preschool children, but, now, since I began to apply Reggio principles, others were becoming interested in my work. Brenda Fyfe, from Webster University, asked me to present the practical aspects of adapting the Reggio Approach with her at the international Merrill-Palmer Institute in Traverse City, Michigan, in the summer of 1993. I was also asked to teach early childhood classes at the University of Missouri at St. Louis and present my work at local conferences.

## *Year 3: Sunflowers*

During the third year, I was beginning to see my teaching in a whole new light. It had become a very personal, intellectual endeavor for me as I tried to teach and conduct my own observational research. I began to understand that, although important, observation of children does not facilitate their learning. I reread Anselmo's (1987) chapters on early cognitive development to focus and refine my expectations of what 2- and 3-year-old children could do and studied Forman and Kuschner's (1983) ideas on how the child constructs knowledge. This study caused me to think about how I might adapt materials and activities to help the children think about their own thinking. I tried to learn more about how children structure and organize knowledge and how the decisions I made could help influence and facilitate this learning. I realized that I needed to improve my questioning techniques as a means of providing scaffolding for their learning.

The process of following an "it depends" (on the children's interests), emerging curriculum was always on my mind. As I had done in the previous year, I kept a journal and wrote down as many observations as possible. I also took rolls and rolls of film to document the process. I became less directive with the children. I encouraged them to follow their own ideas and dig a little deeper into what they wanted to do. It was difficult to keep from interfering, but I tried to facilitate rather than tell the children "how" to do something or do it for them.

Having observed the children's interest in some sunflowers planted by another class, I put dried sunflower heads on the sensory table. I encouraged the children to look at them carefully and feel them. Not sure whether they understood that the dried sunflowers had been on the plants in the garden,

I brought in a fresh sunflower, and we all began to try to put the sunflower "puzzle" back together. During the course of this project, the children drew on the flower, painted on the leaves, and matched sunflower colors. They also dug up a stalk from the garden and examined the roots. As the fresh sunflower wilted, the children noticed the transformation. Questions like "Where's the yellow?" and "How did it go away?" posed by one of the 2-year-old boys as he closely examined the wilted sunflower exemplified the high level of inquiry, inquisitiveness, and insightful thought, clearly evident in these young children.

## Year 4: The Line Project

By the beginning of year 4, I was reading everything I could find pertaining to scaffolding children's learning (Forman, Minick, & Stone, 1993; Rogoff, 1990; Rogoff & Wertsch, 1984; Vygotsky, 1978). I continued to observe the children as they keenly observed their surroundings and take cues from them for generating curriculum. When one of the boys noticed the tracks he had made as he drove through the water on the playground and called them "lines," we invited some of the other 2- and 3-year-olds to notice lines in their world. In order to provide extended thinking about lines, we invited the children to make lines with as many materials as possible. As the experience unfolded, the children painted, drew, constructed, and continued to observe lines in their natural environment. At times we seemed to have gone a step beyond emerging curriculum to coin a new concept "erupting curriculum." They made the connection that little lines can make bigger lines, and there are all kinds of things to make lines from in our room. The Line Project has attracted significant attention from parents, university students, and other preschool teachers because it demonstrates so clearly and dramatically that 2- and 3-year-old children can relate to and make connections to abstract concepts.

In the beginning, I had been overwhelmed with the particulars of how to document the children's work, in both the group project work and their individual growth. We started by constructing documentation boards that displayed "provocations" and finished work. In previous years, I had made prolific journal entries attempting to capture everything that occurred in the classroom. Now, in an attempt to be more efficient, I began to focus my journal entries on children's actions that demonstrated interests that could eventually develop into emerging projects, as in this case "line behaviors." I also concentrated my photo documentation in the same way. As we continued to work on projects, the walls exploded with answers to the children's questions, activities, and various graphic expressions of their ideas and the concepts being investigated. In addition to documentation boards, individual documentation has also evolved. The most striking example is the individual portfolio we compile for each child, indicating his or her involvement in projects and center activities with photographs, dictation, and examples of the child's work. Both the group documentation and portfolios allow us to reflect on prior experiences, contribute ideas for future activities, and communicate in more meaningful ways with parents.

Janet and I worked closely together, deciding on and coordinating the areas of research on which we each wanted to focus. Since documentation is very labor-intensive, we are still trying to understand, prioritize, and accept what we can actually, realistically accomplish in the time allotted. We have been working closely with Lori Geismar-Ryan of the Family Center and Louise Cadwell, our Danforth study group consultant, but we are still struggling to balance what we would *like* to do with what we are realistically *able* to do.

## *Reflections and Future Intentions*

Initially, my study of the Reggio principles was more exploratory, interior, and private, relying on my own subjective experience. By the conclusion of the Sunflower Project, I was beginning to clarify my thinking. Puzzlement and discrepancies were beginning to melt away. Not only was it becoming clear to me, but I could actually explain it in a way that was understandable to others. As my interest has grown, I have been doing more reading, writing, asking questions, and thinking things through. These intellectual pursuits led me to apply and be accepted into the doctoral program at the University of Missouri at St. Louis. Now, the same theories and challenges are weaving like a web throughout the various facets of my professional life: my work with the children, with the university students, and in my own graduate work. From an early foundation in thematic work, I have seen a progression in our project work from tangible subject matter to more abstract concepts. Presenting the results of each year's work, beginning at the Reggio Conference in Traverse City, has helped me reflect on and organize my thinking.

This coming year, Janet and I hope to improve collaboration between children and adults. We want to promote a greater cooperation and a sense of community by including parents more fully as resources for ideas and materials. They are integral to the co-op's functioning, and we want to make their contributions more visible. This past year we had asked the parents for their perspective on the Line Project documentation. We plan to include their ideas in a more formative way as projects emerge in the future.

To summarize my 4 years of intense study of the Reggio Emilia Approach, I have documented my continuing journey of growth in Table 10–1.

**TABLE 10–1**
One teacher's process of change: Working with 2- and 3-year-old children

|  | Curriculum Methods and Materials | Teaching Strategies, Cognitive Goals, and Group Dynamics | Documentation |
|---|---|---|---|
| **Year 1: Before Reggio** | • Teacher driven<br>• Monthly or holiday themes<br>• Prop boxes with materials to support themes<br>• Corresponding children's books | • Careful monthly planning<br>• Behavioral objectives, developmental goals<br>• Work taken home daily, sometimes hung on boards<br>• Centers<br>• Individual process work, parallel play<br>• Limited group work | • Write anecdotal records<br>• Monthly systematic observation sheets:<br>   favorite activities<br>   changes in abilities<br>   social interactions<br>   problem-solving skills<br>   transitions<br>   use of body |
| **Year 2: Seasons** | • Emerging projects generated from both teacher- and child-selected themes of interest<br>• Prop boxes to support project work<br>• Scientifically accurate reference books | • Allow children slow, unhurried time<br>• Use staging projects<br>• Teacher acts as organizer and provoker of thought<br>• Elaborate and extend ideas<br>• Teachers model collaborative learning, conflict resolution | • Document group projects in room by:<br>   using journal to write down dialogues and ideas,<br>   putting dates on all work, and taking photographs of process<br>• Maintain individual portfolios |

| | | | |
|---|---|---|---|
| **Year 3: Sunflowers** | • Continued refinement of emerging project work based on provocation of the children's interest | • Challenge children with more complicated ideas<br>• Teacher taking role of researcher<br>• Help children discover their own problems and questions<br>• See drawing and sensory activities as teaching tools | • Use journal notes to pose problems<br>• Continue to share documentation with children by making it more accessible to parents by hosting parent meetings and to other teachers and the public by supporting visitation and conducting staff development workshops |
| **Year 4: Lines** | • Anticipating where content might emerge by focusing on the children's interests, questions, and hypotheses | • Observe children's reactions and help them act upon their observations<br>• Teach technical skills more directly<br>• Revisit learning experiences<br>• Give opportunities to expand upon work | • Continue authentic assessment portfolios<br>• Collaborate on documentation<br>• Accept what can realistically be accomplished with time and money allotted |

## JANIS'S STORY

### New Thinking About Teaching Strategies

As I recall my teaching style before incorporating the Reggio Approach, I am able to make a few comparisons. Like many of my colleagues and role models, I had fallen into the mode of lecture-style teacher. An increasing amount of curriculum seemed to bog me down and force me into a regimented schedule of exact minutes spent teaching reading, math, spelling, handwriting, and so forth. I was very proud of accomplishing all these things within my school day, but, unfortunately, as with many routines, creative thinking gets lost or pushed to another time.

Realizing the joy children found in expression, I began lingering during the children's weekly art lesson. Somehow, connecting to the art educator became very important to me. I could not help studying and cherishing the creations brought back from the art room. The variety in expression simply fascinated me.

I discovered the Reggio Approach in the fall of 1991 when I had the opportunity to visit "The Hundred Languages of Children" exhibit. Before my visit, I had never heard of or read about this remarkable example of child-centered learning. Afterward, I found myself drawn to the many lectures, classes, and readings that surfaced about Reggio Emilia, and I was fortunate that the superintendent of schools, Steven Adamowski, and my principal, Phyllis Stoecklein, supported my interest by funding my trip to visit those schools in Italy. Upon my return, I was included in a special Danforth grant and worked with Brenda Fyfe to actualize my learning. Once I began to study, I realized that I *could* blend a higher sense of creativity into my daily classroom routine. Better yet, routine would fade away and daily surprise would fill its place.

### The Hornet Project

I would like to share a specific experience that occurred during the first year I implemented the Reggio Approach when I was still teaching at the second grade level. My father had given me a beautiful hornet's nest that hung in his tree (minus the live hornets, of course). I wondered how I could use the nest as a provocation for learning and realized my lesson planning would need to take a decisive change.

The first thing I did was rearrange the classroom setup from desks in rows to desks in connecting tables. I hung the nest from a long rope in the center of the classroom. I wanted the children to be able to see and experience the nest throughout the day. My brother, who had just graduated from medical school, supplied me with lots of trays, tweezers, gowns, and so forth. The children enjoyed wearing the gowns and using the medical tools in their explorations. I invited them to think about the nest, paint representations of it, wonder about its inhabitants, write about its growth (and demise), and, finally, work together to figure out exactly what insect created it. For the final 3 weeks of school, they worked in small groups to come to a better understanding of the nest. I was delighted that they returned to their work the next day, the next week, with continued excitement.

*What the Children Learned.*    I remember dropping in on a conversation a pair of boys were having regarding how the nest was made. Intuitively, I began to write down what they were saying. It was my first effort at documenting our learning and, for me, discovering the importance of asking probing questions to deeply involve the children in the topic. I asked the boys questions such as these: Can you guess how the color orange got into the pattern of the nest? How does the nest feel in your fingers as you explore it? Does it remind you of any material we have in the classroom or at your home? Is there any way *we* could make something that looks and feels like the nest? These questions led the children into deeper thinking and encouraged them to continue to wrestle with their own interesting ideas.

Other children spent days using water paint to copy the lines, patterns, and colors of the nest. One group enjoyed actually dissecting the nest, counting the combs inside, piling up the corpses of hornets, and discovering unborn young. We learned to wear plastic gloves, like surgeons, because the exterminator had used poison to kill the swarm. We borrowed microscopes from the sixth grade to closely examine things found. Magnifying glasses, books from home, and curious parents filled our room. Certainly, the skills of second graders made this process fascinating for me. They could read on their own to find solutions.

*What I Learned.*    I learned not to give all the answers but to trust that with the proper materials, interactions, and time the children would discover solutions on their own. The kind of experience that leads children to think carefully about their own thinking is perhaps the very best kind of experience. The day that a student matched a dead hornet to the "Baldheaded Hornet" in the encyclopedia was truly delightful. Arriving at that answer took many hours of discussion and careful posing of questions from me. When a student wanted to call the insects "bees," I would not accept the quick answer. I asked that child to find out about bees. "Let's look at bees when we go to recess," I said. (Bees were common on our playground, visiting clover and empty juice boxes.) Then I asked the child to write down every detail about bees that he noticed. We began to carry notebooks and pencils to recess for the chance to draw and jot down observations. We compared the body structure, wings, legs, color, behavior, everything that we could, in order to see whether our nest belonged to a bee. Of course, we quickly learned that we did not have a bee's nest at all. I asked the children questions like "If this is not a bee's nest, then what kind of nests do bees have?" and "What makes it possible for a hornet to build this kind of nest?" Even I began to wonder about the structure of a bee's mouth as opposed to the hornet's mouth! Each discovery led to another question. I could not have planned a more complete lesson!

As a group, we all rejoiced in this new way of learning. I can only imagine discovering hornets the old way—through lecture or textbook. We learned to use textbooks as tools and resources, only after stretching our own thinking. Yes, it is an exhausting effort, but absolutely worth it. After school ended that year, during my lazy backyard days in the summer, it occurred to me that those children invested in the tasks of reading, writing, researching, recording, counting, and sharing more during the Hornet Project than they had done in other topics the rest of the year.

One of the most rewarding memories I have is of a young boy who invested very little interest in school during the course of that year until the Hornet Project. He came to the room so excited each day and even took quite a leadership role in the group. He put himself "in charge" of the nest dissection, handing out job assignments reasonably to other children. His eagerness to work and sustain his efforts delighted me.

During our Hornet Project, I began to realize that collecting the drawings and conversations would, over time, become dramatic data that would help me better understand the children's theories. Unfortunately, I did not keep any of the documentation that I started. How much I regret that I did not take any photographs; I made no memory of that experience whatsoever. The children carried their drawings and paintings home in their backpacks. This experience taught me the importance of documenting all magical learning.

## The Value of Documentation

Documentation is more than a memory board, book, or beautiful panels. It is validation for the hard work of all involved. It documents the very process of learning. Now that I am teaching kindergarten, I find that children do enjoy looking at panels showing photographs of their efforts. They have learned to search for their names in type, because "Mrs. Dillon loves our words." The children know that I value what they do each day in class. If they see me sitting with a clipboard near a group of block builders, they know that I am interested in what they are doing. I validate their love of learning every time I engage in a conversation about what they have chosen to do.

A discovery is made each time the teacher takes the energy to listen carefully to children's conversations. We can learn what is important to them, what occupies their thinking, and what possibilities exist for further discovery. Parents know what has occurred in the classroom because I can show them through documentation. It truly is a celebration of the things we choose to explore at school. I cannot imagine continuing teaching now without documenting certain projects. Bulletin boards in my classroom are no longer for sheer decoration. Each board has a definite purpose and meaning. The whole concept is enormously respectful of the entire learning process. My classroom is now a place that not only supports and facilitates learning but also displays and explains learning as it transpires.

## My Biggest Headache

The most significant issue for me as a public school educator in America is our society's expectation of what curriculum should consist of and the need to balance those expectations with the Reggio philosophy of the emergent curriculum. For as long as schools have existed in the United States, educators have decided what subjects and lessons should be taught.

In place of that conventional approach, Reggio teachers have dramatically involved children in taking responsibility for their own learning, and they have successfully incorporated parents into the school program also. In Reggio Emilia, parents, teachers, and children choose the curriculum, by collaborating together, and teachers take the responsibility for weaving in an interest in early reading, writing, and counting activities.

## Integrating the Designated and the Emergent Curricula in a Creative Way

The way I have resolved the problem of honoring both approaches in my classroom has been to look carefully at our designated curriculum and find what within that curriculum excites, invites, and involves children. In this way, the designated curriculum can be blended with the emergent one. I carefully dissect the required units before they are taught to see how I can best incorporate the children's interests. If, for instance, I am charged with teaching about winter, I could easily make a project study of ice crystals if this reflects an emerging interest of the children. I could provoke their curiosity by inviting them to wonder about how icicles form. I might ask them to create patterns similar to those found on the windows using clear materials like plastic, wire, or lace. Some questions might be "Why do I see these patterns when it's cold and not when it's hot?" or "Can we find similar designs anywhere else in our world?" or "In your opinion, tell me how you think these beautiful designs got on this window?" Or even, "Can you show me how this icicle got so long and pointy?" If the children were unable to

respond to my questions, I would know to change my questioning or provide an experience to help them think things through.

## Including Parents in the Classroom Helps Them
## Understand the Value of the Emergent Approach

Parents and community members contribute enormously in my classroom.
The Reggio teachers have shown me that involving these important sources
enriches everyone's view and understanding of school. Parents need to
understand the differences between this newer approach to teaching and
the way they were taught long ago. Parents who are involved in the classroom will see their child's interactions and quickly see how the approach
strengthens and supports the child's own curiosity.

In my classroom, parents are invited to help in many ways. They can
sign up to be a parent volunteer in the classroom setting. These parents can
come as often as they wish, and they are scheduled on a master calendar for
my planning needs. When in the classroom, parents work with children in
small groups. They are taught to jot down conversations, ask probing questions, assist in project work, and enjoy the many interactions of the children. Other parents choose to help me compile, arrange, and display documentation. Those who are unable to serve as volunteers help me collect
materials for the classroom, provide film and processing funds, type conversations for documentation, and support us in any other way they can. I
make sure there are plenty of opportunities for parents to hear and read
about the Reggio Approach. I want and depend on their support, interest,
and involvement. The result is that I could not ask for a more interested,
involved group of parents. Each year, I gain more supporters of this
approach.

## What Is the True Meaning of the Hundred
## Languages of Children? The Rat Project

I would venture to guess that most teachers who first encounter the schools
of Reggio Emilia would say that this is an "art" curriculum. I have to admit
that I, myself, was first drawn to the schools purely because the creations
and representations of learning are displayed in such a beautiful, artistic
manner. The documentation does have a museum-like quality. However, the
longer I study this approach, the more I realize that what the teachers are
searching to hear and see are the hundred ways youngsters can learn and
explain what they know.

I believe that I gained a further understanding of the concept of the hundred languages this year when my class pursued a study of rats with my student teacher, Sylvia Bronner. Having the opportunity to sit back and observe her interactions with the children and their various methods of gaining understanding was fascinating! Sylvia engaged the children in many large- and small-group conversations regarding the possibility of having a rat for a class pet. She asked them difficult questions to force them to think seriously about this pet. She said, "People are usually afraid of rats. We have to find out *why* and if we should be afraid, too." In our planning for this project, Sylvia and I spent hours thinking of important questions to raise with the children. We met each afternoon after the children went home to review what had occurred that day. Early in the process, she asked them, "What kind of home does a rat need?" and "In your opinion, how will we manage feeding and keeping the rat's home clean?" We were thrilled by a child's question "How will we know if our rat is happy?"

After we had the pet for a few weeks, we were faced with the dilemma of finding suitable exercise for the rat. Sylvia presented the problem to the children. "We have to find a way for the rat to run around and still be safe. How can we do this?" The children worked through models using the wooden blocks and classroom furniture. Eventually, they came up with the idea of transforming a refrigerator box using smaller boxes, rocks, yarn, and other found materials. At this point, the group brainstormed how to get some parents to help. They invited parent volunteers to help them with the construction. When the rat jumped out of the box, they had to wrestle with the idea of using a lid. It became important to the children to find a clear or see-through lid. A helpful parent provided an old acrylic storm window. Each challenge led to a new discovery and a new activity. The box contained an elaborate maze, stairway, and even a simple elevator! When their box was completed, they showed it off at a whole-school open house.

Even though most parents were not crazy about handling the rat, they visited our classroom often and listened as their children shared new information. The children enjoyed fictional and factual stories. We photographed their every step and watched the experience unfold.

*Meeting Expectations.*   Skills acquired were documented for the teachers and parents. Specifically, the children learned to measure with a ruler, make predictions, and find information within an encyclopedia. The rat study gave them a reason to learn to measure. We noticed, in addition to these newly acquired skills, a marked increase in interest in the school library. Children read more often both to find information and just for fun. An experience like this contextualizes learning in a meaningful way. One of the most rewarding aspects of this project was seeing the ownership of the work in the children. They would teach and share all that they knew with any classroom visitor. In the end, I came to the realization that the project from start to finish was expertly managed and maintained by the children with support from the teacher. There were so many ways to reach an understanding of rats!

## *Final Thought*

The Reggio teachers have made it clear that they do not wish to be a "model" program for others to duplicate. Rather, they insist on growing and adapting each year themselves as they become more knowledgeable about children and the needs of their community. I intend to continue to follow their lead and work to learn and study as much as I can, also. It has been very rewarding to know and involve my community as I learn. Most valuable of all has been the drawing together of wonderful educators in pursuit of better education for everyone.

# 11

# *Implementing Reggio in an Independent School*
## What Works?

*Barbara Geiger*
Director, Overfield Early Childhood Program, Troy, Ohio

The Overfield Early Childhood Program was founded in 1960 as the Overfield Nursery School by Troy, Ohio, resident Julia D. Hobart as a direct result of the lack of an appropriate nursery school for her 3-year-old daughter. As a professionally trained early childhood educator and person of unique insight and vision, she saw the need for a developmentally appropriate program that would be unique to the area (a small town located 25 miles north of Dayton, Ohio).

The school began with 12 students in two back rooms of the Overfield Museum and remained there 29 years, while growing to an enrollment of 60 students and becoming accredited by the National Academy of Young Children. The expanded program, renamed the Overfield Early Childhood Program, moved into the historic Edward and Martha Hobart home in the fall of 1989 and now serves 175 students (ages 3–6). Classes for preschoolers are offered two, three, and five half-day sessions per week, and kindergarten classes are offered five half-day sessions a week. Extended care is also available.

## HOW CHANGE BEGAN

Overfield's approach to early childhood education has always been eclectic—a constant examination of new theories and ideas and incorporation of them when appropriate. So, we were intrigued when we heard that "The Hundred Languages of Children" exhibit was coming to the Dayton Art Institute in 1990. Staff members attended the many workshops held at the Institute in conjunction with the exhibit. While there, they found many examples of developmentally appropriate practices in the Reggio Emilia Approach, but they also realized that children were capable of far more in-depth exploration and investigation than they had previously thought. Children could also show what they had learned, share this information with others, and continue their investigations through the use of symbolic languages. The idea of incorporating this possibility into what was already being done at Overfield was exciting, and the first consideration for change was the "image of the child" because staff felt the image is the key to any attempted American interpretation. Loris Malaguzzi (1994b) said, "It's necessary that we believe that the child is strong and beautiful and has very ambitious desires and requests. This is the image of the child that we need to hold" (p. 61).

## A DELICATE BALANCE

Acceptance of this image is just the first step. Knowing how to act on it is vital and takes time to understand. We found it difficult to know just how much teacher input should be contributed. We knew that we were supposed to observe and take the lead from the children and that doing this involved observing carefully and extensively and making critical decisions. For a while we were afraid of imposing our own ideas on the children. We knew they were not just empty vessels, but we were not quite sure what to do. Gradually, we progressed from just watching them and thinking, "They're not giving us anything to go with," to trying to achieve a delicate balance between teacher input and student input. Teachers now plan for worthwhile experiences while still honoring the children's input. The ideas may come from the teacher (e.g., they know there are tadpoles in a pond near the school each year and that some aspect of this will be explored), the children (e.g., a child may ask, "What does a squirrel eat?"), or a chance occurrence (e.g., a bird builds a nest in a tree outside a classroom window). Teachers plan ahead, make appropriate preparations, and then make adjustments as needed. This, however, is easier said than done. We are still working on that delicate balance.

## CHANGES IN PARENT INVOLVEMENT

We had always had a lot of parental involvement (helping in classrooms, fund raising, end-of-year festival, etc.), but my image of the parent changed when I attended the study seminar in Reggio. "I am the teacher; you are the parent; I'll explain education to you" was no longer valid. Parents, too, bring things of great value to the learning situation. They, like the children, are not empty vessels—we all must construct our learning together.

End-of-year evaluations filled out by parents had always been carefully considered, but it now became important to have their input at the beginning of the school year as well. In the fall of 1994, I distributed a questionnaire to parents, asking them to describe their expectations for the school year and the experience they would like their child to have. Responses were carefully studied by teachers and discussed with parents. We also began looking at the child as a part of a group as well as individually. I feel this is very important in planning for the growth of the "total child." We still have two individual parent-teacher conferences each year, but we added two parent group meetings during the 1994–95 school year. During a parent group meeting, all parents of an individual class meet with a teacher in the evening to discuss what is happening in class and plan together. This approach has been so successful that parents have requested that we add a third parent group meeting for next school year.

## CHANGES IN CURRICULUM

Good things were happening with the curriculum in our school as we discovered opportunities for in-depth explorations. However, we were still feeling somewhat "fragmented" and "overworked" because of our schedul-ing and the fact that these in-depth experiences were happening within one class, with little or no carryover to other classes. The teachers became exhausted trying to keep separate major investigations going on in many separate classes. So, we had to figure out a more realistic way to deal with that problem.

## COORDINATING A PROJECT THAT INVOLVES A SHIFTING POPULATION OF CHILDREN: THE CASTLE PROJECT

During the 1994–95 school year, a Castle Project evolved that was particu-larly exciting because it involved 3- and 4-year-old children from four differ-ent classes: Red Group (MTW morning), Green Group (MTW afternoon), Yellow Group (ThF morning), and Blue Group (ThF afternoon). The investi-gations progressed from Red Group to Green Group to Yellow Group to Blue Group and back to Red Group, with common experiences such as liter-ature, songs, environment, and changes that the children and teachers made to ongoing activities and materials included for everyone. The com-mon core experiences were done by all the groups and bound the experi-ence together. Changes and progress by intervening classes were viewed by the children as "surprises" and added an impetus to their play and explo-ration. As the project continued, children from additional classes floated in and out of the project while finding it fun and rewarding. It unified the interest and experience of the whole school.

In late October, teachers noted an interest by the Red Group in build-ing castles in the block area and talking about castles:

P.J.:      It's a castle for a person who is a princess.

Ann:      Guards stand by the door.

Children began using blankets and tablecloths from the housekeeping cor-ner for stately robes, indicating an extended interest. During this time, the teachers and I had many conversations about assessing interest, knowledge, and availability of resources to sustain an in-depth study. The teachers pre-pared some questions to ask the children in the Red Group to determine interest and/or direction of interest: "Do you think we need to know more about castles?" "Where can we find out?" The children's answers indicated they wanted to know more about castles, and they felt that books would give them the needed information. A small group of children helped a teacher find some books in the school library, the teachers brought in books, and some children brought books from home. Meanwhile, teachers contin-ued to listen carefully and document what was happening in the castle area.

When teachers and children returned in January, after a 2-week break, the children's interest in castles was still there:

*Katy:*     Kings live in a castle.

*Jody:*     The queen lives in the castle. And the maid.

From discussions with the children, teachers determined that there was an interest in the castle as a place to live.

Experiences with castle shapes on the light table were introduced, and shadow play with castle shadow outlines on the wall provided a backdrop for dramatic play. It took a full 2 weeks to introduce these activities to all four classes.

At a parent group meeting in mid-January, the teachers discussed with the parents what was happening in the Castle Project and shared some documentation with parents. Parents volunteered to send in costumes and did so the very next day. The arrival of the costumes made the children very excited. They noticed the similarities in their costumes to costumes pictured in the books and started making accessories (crowns and flags) seen in their books. This activity was happening in all four classes. The teachers noticed that the children loved dressing up in the costumes but then did not seem to know what to do.

The teachers decided the children needed more information to extend their role playing. They asked the children in the Yellow Group what else they needed. "A castle" was their reply. The teachers then asked what could be used to make a castle. The children decided to use large blocks to define the castle boundaries and a familiar piece of play equipment (the rocking boat steps) as an entrance to the castle. The Red Group was delighted to discover this on their arrival the following Monday morning. In all four classes, then, a lot of play centered around the castle entrance, and castle guards became very important in granting and denying entrance to the castle: "We have to guard the castle from people" (Jake).

When a teacher asked Jake and a small group of children about the identity of the people who might be coming to the castle, the children replied, "Bad guys." To introduce more people involved in castle life, the teachers acted out "Sing a Song of Sixpence" and "The Princess and the Pea" for all four classes. More castle books were added. Children in all classes began spontaneously acting out these rhymes and stories, employing props that teachers had added, as well as props that they themselves had decided to make.

Some children from the Yellow Group then expressed the desire to have the castle look more like the castles in the picture books. On January 20, they worked together to make a more realistic castle. After looking at books and brainstorming, the children chose cardboard as their construction material to make a child-sized model. It was constructed, painted, and much admired. One child in the Blue Group decided it needed a drawbridge. "A door that goes up and down with ropes. You tie ropes. We can make a hole with a needle for the ropes and tie them on the door" (Scott).

A teacher asked Scott where he could get materials for this kind of drawbridge. He suggested going to the school's basement where many materials were stored. He and the teacher went to the basement and found the needed materials: a large piece of cardboard, clothesline rope, and a large tapestry needle. The drawbridge was made according to his directions. When making the hole for the rope, he discovered the needle could be pushed through the cardboard but would not make a hole large enough for the rope to go through. The teachers asked him what else could be used to make the hole, and he suggested scissors. When the child-sized blunt scissors did not work, the teacher asked him whether he could think of a different type of scissors that might work. He suggested the large, point-ended scissors used by the teachers. This solution was successful. On its completion, the drawbridge could actually be raised and lowered, which gave additional duties to the castle guards.

After school, the teachers set up two throne chairs draped with luxurious-looking fabric in the castle and added stick horses as a surprise for the children. The surprise was a great success! About this same time, two children in the Red Group decided to make a treasure chest similar to a chest in a castle book. This gave the king and queen something to do while sitting on their thrones: they counted their money.

The children in all four classes were delighted with these additions and used them joyously. They came in every day excited about changes they observed and then added information and ideas of their own. On January 24, a child expressed dissatisfaction with his stick horse. He wanted it to look more like the "castle horses" draped with accoutrements as pictured in the castle books. A trip was made to the basement to search for materials. He chose a wooden saw horse as the basic structure. He decided that accoutrements could be made with paper and materials available in the art area. Three other children expressed interest and started to help. Some older children (4- and 5-year-olds) from another part of the building who had also expressed interest in the castle horse were invited to help and soon were very involved in the work. The castle horse was fancy, but the children soon discovered it to be stationary. When the teacher asked, "What shall we do?" they decided that the castle horse would remain as a decorative example of a castle horse, and they would continue riding the stick horses.

By the end of January, virtually everyone in the school had some interest in castles. Children from all over the building were interested in what was happening in the four classes where the project originated and would stop by to observe, offer help and suggestions, and play in the castle. Parents were coming to school specifically to see those "castle things." Children in the Red Group were observed eating a lot of bread and honey during dramatic play. Teachers observed this interest and felt it could be used to offer the children an experience with mixed-age grouping and occasions for learning together. When the teachers suggested hosting a bread and honey feast, the proposal was immediately accepted. They decided to invite the morning kindergarten class because some were older siblings, and some had helped with previous castle work. A small group of children dictated the invitation to the teacher, decorated it, and delivered it to the kindergarten class. After a short class discussion, the kindergarten students decided they would like very much to attend. One kindergarten girl suggested they wear costumes. Another kindergarten student acting as scribe wrote back accepting the invitation and asking whether they should wear costumes. The Red Group discussed the matter of costumes. A message was dictated, decorated, and delivered saying yes. The kindergarten children researched and made costumes to wear; the younger children baked bread for the feast; and a good time was had by all.

On January 25, the Red and Green Groups showed an increased interest in dragons. Children had seen dragons in their castle books and enjoyed singing "Puff the Magic Dragon." A teacher noted they had been singing it in the castle area and then started discussing dragons in a factual way:

Ken:      Dragons live in water.

*Ann:*     Dragons don't live in the castle—they live outside and try to get in.

The next day the teacher initiated a discussion of dragons and ascertained a real interest with little knowledge. When children were asked where we could find out more about dragons, their answer was "books." For this particular project, books were our main source of reference. Ordinarily, when children are asked where we can find out more about a specific subject, the answers are usually much more varied. Someone will suggest a person we can ask, a place we can visit, or somewhere we can write for answers, or some children will say they can bring something from home. Unfortunately, we could think of no one with personal experience of dragons. Additional songs and books about dragons were found by teachers, students, and parents and were brought into the classroom. All four classes began drawing dragon pictures; some children started drawing spontaneously and others after observing other children's interest and drawings. Some children used the copy machine to enlarge their drawings. They fit their pieces together carefully and painted them. Several of these children continued to explore dragons through clay. Showing much wear and being in poor repair, the castle and drawbridge were removed from the play area the first week in February. The children's focus was now on dragons.

Children in the Green Group decided they wanted to make a dragon and started what was to be the culminating activity of this project. With the help of teachers, other classes, kindergartners, and children from extended care, the children constructed their own dragon. A small group from the Green Group went to the basement to choose materials to begin. They picked big wooden spools for the dragon's legs but then decided they were too much fun to sit on. So, they decided to nail them together.

When the neck became too weak to support the head, a letter was written to several older children (in a class of 4- and 5-year-olds) who had been observing the progress. The letter requested their help with the neck. Help was soon given. They decided to use a strong cardboard tube for the neck, and one of the older children used a saw to cut the tube, which was then used successfully to reattach the head.

Many children became involved in plastering the dragon (with gauze and plaster normally used to make casts for broken limbs). A teacher had proposed using these materials, and the children had agreed. One afternoon, a morning kindergarten child from extended care had come in to help with the dragon when the casting supplies ran out. She said her father was a doctor, and she would bring in more supplies the next day. She did. The children added facial features, spikes, front legs, and wings (using books as references) while continually assessing the dragon construction from day to day and class to class to determine what work remained undone. Groups of children formed and then reformed while work was in progress. Some would stand by giving advice, and sometimes a child would stand with an open book showing workers how a particular feature should look. On February 15, the dragon was completed and placed in the play area of the classroom. It was declared "magnificent," and the whole school took pride in its completion.

This project held high interest and satisfaction for teachers, students, and parents. At the beginning, the teachers first noticed the children's interest; listened to their words; collaborated with children, staff, and parents; asked questions; planned; presented materials; and set the environment—meanwhile documenting all that was happening.

Parents sent in materials and stopped in frequently to see what was happening. They felt not only an interest in what was going on but also an inclusion in the project. The documentation posted on the classroom walls remained a source of great interest.

Teachers learned from the experience:

❑  the importance of daily observations and documentation,
❑  the importance of daily collaboration with other staff,
❑  the importance of planning carefully and remaining flexible,
❑  how to proceed and build on investigation with four separate classes,

❑ how students from other classes could be a part of these investigations, and

❑ that not every child must have the same exact experience to be a good experience.

Children gained from the experience:

❑ time to explore fantasy versus reality,

❑ opportunities for role playing,

❑ social skill development,

❑ cooperative learning through group work,

❑ problem solving,

❑ how to use books as sources of information,

❑ how to put ideas into graphics,

❑ how to translate graphics into concrete experiences, and

❑ heightened self-esteem by sharing work and skills with older children.

Children used many expressive languages to demonstrate their knowledge and understanding:

❑ dramatic play,

❑ verbal language (talking among themselves and with adults),

❑ graphic language (descriptive drawing and writing),

❑ three-dimensional materials (clay, collage, construction),

❑ songs,

❑ movement, and

❑ shadow play.

The experience of attempting an American interpretation has been frustrating at times but always rewarding. Each discovery brings a thirst for more knowledge. When I first started studying the Reggio Approach, I found much that was familiar—things that we already knew about developmentally appropriate practice. It was not a matter of throwing out everything and starting over. Rather, it was a matter of recognizing that what we were doing was good but could be made even better by incorporating some of the Reggio Approach. At the same time, we also recognize that the approach at Overfield will always reflect our own culture and history. In this way, the Reggio Approach can become an American interpretation reflecting great respect for the Italian inspiration and our own American heritage.

# IV

# Working with Staff to Bring About Change

Part IV shifts the discussion from making direct changes in the classroom to bringing about changes at the organization level. In contrast to Barbara Geiger's description of Overfield, Karen Haigh's chapter takes us to a very different setting in inner-city Chicago. As director of a child development program providing care for 970 children at 8 different sites, her problem was how to inspire her staff to take an interest in the Reggio Approach so they would teach the children that way. Undaunted by situations many of us would find disheartening, she concludes with a long list of future hopes as she envisions her staff and children gaining empowerment from using the Reggio Approach.

Like Haigh, Rosalyn Saltz also wished to bring about change in her staff, but this staff consisted of teachers at the University of Michigan Child Development Center. She reviews some fundamental tenets of the Reggio philosophy and explains how the teachers incorporated them into their teaching. Then she cites some roadblocks that have occurred along their journey and explains what they did to solve them.

Finally, Fran Donovan takes us away from the traditional educational setting of children's centers and schools to an interesting variation of that educational theme as she shows how Reggio can influence the learning process in a children's museum. She draws some interesting comparisons between children's museums and the schools in Reggio Emilia and then describes how applying the Reggio philosophy brought about changes in the way the museum offered learning experiences to children and their teachers.

# 12

# How the Reggio Approach Has Influenced an Inner-City Program

## Exploring Reggio in Head Start and Subsidized Child Care

*Karen Haigh*

Director, Chicago Commons Child Development Programs

Chicago Commons is a 100-year-old settlement house that provides multisocial services at various sites throughout Chicago's
Near Northwest, Near West, and South Sides. Its Child Development Program provides care and education for 970 children
at 8 different sites. Types of programs include Head Start for 3-
to 5-year-olds, subsidized child care for infants through 12-year-olds, state
prekindergarten for 3- to 5-year-olds, and a day care homes network for
infants through 3-year-olds.

Commons' Child Development Program serves mostly Hispanic and
African American populations. Each site is unique as it represents the community it serves. Most sites have common community problems such as
high rates of unemployment, illiteracy, substance abuse, domestic and community violence, along with inadequate health care and housing. However,
some communities we serve have more severe problems than others. For
example, one site, Mile Square, is located in Henry Horner Homes, a
Chicago housing project written about extensively in the book *There Are No
Children Here* (Kotlowitz, 1991).

Each site has a site director, a family worker, teachers, and support
staff. The central office has a child development director (my position), two
education coordinators, two support services coordinators, a health coordinator, and administrative staff. Many of the staff reflect or come from the
communities they serve. As a result, staff may spend a great deal of energy
and effort supporting children and families with extreme challenges
because of a lack of resources and opportunities only to go home and face
many of these same challenges themselves! Staff education and background
vary tremendously. Some teachers have bachelor's degrees, some have their
CDA (Child Development Associate) or are working to earn it, and some
have only 30 hours in child development. It is extremely difficult to find
degreed teachers to work in our programs because of the low salaries and
challenging communities. Sometimes interviewees do not show up for initial interviews once they have sized up the neighborhood.

## HOW INTEREST IN REGGIO BEGAN

I have been fortunate to visit Reggio Emilia to study the early childhood
program twice in the past 4 years. After returning the first time, I really had
no idea how any of the Reggio elements could be applied to our programs.
Reggio Emilia and the inner city of Chicago are so completely different.
However, I did continue to think about Reggio frequently, especially since I
met regularly with Fran Donovan (former museum education director, current teacher), Dan Scheinfeld (researcher), and Lynn White (teacher) to
reflect on our trip to Reggio and discuss what each of us had been doing or

thinking about with regard to the Reggio Approach. These bimonthly meetings have been invaluable to me as an administrator. Often administrators are so overwhelmed in dealing with bureaucracies, personnel problems, program crises, and inadequate funding that having the time to reflect and think about such areas as curriculum and the learning process, philosophy, the role of the teacher, and so forth, is a luxury.

I did do a presentation of my first trip to Italy for Commons staff that included a variety of slides and overview of the Reggio Approach. Then Fran, Dan, and Sue Sturtevant (a children's museum director who had gone on the first Reggio tour with us) did a 3-hour presentation on shadows for Commons staff. Staff seemed to show a great deal of interest in studying shadows as a result.

Because some Commons staff showed even further interest in studying Reggio, they were sent to more in-depth seminars on its approach. Eight staff were sent to a week-long seminar in Traverse City, Michigan, and eight to a week-long seminar in Chicago. It was after these seminars in July 1993 that staff began to say, "When are we going to begin doing something with Reggio and our classrooms?" I was waiting for them to show an interest. Now the desire was there, and I began to plan ways to explore the Approach with staff.

# THE FIRST YEAR

## Exposing Staff to Reggio and Assessing Interest

It was decided to have any Commons team interested in exploring the Reggio Approach fill out one questionnaire together as a team. A team consisted of a site director, a head teacher, an assistant teacher, and a family worker. I really wanted to emphasize a more collaborative approach by having directors and family workers participate as team members with teachers. Usually these people have not been directly involved in any new curriculum approach, but I think their involvement is essential. The first year 7 teams applied from 6 sites, while 10 teams from 7 sites applied the second year. We chose to work with teams who volunteered because we did not have enough support staff to include all 160 Commons child development staff. Plus I have found that it is more successful to allow some staff to volunteer to participate in something this complex than to mandate that all staff study a new approach. When curriculum approaches are mandated by administration with little staff interest or initiation, there is often much resistance. It is also important to note that just as teachers should be encouraged to see and use opportunities to facilitate children's study of an interest or topic, administrators should be encouraged to see and use ways to facilitate teachers' study of children and the learning process.

## Constructing a New Building Using Some Reggio Influences

Two new sites were built within the first and second years of Commons' exploration with the Reggio Approach. Nia Family Center was newly constructed in 1994, and Guadalupano was renovated in 1995. There were great limitations in what we could construct or renovate.

Nia was a very special project funded by the Illinois Facility Fund (a nonprofit agency that provides funding for the purchase of new buildings or building renovations) and the State of Illinois. Seven new child care centers were built in Illinois. Commons was one of three agencies chosen to have a new facility built in Chicago. Some conditions of the program were that at least 150 children be served and infants and toddlers be served, it must be in a needy area, and many limitations were set on size and costs.

The name *Nia* is associated with the African American celebration Kwanzaa. It means "to have a sense of purpose and to bring the community

*The studio at Nia Family Center is intended to facilitate studying life as well as enjoying art.*

back to its sense of greatness." After being exposed to Reggio, I have given greater importance and value to the process of choosing a center name. In the past, a name was thought up quickly by relating to the name of the community area.

Nia was the first building built in 20 years within this West Humboldt Park community. The community had felt ignored and deprived of basic services and resources for years. It was even difficult for them to believe we were actually going to build a child care center. They believed adamantly that we were going to build housing projects. Clearly there was a lack of trust that anything good would be built within the community. We developed a committee of board members and people from the community to work together to address issues such as the name of the center and program planning. I believe that it was well worth taking the extra time to go through the long process of deciding on a meaningful name. Nia really represents a new hope for the community.

Nia has 47 staff of which approximately two-thirds were hired from the community. Many of the staff had jobs for the first time and needed a great deal of guidance on what is appropriate work behavior.

The center provides care and education for 156 eligible (publicly funded care for low-income families) children from 6 weeks to 12 years of age. It also serves 68 Head Start children, aged 3 to 5 years.

The building had to be built quickly (within 6 months) because of the time frame that the Illinois Facility Fund was mandated to meet. I had my first meeting with the architects in November 1993, and the building was completed in May 1994. Fortunately, our assigned architect, Heidi Hoppe, had read some articles about Reggio and was very responsive to my requests for Reggio influences. However, many disappointments arose because of funding and time limitations and code restrictions. For example, I had tried to get a separate room for lunch, but it was too costly. A piazza or "common area" was planned, but the fire department would not approve it. As a result, the common area had to be walled in as a separate area.

Despite these restrictions, subtle Reggio influences are included throughout the building. More soft, subdued, or earth-tone colors were chosen throughout for the building's walls and flooring. We have been especially influenced by a comment Lella Gandini made while visiting our centers: "The children will bring color to the program." Our eyes should be drawn more to the children and their work rather than the color of the walls or the background of the bulletin boards.

We wanted to have as much natural light as possible. Natural light is not common in many of our centers. Windows became an issue as the architect wanted to have floor-to-ceiling windows so there could be an abundance of natural light. However, Nia is in a neighborhood that endures frequent graffiti and violence. Large windows can become an easy target. We negotiated and decided to use glass block windows. They are safer and less costly to replace if damaged. I was concerned that they would look too institutional, but they turned out to be especially beautiful. Small skylights were also put in some of the hallways. At times we notice children moving under the skylights and looking up.

We wanted to offer children opportunities to see what was happening in other rooms, as well as what others were doing. Therefore, small windows were put between rooms, and many were placed between the walls of the large motor room or "common area." The present windows between classrooms are very small, 1 × 1 foot, and should have been made much larger, at least 2 feet wide. I thought windows would not be necessary in the infants' rooms. I was very wrong. Windows seem to be a very popular activity for infants as they begin to crawl, stand, and walk. They frequently are interested in watching what others are doing or trying to engage others. I keep recalling comments, from a Reggio seminar, that emphasized how infants show interest in socializing not only with their parents but with others in general. I see infants' great interest in socializing every time I go to Nia. The infants often go to the windows by the doors and attempt to engage and interact with people going down the hall. It is clear that the infants should have windows between their classrooms. Staff have requested to have the additional windows installed between the two infant rooms. We hope to make this change in the near future.

We were able to build a "studio" with such things as a large magnifying glass (the size of a child), pictures of families from the community that someone had thrown out, fish and plants, shelving and storage for a variety of free, found materials, a woodworking table, a work table with chairs, a large easel, an old bicycle wheel with crepe paper woven between the spokes, and a variety of art media. We are trying to remember to use the term *studio* instead of *art room* or *art studio* because it is a room that facilitates studying life, not just art.

We have spent and continue to spend time reflecting on sizes, types, placement, and use of documentation boards. It is important to note that while only some staff explore with the Reggio Approach, changes in or reflections about the environment tend to affect most staff in the program.

## *Working with Staff the First Year*

The first full year of exploring with the Reggio Emilia Approach began with a 3-day seminar focusing on some of the key elements: environment, image of the child, use of materials, the role of collaboration, emergent curriculum, the project approach, and documentation. We spent time discussing the anxiety of exploring something new. We reviewed some of the aspects of each of the previously mentioned elements. We allowed staff to explore with clay. We had Lynn White, a first grade public school teacher in Winnetka (an affluent North Shore suburb), do a presentation on her current work with children. We tried to have presentations, active experiences, discussions with much reflection, and team planning during those 3 days. Each team was asked to focus on some of the elements they would like to explore throughout the year. I am aware that the elements are integrated and work together, so it is difficult to separate them out and center on just one or two. However, staff were too overwhelmed to try to think about more than two or three elements at once. It turned out that some staff only wanted to choose one element to explore.

I must also note that all the teams exploring Reggio are working with 3- to 5-year-olds. We hope to one day be able to explore with school-age and infant-toddler programs but currently do not have enough resources to do so.

We planned that the main avenue for exploring Reggio with the teams would be conducting weekly team meetings with the team and a facilitator. A facilitator would be a central office education coordinator or me. I felt it was very important that someone other than the team be there to help staff focus and bring in an outside perspective.

Monthly group meetings, open to anyone, focused on some general topic, while the weekly meeting centered entirely on what was happening in the classroom of that particular site. The totally voluntary monthly group meetings were after hours because no other time was available for additional meetings. We always try at least to offer a meal to staff attending.

Both weekly and monthly meetings have been essential for staff to have the opportunity to discuss and build their knowledge of the learning process, the child's abilities, the teacher's role, and the parents' role. Making sure these meetings get scheduled and occur has been a very big challenge. I have had to make them a high priority. During the first year, having enough central office support was particularly difficult. Our education coordinator had to take a leave and was not available, which affected our ability to have enough facilitators, but we managed.

Some highlights of the first year were that staff were really overwhelmed and nervous about trying to explore Reggio. They chose to go very slowly and often only to focus on one element. Some teams considered the image of the child, and some tried to do miniprojects that included studying birds and nests, signs, clouds, and buildings. We learned that even in the most desolate places of the city, interesting topics can arise for children and teachers to study. Some staff also began to do presentations in which they shared their experiences and learnings with others. Finally, I will always recall a comment made by a visitor attending our monthly meeting: "It seems like the Commons teachers really like their jobs." A clearly deepened sense of commitment has emerged from staff.

# THE SECOND YEAR

Two major challenges occurred within the second year. First, we had experienced major, rapid growth, which caused great stress to our program. We had grown from approximately 625 children to 975 children, with both Nia and Guadalupano Family Centers beginning program operations. Second, we experienced a severe shooting at Mile Square as a staff member (a maintenance worker) was shot. Such an incident is very upsetting to children, families, and staff. We now have a psychologist who is available to support staff when violent crises occur.

## Renovating Guadalupano Family Center

During our second year exploring Reggio, we renovated Guadalupano, a new site in Pilsen, a Hispanic neighborhood. We were influenced by Reggio as we were able to choose more earth-tone colors, install windows between classrooms, and include a studio. Guadalupano is off a plaza used by the neighborhood as a gathering place. An amazing amount of community involvement is evident here. Indeed, it was the community working together for the past 3 years that caused the center to be built in a former Catholic school. We were sought out to manage the program. We are adding a team from Guadalupano to explore Reggio next year.

## Reggio Emilia Revisited

I was fortunate to attend a 2-week seminar in Reggio Emilia. Dan Scheinfeld and Fran Donovan also attended, which meant that Dan, Fran, and I could continue discussing our trip regularly. One memory of the trip that stands out for me were comments made by another participant, Gunilla Dahlberg from Sweden. She said that she had been studying Reggio with staff for the past 5 years. They made all kinds of changes in their environments, yet not too much seemed to be happening. Then, she said, they began to focus heavily on the image of the child. They began to videotape children and study them, and that step greatly impacted their programs. This information was very helpful as I planned the second year.

## Exploring with the Reggio Emilia Curriculum Approach

We began our second year with a 2-day seminar for our Reggio teams, including an additional team from our new Nia program. We spent some time reflecting on the past year. It was decided that there would be a common focus on the *environment* and the *image of the child*. I firmly believed that in order to fully implement some of the Reggio elements, we had to take the needed time to look at our former image of the child and change it to include recognition of the child's capabilities, interests, and potential. We began to videotape children and observe 10-minute videos in our monthly Reggio meetings. Some sites began to do their own videotaping to view and discuss at their weekly meetings. The videotaping process led us to two realizations. First, we had a very poor inventory of audiovisual equipment. I used to think that AV equipment was an unnecessary expense, but now I see how it can help children and especially teachers in the learning process. We only had one camcorder for all eight sites. We realized a great deal of new equipment such as camcorders, slide projectors, overhead projectors, VCRs, and cameras was needed at almost all sites. We spent months assessing what was needed, searching for funds, developing security plans, and finally ordering, purchasing, and delivering the audiovisual equipment. We used general agency inservice time to introduce different kinds of equipment to staff.

Second, we realized that when looking at videos of children, we were constantly on the lookout for what was wrong: what was wrong with the classroom, what the teacher should have done, and so forth. Ayers (1994) has said that "it is much easier to notice what is wrong than to notice what is right." That is so true. It is much more difficult to focus on what is going well. I think we are trained from early on to focus on the deficit, on what is wrong and what needs to be fixed. Many times we focus on a child's growth by noting what he cannot do as opposed to what he can. We have just begun to be amazed by what the children we videotape *can* do. Our goal is to become real listeners and real observers of children.

Paley (1995) states that one essential lesson learned after teaching 37 years is "to take very seriously the things that children say and take equally seriously the things you say to children" (p. 14). We plan to continue to develop skills and knowledge in listening to children. Our next goal will then be to pay more attention to what we say to children, taking our comments more seriously and developing better skills in talking with them as we support their construction of knowledge. We want to become better at truly building on children's strengths.

During the second year, we also worked hard at becoming more consistent with our weekly team meetings. For some reason these meetings can easily be canceled. Because of their value, we have to treat these meetings as the most cherished of all meetings, yet it sometimes becomes difficult to be consistent. At times staff have needed to be pushed a little to try something new. It can happen that staff will continue to talk and talk about children, activities, and their classrooms and never actually apply new aspects of Reggio elements unless given a great deal of encouragement and sometimes a push.

Some topics children studied were homes, offices, beds, doctor's offices, and how to decorate a cubby. Children took weeks to think about, plan, purchase, bring from home, or make items to put in their cubbies. This was an excellent example of looking at the image of the child. Most often the teachers decide what will be in the child's cubbies, usually some type of sign for a name or some kind of symbol; but when thinking about children's capabilities, if children are supported and their ideas are respected, they are more than capable of planning and decorating their own cubbies. This is a small example of allowing the children to do for themselves what they are capable of doing and not robbing them of an opportunity. The children had many ideas for their cubbies as evidenced by photos of families, drawn pictures, cut-out pictures from magazines, miniature mobiles, miniature painted wood cut-outs, stuffed animals, and mirrors. Everyone wanted a mirror installed in their cubby.

## Hiring a Studio Coordinator

Our second year led to a brand-new position developed at Commons and influenced by Reggio. It was the position of studio coordinator, which is somewhat like the Reggio *atelierista*. It took us months to decide on a name for this position, and finding the right person to fill it turned out to be very

*The children took weeks to think about, plan, purchase, bring from home, or make items to put in their cubbies.*

difficult. We wanted someone with not only a background in the visual arts but also a respect for the learning process that allows children to explore, predict, analyze, and problem-solve while spending more time and focus on the process rather than the end product. Dave Kelly, who had a background at a children's museum, was hired. Dave is stationed at Nia but works with all the other sites. He has helped staff tremendously in looking at their environments and making dramatic changes such as adding lighting, making large easels, changing colors to be more soft and subdued, putting windows between rooms, installing mirrors, making and installing documentation boards, and adding studios with free, found materials, plants, and fish. Our goal for next year is to involve Dave more with some of the weekly meetings so he can plan and implement collaboratively with the teams. We desperately need an additional coordinator.

## Five Staff Attend a Study Tour of the Reggio Program

I had been the only person at Commons actually to see the schools of Reggio Emilia, and I wanted others within the agency, especially teachers who work on the front line, to see them too, but we did not have the money to send them. As a matter of fact, we have had no additional funds to explore any Reggio elements.

The staff agreed to have a major raffle to raise enough money for the trip. We raised $7,000, plus we had existing funds from a previous fundraiser. Thus, we were able to send five staff to Reggio Emilia on a study tour in April 1995. We went through a process that entailed applicants completing an intensive questionnaire. After reviewing the answers, the applicants' level of involvement, and their site location, the committee, composed of central office staff and a parent, selected the studio coordinator and four teachers. The parent commented on how difficult she felt it was to decide on who should go.

This was a very exciting time, since most of the staff do not have opportunities to travel extensively. They returned with a better understanding of Reggio. I was glad that now others besides myself could share their experience in Reggio. Although most of our staff work and live in communities with fewer resources than the Reggio program, it was interesting to note that staff did not emphasize all that the Reggio programs had that the Commons program lacked. It is very easy to notice all the things that the Reggio schools can do that we cannot do. Our staff seemed to see beyond that and focus on understanding more about the learning process for the child and what could be applied to our program. Again they were looking to see what *could* be done and not centering on what would not work.

## Parents

Determining how to include parents with regard to Reggio has been diffi-cult, and this issue raises the most questions among area staff. We are still so unsure of ourselves that it is uncomfortable to involve parents, but we are making a beginning. What was done with staff initially is being done with parents now. We are providing them with opportunities to become inter-ested in Reggio and waiting to see what happens. One encouraging inci-dent has already occurred. While interviewing an applicant for a central office position, a parent asked the applicant if she was familiar with the Reg-gio Emilia Approach. I was so surprised she asked about Reggio.

I think we spend too much time trying to explain Reggio instead of helping parents hear and see their children's work and ideas. When chil-dren's work has been displayed, some parents were pleasantly surprised by their children's thoughts and feelings. We will continue to look for opportu-nities to include parents more directly. I have a strong sense that the family worker, who is part of the team and often does not know quite how to fit in with Reggio, has the potential to develop a new image of parents and really work with them in a different way that looks at their capabilities and strengths. Unfortunately, the family worker position is currently bogged down with paperwork. We must find a way to address this issue.

## Staff Development

Our staff deal with numerous and sometimes extraordinary challenges within the program and sometimes within their own personal lives. Because of these circumstances, it sometimes can be difficult for them to have enough enthusiasm or interest to continue to study a new approach like Reggio. I believe that the administrator can play a great role in motivating people.

Administrators need to keep work exciting, interesting, and new. For example, I think each year the directors and I must find new activities to help maintain a high enough level of enthusiasm. Sending staff to a week-long seminar in another city or on a study tour to Reggio Emilia or involv-ing them with Erikson Institute's research are examples of contributions to enthusiasm.

For any curriculum approach to stay alive, teachers and staff must have frequent opportunities to reflect and discuss with each other. It is simi-lar to the collaboration with others that children need in order to construct or build knowledge. Because teachers and staff need these consistent oppor-tunities, administrators must assure that adequate meeting times are estab-lished. (I recall recently talking to a teacher who had attended a Reggio seminar a couple of years ago. She said she was never able to follow up and really work on it because she had no one to talk to about it.)

I have come to believe that it is important to help staff become better reflective practitioners. The education coordinator and director should both provide scaffolding or a framework for teachers to reflect on their role, the child's thinking, and the child's capabilities, interests, and potential. Taking time to reflect and look back at such things as how teachers or children became interested in an activity, how it began, what happened, or what has changed over time can serve as a tool to help staff develop a better understanding or new knowledge about children and learning or even adults and learning. It is true that you cannot go forward until you look back.

During the past year as we have studied the Reggio Approach, the staff and I have been looking at our image of children with the intention of seeing their capabilities, not their deficiencies; seeing their interests, not the adults' interests; and seeing their potential for learning, not their potential for making mistakes. It is difficult for teachers to become listeners and observers who notice children's capabilities and interests and then plan or wait for opportunities to support their learning. It is difficult for teachers to know when to step in and offer a challenging question, when to offer advice, when to stand back and watch and let the child discover, when to set limits, and when to support opportunities for children to advance on their own. These are some of the most challenging aspects of teaching.

Just as we look at the image of children, so it is also helpful to look at the image of teachers. How do we view teachers? Do we see them as listeners, observers, researchers, facilitators, problem solvers, learners? Or do we see them as the problem, or people who have fun jobs with cute, small children, or as people who no longer have anything left to learn? Like the teachers, we administrators also have a challenge. Just as teachers may be rethinking their image of children, we should be rethinking our image of teachers' capabilities, interests, and potential. We need to know when we should step in and offer support, suggestions, guidance, limits, or a new framework and when we should wait and allow teachers to discover a solution for themselves.

## LOOKING TO THE FUTURE

### The Erikson Institute

Dan Scheinfeld, Gillian McNamee (both of Erikson Institute), and I have met over the past year to discuss the development of a collaborative effort between Commons and Erikson to provide ongoing staff development and research as we explore with elements of the Reggio Approach. Although it has been difficult to acquire funds for this collaborative project, recently the Spencer Foundation has awarded Erikson a small grant to begin research on "Evaluating Educational Innovation in an Inner-City Setting Inspired by Principles from Reggio Emilia." Teacher, classroom, and child assessment instruments will be developed and used to evaluate the beginning process of Reggio explorations. What is particularly exciting about this new project is that a committee of Commons staff and the Erikson researchers has been formed to develop the instruments collaboratively.

## Hopes for the Future!

Many obstacles have stood in our way, including lack of space, programs that are too large (it is more cost-efficient to operate a large program, yet it is easier to manage smaller ones), lack of adequate funding, lack of meeting time, lack of adequate staff development support, inability to have coteachers, severe community problems, and lack of resources. Despite these hardships, I find it amazing that our program is able to continue our exploration. One key is to look at what *can* be done and focus on the program's capabilities and potential just as we must do with children, staff, and parents. If we focus on all of our obstacles, we would never accomplish anything.

Our hopes for the future are to:

❑ continue research with Erikson Institute and obtain assistance with professional development;

❑ continue to make the most of the weekly team and monthly group meetings;

❑ experiment more with a variety of AV equipment along with building a darkroom;

❑ acquire funding for another studio coordinator;

❑ have staff do some more presentations for others;

❑ help further develop the newer, stronger image of the child, the teacher, and the parent;

❑ begin exploring collaboration between children and between adults;

❑ continue to study the children and staff and the learning process;

❑ continue to examine how the environment can or cannot support learning;

❑ use local field trips to help support and expand children's knowledge base of a topic of study;

❑ reexamine our activity plan format to reflect the influences of the Reggio Approach;

❑ adapt the daily schedule to accommodate the child's sense of time;

❑ involve parents more and look at the family worker's role with Reggio;

❑ begin exploring Reggio influences within infant-toddler and school-age programs; and

❑ think more about the role of advocacy and what we are learning from Reggio.

I have been interested in finding ways to help teachers become more knowledgeable and supportive of the child and the learning process. In addition, I am always looking for ways to help directors become more knowledgeable and supportive of the teacher and the learning process. I believe the Reggio Approach is exceptional in that it respects the learning process, the child, the teacher, and the parent. It is an approach that has the potential to empower children, teachers, and parents—and where else is empowerment more needed than within the inner city?

Besides empowering children, staff, and parents, Reggio influences have given our program a sense of hope—hope that we can find better ways to support children, teachers, and parents so that they can live a more rewarding life.

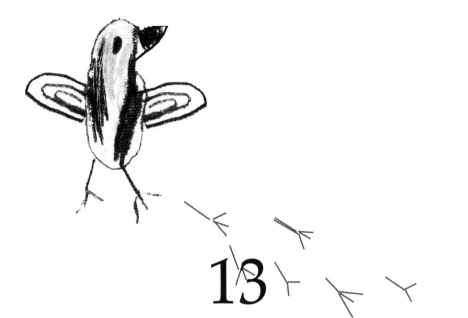

# 13

# The Reggio Emilia Influence at the University of Michigan–Dearborn Child Development Center

## Challenges and Change

*Rosalyn Saltz*

Professor of Education and Director, University of
Michigan–Dearborn Child Development Center

This chapter focuses on the issues that arose when educational strategies inspired by the Reggio Approach were introduced at the University of Michigan–Dearborn Child Development Center. How and why were the teachers motivated to introduce changes based on the philosophy of Reggio Emilia in an already successful early childhood education program? What were some of the problems encountered along the way? What supports by the center administration enabled the teachers and their staffs to continue the process of change and development of program in Reggio-inspired directions?

To understand the issues involved in this process of encouraging change, we must first learn a little about the background and philosophy of the University of Michigan–Dearborn Child Development Center.

## THE UNIVERSITY OF MICHIGAN–DEARBORN CHILD DEVELOPMENT CENTER

The Child Development Center (CDC) serves as a teacher education and child study facility as well as a campus child care center. Approximately 120 children, 1 to 6 years of age, are enrolled each term. These are the children of students, faculty, staff, and community families of diverse cultural and ethnic backgrounds. Preschool children attend the center according to individual schedules, ranging from a minimum of two half-day sessions to five full days per week. Approximately 30 college students use the center classrooms each semester to fulfill practica and observation assignments for various classes. The center's permanent staff includes its director; a senior member of the School of Education faculty who heads the early childhood education program area; a full-time education coordinator, holding at least a master's degree, elementary teaching certification, and an early childhood endorsement, who supervises the center's teachers and its daily educational operations; and lead teachers for each of the four center classrooms. The lead teachers must hold, at minimum, a bachelor's degree with Michigan elementary teaching certification and an early childhood education endorsement (or equivalent), and they must either have obtained a master's degree or be working toward this degree.

The program has always had a tradition of exploring, implementing, and studying promising innovative ideas and practices in the early childhood field that appear to be consistent with its basic educational philosophy. From its earliest days, it has had a firm vision of the psychological and philosophical principles underlying its early childhood education programs. The center found Reggio notions adaptable because the Reggio program in Italy (like many excellent early childhood programs in the United States) is grounded on many of these same principles.

Major tenets on which both Reggio Emilia schools and the CDC program are based include (a) an educational approach that rests on the legacy of Jean Piaget (Piaget, 1965; Piaget & Inhelder, 1969), John Dewey (1938), and Erik Erikson (1950); (b) a genuine and deep respect for the center's children, their families, and their cultures, all viewed as integral players in the educational process; and (c) expectations and educational activities that are designed to be developmentally appropriate and based on our knowledge of children's development that take into account individual differences in children and their cultures. Consistent with these principles, the early childhood curriculum has emphasized active learning through play and discovery, individual choice, and extensive social interactions with peers and teachers.

With such a quality program already in place, what, then, did the CDC staff see in the Reggio Approach that could enhance their educational practices further? What was the motivation for growth and possible change in an already successful, highly regarded program?

## REGGIO PRINCIPLES AS A MOTIVATOR FOR CHANGE

At the center, we found that one of the important factors in motivating the teachers to take on and persist in exploring this new approach was ensuring that they understood those tenets that Reggio had added to our common base of principles. The need for clarity and understanding arose time and again in discussions with the teachers. It was important for them to feel confident and comfortable with this new approach, to feel that they understood what the Reggio Approach was and why teachers there did what they did.

The following principles were regarded as being vital ones to comprehend and honor.

## *Image of the Child*

The Reggio philosophy sees every child as "strong and powerful . . . as unique: having rights rather than simply needs," having "potential, plasticity, the desire to grow, curiosity . . . and the desire to relate to other people and to communicate" (Rinaldi, 1993a, p. 104).

Our center, as in all good early childhood programs, has always respected and valued children, their families, and their cultures. However, Julie, a CDC teacher, feels that she now has a clearer image of children's strength and potential for thinking and learning:

I have learned that children have wonderful ideas and are usually able to express their interests and needs to adults. It takes a caring adult to respect these ideas and encourage them to develop their thoughts. I have started to really listen to what the children are telling me and to use their ideas for projects. I ask many open-ended questions to make sure that I am understanding their ideas correctly.

## "The Hundred Languages of Children"

In Reggio, this term refers to the wide range of ways children can communicate and represent their understandings, feelings, and creative selves. These "languages" can be written and spoken words, drawings, paintings, sculptures in clay and other materials, block constructions, drama, movement, dance, music, computers, and more.

This concept of helping children develop and express themselves in their many natural symbolic languages has taken on great importance at the center and has led to an expansion in the variety of classroom materials and equipment available there. It has also sometimes required our teachers and other adults, in the words of Loris Malaguzzi (1993a, 1993b), the founder and philosopher of the Reggio Emilia Approach, to "lend" the children some of their knowledge and skills so as to support and help develop the children's ability and willingness to use their many potential languages, a notion consistent with the currently widely accepted Vygotsky concept of "scaffolding" (Beck & Winsler, 1995; Vygotsky, 1978).

## Collaboration as a Central Feature in Learning

Collaboration is a major feature of the Reggio Approach. At the CDC, the Reggio example has led to increasing collaboration among all those involved in the life of the school. Teachers and children collaborate through large-group, small-group, and individual activities; questions; and discussions, which allow them to learn together, to "coconstruct knowledge" (Malaguzzi, 1993a; Rinaldi, 1993b). Center teachers find rich support and ideas through their regular collaboration with each other, their staffs, and their university practicum students. Families also collaborate with the teachers and children in developing and implementing the educational program, by contributing skills, materials, ideas, and home experiences to enrich the educational process for their children.

## The Emergent Curriculum

An important insight into the Reggio Emilia view of the emergent curriculum concept is contributed by Carlina Rinaldi (1994a). She explains that, for the Reggio Emilia schools, the meaning of "emergent curriculum" was certainly *not* a complete abdication by teachers of their responsibility for planning to facilitate children's learning but rather "the abandoning of rigid programs and plans and excessively planned objectives. . . . *Use the compass and not the train schedule,*" she urges.

Consistent with her advice, at the center, emergent curriculum means that projects, activities, and time frames are made as flexible as possible. The teachers set direction and guidelines for curriculum. Within these broader guidelines, activities and projects develop through teachers' careful attention to the children's interests and cues, exercising their own judgments as to educational values and objectives and engaging in ongoing collaborative planning by teachers and children together. As one example, Sharon, a CDC teacher who for a year or more had been gradually making changes in her teaching strategies consistent with her understandings of the Reggio Approach, said:

> About 3 weeks ago a group of children spontaneously got into building zoos with blocks, which became more and more elaborate over a period of several days. I took Polaroids of their constructions. We revisited some of the photos and brainstormed what the children wanted to do and learn next, and we were off on a new zoo project. The other teachers, lab students, and I collaborated on some ideas too. We're still into it. Last year, I wouldn't have really paid such careful attention to their self-directed play and used it as the basis for an open-ended project.

## The Project Approach

The term *project* refers to long-term group activities, jointly planned by the teacher and a group of interested children. These activities have no predetermined time limits. Completion of one subgoal suggests and leads to a new goal. As a result of exposure to the Reggio Approach and also work by Katz and Chard (1989), this approach has become a major CDC teaching strategy, and, in the context of an emergent curriculum, center projects have focused on a wide range of topics (gardens, zoos, children's dramatic productions, ballet, volcanoes, and the development of a new playground for the kindergarten, among others).

However, project work does not absorb the entire day. As important and exciting as it can be for both children and teachers, the children at the CDC continue to have many daily opportunities (and the freedom) to engage in a great variety of developmentally appropriate activities for the "whole child," along with projects. This is true in the Reggio schools as well (Katz, 1993). However, the range and depth of these activities have been expanded and enriched by the introduction of the many new materials, media, and strategies in the center classrooms as a result of our interest in Reggio.

## *Documentation and Portfolios*

Still another essential part of the CDC Reggio-inspired teaching strategies is documenting both the process and products of the children's work. Documentation highlights turning points of exploration and discovery and summarizes the process and results of individual and group work. Documentation and portfolios include many photos, samples of children's language that capture their questions and hypotheses in the course of their work, videotapes, and children's productions. Much of the material collected is carefully arranged and displayed for children, teachers, parents, and visitors to review, and it is used as a continuing resource for planning, collaboration, and parent involvement. Julie, a CDC teacher, explained:

> I use documentation to tell a story about their [children's] learning. Teacher, parents, and the children use this so-called documentation to piece together the learning that has occurred during a given project. Parents and teachers are able to identify the children's careful planning to reach their goal. The children are able to use documentation as a form of recall and as springboards for further development of their ideas. I have found that documentation can be a useful tool to include everybody in the projects.

## *The Environment as the Third Teacher*

The Reggio Emilia Approach emphasizes the important role of the environment of the school in the educational process (Gandini, 1991, 1993a, 1993b).

Diane and Julie, reflecting on changes in their classroom environments during the past several years, made the following remarks:

*Diane:*    I have made a lot of changes to make the environment more aesthetically pleasing and more welcoming. We've added many live plants, fresh flowers, and have tried to reduce clutter. I added an adult-looking couch, to make it more like home. I also have added many more mirrors and a greater variety of art materials; different types of brushes, pencils, crayons, paints, and oil pastels; and clay.

*Julie:*    I now consider the environment as interactive for the children almost as another teacher. The environment is planned thoughtfully and carefully to encourage children's continued exploration. Often, I consider this carefully arranged environment as my lesson plans. . . . So plants may be placed in front of mirrors so it may create curiosity in the children. Scarves, material scraps, and materials that make interesting sounds would be added to the environment to foster the development of a dance project.

## ROAD TO REGGIO: ROADBLOCKS, MOTIVATIONS, AND SUPPORTS

It is clear that the CDC teachers have by now adopted many aspects of the Reggio-inspired approach as their own during the past 4 years. Nevertheless, roadblocks sprang up along the way to this wholehearted acceptance and implementation of our new Reggio-inspired approach, and many challenges still remain.

What were some of these roadblocks? What do the teachers see as continuing challenges? What is their motivation to persist in spite of difficulties, and what supports have made it possible for them to persist and continue to develop Reggio-inspired educational strategies despite difficulties and challenges?

### Roadblocks

In the beginning, the center staff had been impressed by their director's descriptions and slides of her visit and study of the Reggio Emilia schools. Later, they were awed and excited by "The Hundred Languages of Children" exhibit in Detroit in 1992 and what they learned about the Reggio program at a conference accompanying the exhibit. As their enthusiasm grew, the teachers, working collaboratively with their peers and administrator, began to explore ways to incorporate some of the Reggio Approach into the center. However, especially during the first months, attempts to implement Reggio-inspired changes often proved to be so difficult, puzzling, and discouraging for the teachers that several of them almost abandoned their efforts. Yet they also found their new Reggio-inspired attempts satisfying enough that they felt compelled to keep on trying to overcome the difficulties.

Among the sometimes troubling issues that the CDC teachers encountered in their early efforts were the following:

*(1) Where do we start?* Teachers sometimes felt overwhelmed by the rapid and wide range of changes they tried to make in their classrooms to implement the new Reggio-inspired educational strategies. The teachers now believe, as one said, that "at first we tried to do too much too fast. It's so exciting when you read about what's been done and you read the book [referring to Edwards, Gandini, & Forman, 1993] that you want to do it all at once, and sometimes you jump without thinking."

Our teachers suggest to those who are in the early stages of initiating Reggio-inspired modifications in their programs: Allow time for change, perhaps beginning by simply learning how to listen to children, carry around notebooks and tape recorders, and *start to change the physical environment of your classroom.*

*(2)    What is the teacher's role in a Reggio-inspired educational process?*    Teachers were not completely clear or confident about their role as teachers in an emergent curriculum. What part should the teacher play in the initiation and development of projects and explorations? How can a teacher help children develop and sustain a focus, without taking over the project?

In their initial attempts to introduce a Reggio-inspired emergent curriculum, the teachers now feel they waited too passively for the children to set the course and guidelines for projects. They became puzzled and confused when they tried to follow the children's ideas as they veered off into many different directions, some of which the teachers felt would be unproductive. The teachers now believe that they at first may have misinterpreted the teacher's role in a Reggio-based approach and tended to forget that the teacher is viewed as a *partner,* not simply the children's follower, in a *collaborative* teacher-child learning experience.

*(3)    What goals and expectations should we set for our children?*    Can and should we use as a yardstick the Italian children's products or the quality of their collaborations (as, e.g., illustrated in "The Hundred Languages" exhibit)?

As one of the teachers related, "It's easy to get discouraged when you look at the Italian children's artwork, and it's not happening for you. Like you put out clay over and over and the children don't seem interested, aren't persistent, aren't representing." But then, she explained, after reflection and discussions with her collaborative team, she realized that the center children had not had the advantage of longtime participation in an art-based program such as that which existed in the Reggio Italian schools and had a very different cultural background as well.

She decided to adjust her expectations and strategies to the level and experiences of her own students, rather than those in the Italian centers, and *take it only one small step further.* For example, since her children were accustomed to using markers for drawing, she introduced markers with soft pointed tips, closer to brushes, as *very, very special tools* for special projects, and stressed to her children that they needed to learn to be very careful and gentle with these if they wished to use them. The children's response to this initiative was very reinforcing for the teacher. The children who wished to use these new artistic tools used them carefully and seriously for more detailed work than they had previously produced. (Gradually, over the next several years, she has added a large variety of brushes, as well as clay, and other new art materials, with which many of the children have since become quite comfortable and proficient.)

*(4)    How can small, collaborative peer groups be fostered?*    First, schedules of attendance at the center preschool vary for individual children, so that

the group of children in attendance changes by session and day. Further-more, the children had not been accustomed to working collaboratively in small groups over a period of time toward a common goal, nor were their teachers experienced in fostering such focused, clearly defined small groups (see Chapter 12 for a further discussion of this problem).

After some experimentation, the teachers found that they needed, as one said, *to go back to basics,* to build the foundation for such goal-oriented peer collaboration. For example, this teacher explained, she found it useful to *focus first on helping children learn to stop and seriously listen to one another's opinions and ideas, and then to encourage them to pursue short-term mutual goals in small peer groups of friends.* With time and experience, both teachers and children have become increasingly accustomed to working in a collaborative group framework. The membership of these groups still tend to fluctuate, however, since children's attendance schedules vary, and the CDC program has traditionally allowed children to make their own choices of daily activi-ties from among many that are offered. The teachers are continuing to work on ways they can best facilitate the formation of collaborative groups with a membership that remains stable over a considerable period of time.

*(5)  Can we really implement Reggio-inspired strategies without sufficient space for a central art studio* (atelier) *or having an art educator* (atelierista) *as a member of our team?*   This issue was and continues to be a concern. Since, however, there was no realistic possibility of space or funds to introduce either of these valuable assets at the CDC, it was a question of either pro-ceeding without them or simply giving up the idea of exploring implemen-tation of Reggio-inspired changes in the center program. The staff chose to proceed. They found ways to rearrange the environments in their class-rooms so as to form art centers (*miniateliers*) in each cottage and to enrich these with a great variety of media and materials in addition to those that had been previously available to the children. The teachers have also made many efforts to increase their own knowledge and proficiency in the use of various media and aesthetically pleasing presentation of documentation. Without an *atelierista,* the staff has had to gain such knowledge and skills through other means: inservice workshops, relevant sessions at professional conferences, art classes, publications, and the occasional visits to the CDC of consultants. These activities have been accelerating as teachers gain more information and skills and as more opportunities for these are made possi-ble by their administrator.

*(6)  How can we find* time *for collaboration and documentation?*   Time constraints sometimes stand in the way of the optimal incorporation of Reg-gio-inspired strategies into the fabric of the CDC program. Staff collabora-tion, a problem in many centers, takes place daily, often through exchanges during lunch in the CDC conference room and informal encounters among

the teachers, and the program administrator also schedules meetings specifically for the purpose of Reggio program collaboration, although time limitations prevent these from being as frequent as they should be.

The most persistent unresolved issue related to time constraints continues to be the problem of teacher time necessary for preparing documentation. Nevertheless, the teachers increasingly use documentation in some form as a routine and essential part of their teaching program. They have dealt with the problem of the time required by sometimes sacrificing what they know would be more ideal documentation, in terms of appearance and completeness, in favor of types of documentation they can prepare more quickly. The teachers often capture the process of children's explorations, ideas, and activities in the course of a project by providing "snapshots" of the process (e.g., displays of children's work and photos of them and the objects on which they may be focusing at the time—flowers, insects, clouds, etc.). This informal type of documentation is usually highlighted and supplemented by brief captions or excerpts from transcripts of children's language (sometimes printed by hand with markers instead of typed). Slides and videotapes are also used. In this way, children and their teachers can have access to ongoing documentation to assist them in the process of formulating new ideas and plans as a project goes forward, and parents and visitors can observe and understand the events and process of the children's learning experiences as they unfold.

On the other hand, the staff also considers it very important to try to emulate the style of documentation they have viewed in the slides of Reggio Emilia schools and at the Reggio "Hundred Languages" exhibit. They try to do this particularly on their more permanent "summary" documentation boards displayed around the classrooms. These boards "tell the story of the children's learning" in a carefully designed, clear, visually attractive, and compelling fashion, thereby affirming the value the teachers place on the children's work and on the overall environment of the school (see Figure 13–1).

## Motivations and Supports

What has enabled the CDC staff to keep moving on the road to Reggio in the face of the many potential obstacles described here? Why have they remained so determined to achieve their goals and find solutions to the problems along the way? The answer lies both in the strength of their motivations and in the peer and institutional supports they have received.

*Motivations.*    At this point, after several years of experience in attempting to incorporate a Reggio-inspired approach into the CDC program, the teachers' motivation to continue has become largely intrinsic and self-pro-

**FIGURE 13–1**
The two children and their mother, pictured here, are examining informal documentation, posted on butcher paper that has been decorated by the children with drawings of flowers. The paper has been mounted along the fence behind two garden plots newly planted by the children. The brothers, referring to the documentation, are proudly taking their mom through the planning and sequence of activities in which they were involved during the 7-week project leading to their gardens. Later, the teachers will expand this temporary documentation and carefully arrange it on poster boards, with headings clearly presented in large type. The photos and children's artwork will be accompanied by typed excerpts from recordings of teachers' questions and children's comments, obtained in the course of the project.

pelling. They have acquired new understandings of the teaching-learning process as a result of their study and their experiences in adapting a Reggio-inspired educational approach at the CDC. They are convinced that the changes they have made in the CDC program have had many positive effects on the children as learners, their parents as partners, and themselves as teachers. In response to my question "What would stop you now from continuing and maintaining your momentum?" one teacher answered, with approving nods and comments from the others, "I don't think anything could stop us, but I think that we are always looking for better ways to do it."

Perhaps the prime motivator that has sustained the teachers' Reggio efforts has been the gratifying reaction of the children in response to their new teaching strategies (e.g., the emergent curriculum, project approach). To the question of what motivated them to persist on the Reggio road, the teachers noted the following major effects:

1. *The increased level of the children's interest and involvement in their learning experiences:* "Children's interest and excitement are so contagious that I can't help but be motivated. The way the children focus, their degree of involvement and depth when they are interested in a project."

2. *The children's increased willingness and ability to express their feelings, opinions, and ideas:* "It changes the children. I think that my children are more confident in expressing their feelings to me and the descriptive words they use are much richer than before, . . . and I think the child knows that the teacher 'is really going to listen when I say this, and so, maybe I should really think about what I am saying' . . . that their teachers will ask them questions, like 'What do you mean when you say . . . ?' and *really want to know!"*

3. *The children's increasing collaboration with their peers to reach common goals:* "One of the things I'm really excited about is how the children collaborate with each other now. . . . Collaboration, discussion between children, is at a different level."

The teachers also mention that it is highly motivating for them that the children's families appear to see themselves increasingly as partners with the teachers and children in the educational process, and, accordingly, that parent involvement in the school and its educational activities has become stronger and more widespread than it had been before. The teachers believe this to be a result of their conscious efforts to find a variety of new ways for parents to collaborate with them and the children in their educational activities. They also believe that the documentation posted around the classrooms has contributed much to the parents' increased interest and understanding.

The teachers also report as very motivating the positive impact of their new strategies on their own feelings of self-worth as professionals who are doing something very serious and valuable for children.

*Major Supports.*   What are some of the major supports that have sustained the staff as they increasingly develop and implement Reggio-inspired strategies at the CDC? First and foremost appears to be the mutual respect and support they find in their collaborative relationships with each other.

Some of the teachers' comments in this respect make this point very clear. One said, "There have been times when we were really tired and wondering if it was worth the effort, and someone says, 'That was great, that was good,' and we have that constant push, 'Come on, let's go.'" Another, agreeing, added, "On my former job I missed out on a collaborative team. It made it very hard to keep going [with Reggio ideas]. I didn't have people to bounce ideas off of and to stimulate my thinking with new ideas, saying, 'You're doing fine,' or 'Let's try this and see where it goes,' or 'Have we looked into this yet?'" The first teacher added, "Yes, and *we are constantly going back and forth, giving each other that feedback, and we challenge and question each other to make sure we understand each other, very similar to the way we question the children.*"

Administrative and institutional attitudes and assistance also play a very important part in determining whether new Reggio-inspired ideas will take hold and blossom rather than soon be abandoned. At the CDC, a number of administrative and institutional supports were provided that the teachers feel were vital to encourage them and facilitate the changes they wanted to make in their classrooms. Based on the teachers' reflections on this subject as well as my own perceptions, a few of the most important of these are as follows:

1. *Establishing a general atmosphere that is consistent with the Reggio Approach—an atmosphere of trust, respect, permission for risk taking, collaboration.*   Diane: "I think Reggio is a very open-ended process. It requires a lot of trust. I think the administrator's continued underlying support gives us the confidence to be able to make changes as need be. When I have an idea, I know it is going to be respected just like the children's ideas." Kathy: "We have the freedom to take risks, to explore as a professional, a teacher." Diane: "And it helps too that we know we're *all (including the administrator) in this together, that none of us knows it all. . . . Always having the support that if we are having a hard time, we can figure out a different way to do it. 'Maybe you could try this?' We are always thinking of what needs to change. 'Well, how can we make it change?' Always, like the children, 'How can we answer this question?' rather than saying, 'I give up.'*"

2. *Facilitating a staff's initial and continuing study of the Reggio Approach and its U.S. adaptations.*   As the center teachers put it, We need to know *why* we are doing what we are doing. Administrators can ensure that the staff has ongoing information and exposure to Reggio Emilia principles, practices, and key U.S. interpretations and adaptations of these princi-

ples and practices. This can be accomplished by distributing relevant current publications, videos, and so forth, and holding frequent meetings to discuss these, as well as by encouraging staff attendance and participation in conferences, workshops, and networking with others who are also exploring Reggio ideas and the adaptation of these in their classrooms.

3. *Arranging schedules of the school day so as to provide as much time as possible for teacher collaboration, staff meetings, and the preparation of documentation.* Making this possible may require some additional staff or volunteer assistance in the classroom.

4. *Recognizing the importance and, to the extent possible, making materials and resources available to expand the opportunities for children's use of "100 languages" and for documentation.* In the context of limited budgets, the administrator needs to consider these goals as budget priorities when making decisions about allocating resources.

5. *Serving as a member of the instructional team in the role of an ongoing, trusted consultant* (pedagogista) *for the teachers.* The teachers believe that it is very helpful when an administrator is knowledgeable about Reggio principles and practices and can collaborate with them as a consultant. They believe that, as a trusted member of their team, the administrator as an ongoing consultant is in an excellent position to help them assess their environments, documentation, and projects and to suggest possible improvements or new directions.

In summary, this presentation and analysis of the Reggio Emilia influences on the early childhood program of the University of Michigan–Dearborn Child Development Center has dealt with several years of change in the CDC staff's views and practices relating to how teachers can best facilitate young children's development and learning. It has been an exciting, rewarding, yet sometimes difficult period of exploration, experimentation, and study that has required an open-minded reexamination of some basic concepts in early childhood education (e.g., "readiness," the teacher's role). We feel we have come far but have still a long way to go, as we take steps on the road to Reggio.

# 14

# Using the Reggio Approach in a Children's Museum

**Fran Donovan**
Early Childhood Education Consultant and Museum Educator,
Chicago, Illinois

Walking into a school in Reggio Emilia, I was immediately struck by the beauty, comfort, warmth, color, and light. Through conversations and presentations by the educators, I was further impressed by the solid, consistent philosophy, the collegiality of the learning environment, the overwhelming sense of purpose, and the strength and commitment of the community that supported these wonderful schools.

I soon began to wonder, "Why can't *we* do this?" The approach is obviously right for children and certainly the best I had seen. This is not to say that we should try to duplicate the schools of Reggio, because that would be impossible and even undesirable. Reggio is a place to be inspired by, not a place to imitate. The Reggio Emilia philosophy can inspire us to alter our image of the child, become more thoughtful and reflective about our practice with young children, communicate and collaborate more effectively, and improve the environments we design for and with young children.

At the time of my first visit to Reggio Emilia, I was working as the director of education at the Kohl Children's Museum in Wilmette, Illinois, a suburb of Chicago. I was interested in what I could learn in relation to my work at the museum and was looking for ways to bring back ideas for improvement. In a broader sense, I came as an early childhood professional seeking to learn more of the story of this incredible community of people who seemed to have found a way to put children first.

I came back with more than ideas. I gained a new perspective on educational philosophy and an overwhelming enthusiasm to attempt change. Encountering ideas in Reggio caused me to reflect in ways that changed how I approached my work. It provoked me to rethink my image of the child and the way I related to children and adults. It helped me remember that everyday occurrences are extraordinary to children and are only ordinary to us because we have forgotten to care. It began a journey of discovery.

## SOME BASIC PRINCIPLES

Because the Reggio Approach is very complex and encompasses so much, I will highlight only some of what I believe are the underlying principles. Although defined earlier in the book, they are worth discussing again because of their particular impact on the philosophy of the Kohl Children's Museum and the changes made there.

## Image of the Child

Each of us has within us an image of the child that determines how we relate to children and how we make decisions affecting children. In Reggio, the child is described as capable, powerful, intelligent, and curious. Each child is considered a researcher, explorer, and investigator. Children are respected as unique individuals full of strengths and potential inherently possessing many rights.

## The Hundred Languages of Children

Reggio educators believe that children are capable of communicating in many "languages" that go beyond written and spoken words. Children want and need to represent their ideas and emotions through painting, sculpting, drawing, constructing, collage, movement, music, puppets, and numerous other media. As children express themselves by means of these symbolic languages, they are also learning to see people and objects from multiple perspectives. Often these languages are the vehicle through which children and teachers study a subject in depth, which results in a long-term project. As they engage in project work, children investigate a topic through various media from many perspectives, constantly revising, modifying, and refining their understanding.

## Role of the Environment

The Reggio educator's view of the school environment might best be described by the following quote from Loris Malaguzzi:

> We value space because of its power to organize, promote pleasant relationships between people of different ages, create a handsome environment, provide changes, promote choices and activity, and its potential for sparking all kinds of social, affective and cognitive learning. All of this contributes to a sense of well-being and security in children. We also think that the space has to be a sort of aquarium which mirrors the ideas, values, attitudes and cultures of the people who live within it. (Gandini, 1993a, pp. 148–149)

The environments of the schools in Reggio are simply beautiful because of their thoughtful design of space, careful organization of materials, and appealing use of light and color. Structures, furniture, materials, and tools are set up to promote encounters between children and adults and with objects. In fact, the environment is viewed as a teacher in that it is designed to encourage and support the learning of children. Everywhere there is evidence of the learning, attitudes, and history of both children and adults.

## Communication and Collaboration

These are very broad concepts and difficult to discuss thoroughly here, but I feel it is important to highlight some aspects of them because both are central to the Reggio Approach. The level of communication in Reggio results in the generation of extremely strong relationships between and among children and adults. These relationships form the basis for the high degree of collaboration and cooperation in the school community.

Without a commitment to collaboration, the Reggio Approach could not have been born or continued to exist. It is only because all members of the community are invited and encouraged to be involved in decisions affecting the schools that they have been able to develop a wide basis of support. Parents, in particular, are considered vital to the operation of the schools and are seen as an integral part of the Reggio philosophy. There is a continuous dialogue between the parents and teachers to keep each other informed. Parents are not simply involved in superficial ways but play an important role in decisions on topics ranging from curriculum to budget.

Reggio educators do not steer away from conflict and differences of opinion but rather welcome them as an opportunity for rich dialogue and learning to ensue. There is an emphasis on listening to and respecting the viewpoint of others regardless of whether one agrees or disagrees. Considering multiple perspectives is valued as a strength in working toward a common goal rather than a threatening challenge. This collaborative spirit is also developed in the children. The emphasis on working in small groups provides a balance between developing personal independence and helping children understand their collective role as a member of a community.

Reggio educators communicate this process of learning through the use of documentation. They use transcripts of children's recorded conversations, photographs and slides, videotape, and their own notes to create a record of experiences. Often, this documentation is compiled on beautiful panels hung in the schools. The careful attention given by the teachers and the prominence of the displays demonstrate to the children and other adults the degree to which the teachers respect their work and feel it is important. Documentation also provides a memory and springboard for children, parents, and teachers to revisit an event or a moment of discovery. In a broader sense, the school itself and all that it contains is a form of documentation that communicates the life and history of the children and adults.

## COMPARISON BETWEEN THE REGGIO SCHOOLS AND CHILDREN'S MUSEUMS

It is helpful to begin a discussion of the impact Reggio had on our organization by examining the similarities and differences between children's museums and the schools in Reggio. Of course, some of the comparisons are very obvious—similarities are due to the educational foundation of both institutions, and differences have to do with the fact that museums are by nature very different institutions from schools. Yet, despite the differences, the introduction of the educational principles of Reggio Emilia can have a significant impact on a museum and therefore on other types of organizations as well.

The most evident similarity is the emphasis on environment, and here there are many parallels. Children's museums are generally intended to be stimulating, inviting, and rich with possibilities and often emphasize multiple modes of expression. Many "languages" are used in exhibits and programs to assure access for all children and opportunity for creative expression. For example, museums often provide opportunities ranging from working with paint and clay to dancing and dramatic play to computer and audiovisual experiences. In Reggio, the environment is often referred to as a teacher. Museums also rely on the environment (especially the exhibits) to provide a catalyst for learning. In both settings, children are empowered by the choices that the environment provides and can usually decide how their time is spent.

Differences are also important to note. A children's museum serves from several thousand to up to a million children per year as compared to the 75 or so that make up the population of a school in Reggio Emilia. Museum audiences are usually diverse in age, cultural background, language, and family income and often come from a broad geographic area. Conversely, the children in Reggio derive from a relatively homogeneous background. The museum is a place for informal education where children spend relatively small amounts of time in comparison to sustained and long-term connections that occur in the schools of Reggio. Many children use museums individually, with a parent or friend, but there is little opportunity for the small-group interaction at the level found in Reggio Emilia. The hands-on, interactive nature of children's museums implies active participation. But because they are designed for such a broad audience, museum environments are much less personal than the Reggio schools, which so clearly communicate the personality of a relatively small group of people.

The most important difference between museums and the schools of Reggio centers around relationships. Museum staff see children for a comparatively short time in contrast to Reggio teachers, who are with children every day for up to 3 years. In a museum, there is little opportunity to know the children well and understand them as individuals, whereas in Reggio very strong relationships are developed with the children and their families. Children who come to the museum are called "visitors" or "audience," which implies a lack of ownership. The museum is there for them to visit, to be entertained or educated by, but it does not fully belong to them.

In discerning the ways children's museums and the schools of Reggio Emilia are alike and different, it became clear that certain aspects of the Reggio Approach presented us with more opportunities for experimentation than others did. Yet, in considering adaptations, we were careful not to disregard ideas simply because of the differences. As you will see in the following section, we made changes on many levels. In some cases, these adaptations caused us to alter elements of the museum such as schedule, staffing, or program curriculum but never the underlying structure. In general, our mission statement was our gauge. We attempted to incorporate ideas that we felt were not only consistent with our mission but enhanced it.

## CHANGES INFLUENCED BY REGGIO

Because several of the Kohl Children's Museum staff, including the director (from 1988 to 1993), Sue Sturtevant, and the assistant director of education, Andrea Hill, had been to Reggio Emilia and studied its approach, we had many opportunities for exchanging ideas and interpretations. After sharing photos, articles, and books from Reggio with the staff, we decided to begin by taking a fresh look at our environment.

## The Environment

In deciding to focus first on the environment, we chose two elements we saw repeatedly in Reggio: the creative use of mirrors and an aesthetically beautiful use of lighting. By looking at their reflection in a mirror, children can see themselves as others see them. They become aware of themselves in ways that are not possible without the reflection. Mirrors are a wonderful vehicle for presenting another perspective. They allow children to see differently—simultaneously to see the front and back of an object, for example, or to be able to see around a corner or over a wall. We also paid more attention to the importance of lighting for its power to entice children into a space or turn them away, the way it sets moods and influences emotion, and its capacity to highlight or hide or simply add beauty to a setting.

When we returned from Italy, we were in the midst of creating a new *Art and Technology Center* exhibit space. This provided an ideal setting for incorporating mirrors and lights in creative new ways inspired by Reggio. A beautiful wooden light table was designed complete with rich materials such as brightly colored transparent plastic shapes to arrange or construct with and black paper to insert in embroidery hoops for creating designs with pinpoints. A large tube big enough for children to go inside was fitted with a black light and a curved mirror to provide experiences with distorted images. Children could also crawl inside the giant kaleidoscope—three large mirrors placed in a triangle—which allowed the children to lose themselves in many images. The most striking feature related to light was the addition of a fiber optics "waterfall," a floor-to-ceiling wall of hundreds of tiny tubes of various colors of light against a backdrop of fancifully shaped mirrors (see Figure 14–1).

As we saw how engaging these exhibit elements were, and as we began to understand the importance of mirrors and lighting in an environment, we became much more aware of their value as we planned future exhibits and spaces. For example, at a later point we developed a construction exhibit incorporating blocks and a city skyline with a mirror in the background and on the base. As children built they saw not only the front of the blocks but virtually all sides. The mirrors added depth and dimension, making the constructions much more interesting architecturally for the builder and the viewer.

Another way that ideas from Reggio influenced our environment was in the area of community involvement. For example, in planning an exhibit about diversity at the museum, we organized an advisory board with representatives from local universities, government agencies, and cultural and

**FIGURE 14–1**
A child experiences the joy of a fiber optics "waterfall."
Source: Kohl Children's Museum, Wilmette, Illinois. Used by permission.

community groups. Members of the committee were instrumental in offering their perspective to enhance the design of the exhibit, improve the educational impact of the exhibit, and reach new audiences.

It is important to emphasize that we saw these changes for what they were—a point of entry into interpreting what we had seen and learned in Reggio. We understood that the Reggio philosophy is much more complex than making a few changes in our environment. We viewed these changes as initial steps at the beginning of a very long process—a process through which we hoped to make much deeper and more substantial changes.

## Staff Development

As we considered the Reggio emphasis on collaboration and communication, we reexamined the role our floor staff play with the visiting public, beginning to see them more as facilitators and provocateurs and less as monitors and directors of play. This change marked the beginning of a long process of regular meetings that allowed staff opportunities to discuss an array of topics, ranging from play in general to ideas for effectively engaging children of different ages in a particular exhibit.

In our effort to understand children in relation to the museum, we worked hard to increase staff skills in order to maximize the benefit of each child's visit. We discussed the value of observation as a tool for studying the children and the exhibits. We examined strategies for engaging children ranging from role playing a character to silently provoking a child's thinking by our actions. We considered how what we say or the questions we ask can expand or inhibit children's thinking. Finding the best way to interact with children in a public setting is a very subtle art and inexact science, but by having ongoing discussions and opportunities for sharing ideas, we felt that we improved our methods and therefore enriched the experiences of the children.

Within the education department, which conducts most of the special programs, we began to discuss the grouping of children more seriously. After realizing the advantages of working in small groups, we reconfigured many of the programs so that children spent most of the time involved in small-group experiences. This approach resulted in more interaction and exchange of ideas between children, more opportunity for children to work at their own pace, and less time spent in transition.

## Applying the Reggio Approach to Our City Connections Project

City Connections was a specially funded project partnering Chicago public schools and Head Start with the museum. Because it was our most extensive program, it provided us with many opportunities to incorporate ideas from Reggio. Our original goal was to serve as a resource for inner-city children, parents, and teachers by offering a year-long experience to enhance and complement existing curriculum in the schools. As a result of our exposure to the Reggio Approach, we decided to hire an urban ethnographer and videographer to help us document and evaluate the project. We felt this documentation could serve many purposes. It could provide a way for us to share experiences and engage those outside the program, including children, parents, teachers, museum staff, and funders. It could provide an effective tool for reflection and evaluation, and it could provide a visual history of the program so that our experiences could continue to be shared.

To facilitate the development of relationships with all the participants, we designed the program to include as many occasions as possible to bring people together. A variety of meetings, workshops, and family parties were conducted at the museum and individual schools, sometimes with the children and sometimes without. Although these occasions were less frequent than would be ideal, they resulted in many wonderful experiences. For example, both teachers and parents shared with us that they realized how infrequently they had a chance to discuss the children and their learning with other adults and how much they appreciated the opportunity.

As part of the City Connections program, we conducted workshops with children at both the museum and their schools. Before learning about the use of projects in Reggio, we probably would have presented a new theme for each of these workshops, believing the greater variety the better. After reflecting on the benefits of building from experience to experience on a particular topic, we instead worked with the individual teachers to choose a topic that would be specific to the children's interest in their classroom. We realized that the result would not be a project of the scope done in Reggio because our time was limited, activities had to be preplanned, there was less opportunity for exchange, and our relationships were not as strong. However, we felt it was a more effective approach for us because it gave the children the opportunity to use a variety of symbolic languages as they revisited a topic from several perspectives. Rather than acquiring surface knowledge of a number of topics, the children were able to develop a deeper understanding of one topic.

Throughout the process, Cynthia Gehrie, the ethnographer, documented many of the sessions with videotape and still photography so that in the end we had a history of the year's program. In her words:

Imagery becomes essential in order to cocreate meaning, in order to give the project form and structure. The documentation enabled us to use the imagery to interest and involve those outside the experience—the parents and the museum staff. The video became proof of the power of creative engagement.

We could watch children become focused with a purpose they invented themselves.

In the spring, we edited the video footage and produced a short overview of the program that we then shared with teachers and parents at each of the schools. The videotape was very powerful because it highlighted the strands that ran through the year's programming. In viewing the tapes, parents, teachers, and museum staff could see connections from one encounter to the next throughout the year. For example, our first contact with the teachers in the program consisted of an introductory day at the museum. Teachers participated in a number of hands-on activities that would later be repeated with the children and were given a chance to explore the museum on their own. When the teachers viewed the tape, seeing themselves playing in the exhibits and working with materials, they were able to compare their own experiences with those of their students.

For some parents, it was the first time they had a chance to see their child in school or a museum environment. It provided them with an opportunity to observe their child and their child's teacher in a new way. In addition to allowing them to view their youngsters on film, involving parents in this program was beneficial in other ways. Parents were able to exchange ideas and develop friendships in a nonthreatening environment. They also became interested in using some of the ideas we shared with them for interacting with their children.

To provide an additional form of documentation that was more readily accessible to the teachers, we created a book of photos for each participating school that included written descriptions of the experiences. Some of the teachers also took their own photographs and created displays in their classrooms. Developing these records helped the teachers see the value of documentation and gave them some tools for getting started.

## Daily Activities

Our experience in the City Connections program enabled us to create a documentation structure that facilitated the flow of information about the process to all concerned. As a result of this success, we decided to attempt another form of documentation in order to produce a more useful method for recording and assessing our daily activities programming.

Historically, the Kohl Children's Museum had offered free activities several times a day for visitors. A wide variety of interactive events were included, ranging from celebrations of holidays around the world to topical events such as the Olympics, to seasonal themes and anniversaries. Through these activities we were able to offer children opportunities to experience and experiment with many languages—the visual arts, music, science, math, treasure hunts, dance, live performances, and visiting authors.

In the past we had kept files on all of the events, but we felt that there was a better way to access these ideas. After seeing the many uses of documentation in the Reggio schools, we decided to create a binder containing a written and visual record of each of the daily activities. Each page included the date, title, list of materials, directions, and a Polaroid picture of the activity or event. The convenience and accessibility of that activities book provided the staff with a history of their accomplishments and evidence of all the wonderful experiences that had taken place. It became a method to evaluate what worked well and what did not. In this way we used it as a reference from year to year as we planned future programming.

In relation to daily activities, we also felt it was important for the children to have a tangible memory of the experience to take with them. Therefore, whenever possible, as part of the event, children created something—a painting, sculpture, piece of jewelry, drawing—that served as a kind of documentation, a symbolic memory of their visit to the museum. By having a memento, children could revisit their experience and share it with other family members and friends.

Additionally, in an attempt to develop a sense of community, we began to plan more opportunities for children to be involved in group experiences. This ranged from creating murals or large sculptures as a group to providing opportunities for children to take part in musical, dramatic, or improvisational experiences. For example, we organized a Martin Luther King Dream panel to which many children contributed. As part of an Earth Day event, we brought in a sculptor who worked with recyclables. Children worked side by side with him to create a group sculpture. When possible, these creations were hung in the museum for a period of time so that as children returned they were able to see their contribution to the piece. We often hired performers who involved the children in their music, drama, or dance and were fortunate to have many creative staff members who included children in improvisational dramatic experiences.

## Symbolic Representation

We developed a recycle arts room that served as a studio space similar, in some ways, to the atelier found in the Reggio schools. The Reggio educators had described the atelier as "not a place to visit, but a place to be." Our recycle arts studio became an art materials library, a rich environment offering many possibilities. It provided a place where children could choose from many materials to describe or express themselves and their ideas or create representations of their learning.

We reevaluated our class offerings for families and schools and redesigned them to include more opportunities for using symbolic languages. For example, we decided to initiate a painting and sculpting class that included nonconventional paintbrushes and an opportunity to sculpt with sandstone and clay. A new lights and shadows program incorporated experiments with transparent materials and a giant shadow screen. In our existing programs, we added "real" elements such as authentic artifacts and the chance to prepare and sample recipes.

## BEYOND CHILDREN'S MUSEUMS

In addition to children's museums, many other professions and settings would benefit from the study of the Reggio Approach. In revisiting the principles outlined earlier, we should consider how these ideas could influence anyone working with children, from parents and medical staff, to librarians and social workers.

## Image of the Child

To perceive the child as powerful and full of rights is the most important lesson we can learn from Reggio and the only place to start. This image of the child puts the adult in the position of being a learner alongside the child and not simply a teacher or one who supplies information. No matter what setting the early childhood professional works in, without this as a basic tenet and point of view we can only be less than effective.

## The Hundred Languages of Children

We need to trust children's ability to communicate in many symbolic languages and offer them as many opportunities as possible to express themselves and their ideas. This step involves supplying the materials and environment conducive to creativity, paying more attention to their drawings and other creations, listening carefully to what they say, challenging them to further their thinking, supporting them in their uncertainties, and becoming more open to using a variety of symbolic languages ourselves.

## Role of the Environment

Studying the environments in Reggio Emilia can help all of us reflect on the importance of surroundings for everyone—children and adults alike. Anyone can be more creative, more productive, and happier in a beautiful, stimulating environment. Environments can also become more meaningful and personal by involving children in the process of designing the space and by displaying work done by the children and documentation about the children.

Every environment is a "teacher" in that it sends messages to children. We need to be consistently aware of the messages we send by what we put in that environment. On the simplest level, for example, the beauty and personality of the Reggio schools send the message that children are highly valued in their community. At a glance on entering a school in Reggio, one encounters many messages—newspaper articles showing the community's involvement in the schools, beautiful work by the children thoughtfully and artistically displayed, a multitude of photos of the children, teachers, and parents showing the life and history of the school. Putting children in a less beautiful, more anonymous space, on the other hand, can send an equally strong negative message. In preparing spaces for children, we may not always have choices about such variables as the size of the room or number of windows, but there are always ways to improve and personalize space even without changing the architecture or having a large budget.

## Communication and Collaboration

There is much to learn from Reggio about communication and collaboration, the core of which is the importance and value of developing strong relationships with children, parents, and coworkers. In developing stronger relationships, adults can understand children and their families better, and a higher level of trust is established. This relationship building results in a much more effective learning environment.

Although a collaborative project takes more energy, more coordination, and more time, I have come to believe it is well worth the effort. The process is enriched by the group effort and input from many perspectives. Being part of a group with a common goal is fulfilling, rewarding, and very enjoyable. Involving people outside the organization is also important to build support and broaden ideas.

After learning about a number of the long-term projects done in Reggio, I became more aware of the value of the small-group process. A group size of four to six children was very effective for maximal interaction while allowing for a manageable number of differing points of view. Each member of the group is important as a contributor of ideas to the group and also as a benefactor of the process. This arrangement could be translated into any setting for children or adults.

## CONCLUSION

As with so many of the attempts at adapting the Reggio Approach in the United States, those in children's museums have just begun. In addition to the possibilities already enumerated, following are some thoughts for places to start experimenting with change in the museum setting:

❑ We need to strive to understand children better to provide the best environment and programming possible. To this end, more research needs to be conducted to understand children and their behavior in the children's museum setting.

❑ We need to develop more sustained programming to build stronger relationships between and among museum staff, parents, and children.

❑ We need whenever possible to involve children in the design of the museum environment as well as in decisions that affect them.

❑ We need to serve as a place for teachers to get support and conduct research.

❑ We need to increase and improve the use of documentation, not only as a learning tool for museum staff and children but also as a way to prove to funders and the greater community the learning and growth that take place in the museum setting.

Looking back at our experience at the Kohl Children's Museum, it is difficult to determine exactly where the influence of the Reggio Approach began and ended. Many of the ideas had been in place in some fashion before our visits but were richly enhanced by our exposure to the Reggio educators. Our experience with the Reggio Approach affirmed much of what we were doing, gave us the confidence to challenge our assumptions, and helped us better articulate our own approach.

Just as with children, the learning process for all of us is a spiraling progression. We cannot know something without revisiting, refining, and reflecting on it many, many times. Most of us find little time for reflection, but we need to carve out time to document, examine the documentation, discuss possibilities, and reflect on our actions and the actions of others. Without such reflection, we cannot learn from our mistakes or even our successes. Too often we are distracted by continuously looking ahead to the next project, but, in forgetting to look back, we miss so much.

The ideas coming from Reggio Emilia are complex and have developed over so many years that I feel I am only beginning to comprehend their journey and discoveries. It is only by revisiting these ideas over and over again and adapting them to our own circumstances, our own culture, that we can get the most from our journey, which, with Reggio's guidance and inspiration, will take us to many wonderful places.

# V

*Working with Student Teachers to Bring About Change*

 The reader may recall that in Part II Eva Tarini cited documentation as being one of the most fundamental concepts of the Reggio Approach. Although many of the authors in this book have alluded to documentation's value and described how they are including it in their programs, it is in Chapter 15—by Jeanne Goldhaber, Dee Smith, and Susan Sortino—which is about teaching student teachers, that we experience the fullest flavor of what documentation can be and how richly rewarding yet difficult it is to do successfully.

While the previous chapters have made it clear it can be difficult for an individual teacher to make even moderate changes in her own classroom or for a director to inspire a staff to do so on a broader level, the mind boggles over how difficult it can be to inspire student teachers not only to grasp but to put into practice these Reggio concepts—concepts that run so counter to the way they were taught while in school. Yet that is what Mary Jane Moran decided to do. In short, she decided she could not be satisfied with telling her students to "do as I say" unless she practiced what she preached and taught them to "do as I do." The intricacies of how she changed her teaching style to set that example complete the final chapter in Part V.

# 15

# *Observing, Recording, Understanding*

## The Role of Documentation in Early Childhood Teacher Education

*Jeanne Goldhaber*[*]
Early Childhood Human Development Program, University of
Vermont

*Dee Smith*
Director, Campus Child Care Center Infant/Toddler Programs,
University of Vermont

*Susan Sortino*
Lecturer, Department of Integrated Studies, University of Vermont
Early Childhood Program, University of Vermont

[*] The authors would like to thank Barbara Burrington, Wendy Hobbins, and Judy Harvey for
their invaluable contributions and limitless enthusiasm.

Like so many early childhood professionals, we have spent the last several years trying to figure out how to integrate the Reggio Emilia approach into our program. We read articles (Gandini, 1984; Gandini & Edwards, 1988; New, 1990), attended the Reggio Emilia exhibit "The Hundred Languages of Children" (City of Reggio Emilia, 1987), and listened intently to formal and informal discussions of Reggio Emilia at the 1990 National Association for the Education of Young Children Annual Conference. We knew from what we were hearing and seeing that there was something quite special about the kinds of experiences children were having in Reggio Emilia.

In the spring of 1991, four of us from the Early Childhood Program at the University of Vermont joined a delegation to learn firsthand about the Reggio Emilia Approach. We wanted to know what of the Reggio Approach should and could be incorporated into both our academic courses and on-site child care facility. Returning both inspired and overwhelmed, we shared our thoughts, observations, slides, and videotapes with colleagues. We spent the year dabbling in some of the most obvious Reggio strategies, hanging plants, taking photos of children painting, and managing a few projects that were relatively short-lived investigations. We just could not get beyond the superficial.

Two of us returned to Reggio Emilia a second time the following year. We were determined to figure out how to bridge the cultural, aesthetic, and pragmatic gaps between our two programs. We came back having a somewhat better sense of how to accomplish this goal. First, we knew that we would have to give ourselves permission to move slowly. Perhaps the primary lesson Reggio teaches is that children and adults must have ample time to explore, hypothesize, take risks. We also knew that we would have to limit the scope of our activity. For this reason, we decided to commit ourselves primarily to exploring the role of documentation in our teacher preparation program.

## A FOCUS ON DOCUMENTATION: A MEANINGFUL MATCH

While our interest in exploring the use of documentation had many sources, the most compelling resided in our theoretical orientation. Our academic courses and on-site children's programs reflect a constructivist view of development that stresses the importance of observing and interpreting children's efforts to understand their world (Goldhaber & Smith, 1993). Reflecting this perspective of constructivist teaching, we were eager to explore the potential of documentation as a tool to teach our undergraduates to be keener observers, more reflective interpreters, and more individualized curriculum planners. Moreover, we hoped that Reggio Emilia's strategy of documenting children's work through panels of photographs accompanied by explanatory notes, samples of children's work, and transcripts of children's comments and conversations would engage our students in conversation and reflection both among themselves and with children, resulting in more individualized, child-sensitive practice. Finally, we believed that documentation could provide students with an effective way of communicating to parents and visitors the meaning and value of children's play and exploration.

## THE NEED FOR COLLABORATION IS IMMEDIATE

Having decided "what" of the Reggio Emilia approach to explore, we next had to figure out the "how." We were lucky. As a training program, one of our primary resources is people. Several of us incorporated documentation assignments into our undergraduate courses, so that as a group we were able to explore not only different documentation techniques but also the relationship between technique and the students' level of training in the program.

With the overlapping focus on documentation in our courses, we rediscovered the importance of collaboration. Certainly collaboration has always been a part of our program's belief system, but over time we had evolved into friendly but primarily parallel teaching practices. We occasionally lectured in each others' courses, walked to lunchtime aerobics classes together, commiserated over classes that were not going well. But with the new challenge of including documentation into our courses, we became increasingly interested in each other's experiences and perspectives, and more reliant on each other for support and advice. Along with our students, we too were trying to develop appropriate strategies to support learning. This was indeed an experience in knowledge co-construction!

But reality, as is so often the case, tempered our efforts to collaborate. Reflecting the ever-present and always changing demands of our professional and personal lives, we met to discuss our work with varying degrees of intentionality and regularity, with many rushed but no less valuable exchanges taking place in the corridors and parking lots outside our offices. For us, collaboration was a messy but essential ingredient.

## A ROAD MAP TO FOLLOW OUR STORY

Clearly, the story of our journey, our students, and ourselves is not a simple or linear one. In the interest of clarity, we will first describe the various documentation techniques we explored with our students and the relative advantages and disadvantages of each. It is important to keep in mind, however, that students often combined techniques for documenting a particular experience. For example, students often used video prints and samples of children's work in their panels, or audio transcripts and Polaroid photographs.

While investigating the different documentation techniques, we engaged in many conversations about what constituted a "good student panel." As we pored over the student panels each week, we began to develop a set of descriptors that evolved into a list that we eventually entitled "Essential Elements of a Panel." We will share this list, with the caveat that it represents our *emerging* understanding of how to support students in their efforts to document children's thinking and problem solving. Finally, after sharing our thoughts concerning the very complex relationships that exist among documentation techniques, the student documenters' knowledge base and skills, and the nature of the documented experience, we will offer a set of recommendations to early childhood teacher-training programs interested in pursuing documentation as a vehicle for professional development.

## DOCUMENTATION TECHNIQUES

In general, several documentation techniques emerged. They consisted of (a) Polaroid photographs with labels for short transcripts or descriptions, (b) audiotape transcriptions with samples of children's work, and (c) videotape prints with transcripts (often accompanied by children's work).

As we explored the various documentation techniques with our students, we were constantly questioning whether the use of documentation was furthering our students' skills and knowledge. Their feedback often gave voice to frustration and disequilibrium, yet the issues they raised reflected a growing understanding of the elements of best practice. For example, when the students demanded that we give them more time to work on their panels, we could not help but feel gratified by their understanding that best practice takes time and effort. When they worried that their panels did not reflect meaningful experiences, we rejoiced that they were beginning to grapple with the "meaning" of children's play. When they complained that parents were not reading their panels, we realized that the process of documentation had expanded our students' consciousness of their roles in relationship to the children's families. Consequently, even when the students were their most negative, we took comfort in their simultaneous learning and hastened to make revisions to create a more positive learning experience. This somewhat antagonistic situation was no more evident than in our use of Polaroid photographs as a form of "instant documentation."

## Polaroid: "This May Be Pretty, but Polaroids Just Don't Seem Aesthetic."

After introducing a group of second-year students to the Reggio Emilia Approach through readings and class discussions (Edwards et al., 1993; Gandini, 1993a, 1993b; New, 1990), we assigned them to teams of two—one student interacting primarily with the children, the other as the primary observer/documenter—for 2-week rotations to specific classroom areas for a 2-hour block every week in the preschool. We asked the students to document an experience of a child or children who were engaged in an active investigation or exploration of the materials by taking approximately three Polaroid photos and writing short observations or transcripts of the children's comments or conversations on small self-adhesive labels.

We assigned them to areas, such as play dough and blocks, that make few demands of students' management skills. Wanting to challenge our own tendency to spend hours working and reworking our panels, we told the students to delegate only 20 to 30 minutes of their 2-hour block to create their panels. To further simplify the documentation process, we stored the camera, 18 × 24-inch poster boards, labels, and markers in a basket in the observation booth adjacent to the classroom.

This method of documentation produced mixed feedback and results. The multitude of factors involved in the documentation process—being in the classroom for the first time, interacting with children while focusing on the meaningful aspects of the interaction, dealing with the logistics and limitations of a Polaroid camera, and handling the imposed time constraints—contributed to a high level of student frustration and anxiety and a low level of documentation!

For example, many of the panel observations were general and subjective, conveying little information that reflected what children were trying to understand or accomplish. Although these students had spent the previous year in a two-semester course observing and recording the exploration and play of infants and toddlers, the new setting and documentation assignment had apparently challenged their observation skills to a degree that surprised and worried us.

We also learned that the expectation of a panel after every session conflicted with another of our requirements—that the panels represent a meaningful experience on the part of the children—with students making what appeared to be random choices in terms of what they chose to observe and document. Students were also unanimous in the view that 30 minutes is not enough time to create a panel. And, finally, as one student stated very plainly, Polaroid photographs, often dark and fuzzy, just are not a very aesthetically satisfying medium.

Clearly, students were struggling with the assignment. They needed more time and flexibility to create their panels. The expectation that they would document an experience every time they were in the classroom had potentially engendered an attitude that they should document something, *anything*, so they *could* then be with the children. Although we knew that *we* were able to use this limited documentation technique to create panels that were effective representations of children's theory building, it was less clear that our students could use this format effectively. Student feedback, as well as a number of panels that were indeed hastily constructed and reflected what appeared to be relatively insignificant classroom experiences, suggested that we revise our expectations, as well as revisit the question of what a documentable experience *is*, when introducing the second documentation strategy involving the practice of audiotape recording and transcribing.

## Audiotape Recording: "I Listen More Carefully."

The use of an audiotape recorder seemed particularly suited to the work that children do in the area of the room referred to as the "round table." This area includes a very low 48-inch round table equipped with a wide assortment of paper, tape, and writing materials. Children kneel around it to draw, dictate, and illustrate stories or books, or sometimes to watch and talk. It is a very social place, where children question their assumptions about the world, such as whether wedding cakes have to start with the biggest layer first (after much deliberation, the answer is yes), or solve problems such as how to draw a frontal view of Batman that includes the insignia on his cape (draw the cape on the other side of the paper and hold it up to the light). The round table area, equipped with an audiotape recorder, seemed the perfect place for documenting children's literacy experiences through careful listening and observing (see Figure 15–1).

Before sending the students back into the classroom, we shared more information about how and what to observe. We reviewed the fundamentals of running records: write what you see; be specific, detailed, and objective; write in the present tense; include a description of context, a time frame, and date. To help them decide what to observe, we assigned readings about emerging literacy (Hayes, 1990; Van Hoorn, Nourot, Scales, & Alward, 1993) and reminded them to observe children who appeared to be engaged and intentional by paying attention to children's affect and facial expressions and the amount of time they were spending in the area.

In response to student feedback, we also allowed more time to document the children's experiences both at the round table or in other areas if

**FIGURE 15–1**
The students found that the use of an audiotape record was very helpful as a resource for documenting the children's conversations.

appropriate and the option of not submitting a panel every week. They were asked to type the observations and audiotape transcripts used in the panels and to include samples or copies of the children's work.

Students' responses to the observation review, changes in expectations, and use of an audiotape recorder were quite positive. They reported a new appreciation to the role of listening, of "listening more intently" to children's conversation. The issue of the meaningfulness of the observed experience was also revisited, with comments such as Toni's observation that "it is through the child's speech that we all can begin to understand what it is that the child is getting from a situation."

The students also agreed that having more time was a significant factor in their ability to create more effective panels. By being allowed more time, the students were able to give much more thought to what they included in the actual panel. The text was typed, making the panels neater and easier to read. However, our flexibility concerning the time frame for creating a panel also produced some procrastination and indecision. For example, in response to the assignment to document examples of children's emerging literacy development, several students reported that there were no literacy behaviors to document and, consequently, did not submit a panel. However, through individual and class discussion, students began to understand that literate behavior does not have to look like conventional writing. They began to recognize literate behavior in the children's maps to the fire in the dramatic play area and in their signs that say "SV" in the blocks. The students were becoming more appreciative of the depth, dimensions, and meaningfulness of young children's play.

Students were also beginning to recognize and reflect on the skills they had already acquired and the role that their skills played in the documentation process. One student wrote that she initially had "no clue as to the process of documenting an activity" but later acknowledged that "an enormous amount of experience in describing every detail through observation in all my other courses" was "extremely helpful" in her efforts to document. Another student wrote that one of her greatest self-revelations was that she did not really "have such a great memory" after all.

Not only was student feedback encouraging, but the quality of the panels also improved. For example, one panel that included a detailed transcript of a child's explanation of how and why he drew the displayed two-headed minotaur reflected not only the child's growing understanding of the relationship between form and function but also the student's recognition that children's drawing is often a visual representation of their thinking. We were making progress.

## Video Prints

Toward the end of the semester, we introduced video prints as a documentation strategy. For the second-year students who had already explored the use of Polaroid cameras and audiotapes, the use of the video camera represented a natural progression to a more integrated audiovisual format. We asked the students to videotape children's dramatic play, because this form of play is very often the most active, interactive play at the preschool level, and we felt that a video camera would be most successful in capturing the action as well as the language of pretense. Their panels were to include video prints, made from a Sony Color Video Printer (CVP-M3), as well as transcripts taken from their videotaping and samples of the children's work if appropriate.

While students appeared to find videotaping one of the most comprehensive documenting strategies, they also grappled with negotiating the value of videotaping versus interacting with the children. Although teaming provided a partial solution to this dilemma, with one student noting that she was "beginning to understand what is meant by collaboration," the balance of documenting and participating remained a challenge.

Although this form of documentation is one of the most expensive (Video Printers cost approximately $1,000; paper and toner cost approximately $0.64 per print) as well as one of the most time-consuming (like audio transcribing, viewing and transcribing videotapes is a very slow process), it provides the richest and most detailed record of children's thinking and problem solving. Moreover, in reviewing the tapes, one is consistently challenged to rethink suppositions about the nature of a particular child's or group's experience.

This process of "review and rethink" was particularly evident in the panels of a group of senior student teachers in their primary-level field practicum. For example, as one student reviewed videotapes of the children in her group building structures as part of a community theme, she learned that this activity had been not only an active investigation of the concept of community but also a very authentic and meaningful community *experience*, with evidence in the tapes of the children's explicit and implicit sharing of design ideas, construction solutions, and aesthetics. Her panel, displayed with the actual structures, included both video prints and transcripts of the children's conversations with short explanations of how the children influenced each other's building, thus documenting the highly interactive and collaborative nature of the children's experience. It was a very powerful panel and elicited a great deal attention from children, parents, and other teachers during the class's open house.

## ESSENTIAL ELEMENTS OF A PANEL: EMERGING GUIDELINES EVOLVE

In reviewing the student panels every week, we developed a better sense of what we wanted the panels to accomplish as a teacher-training tool and how to identify the extent to which the documentation process was accomplishing our goal. In essence, we hoped the process of documentation would help students be better observers and recorders of children's thinking and problem solving. We wanted students to pay close attention as children worked to make sense of the world around them, to record the children's thoughts and hypotheses so that they could be revisited and perhaps challenged, as well as shared with families and other teachers, and to be careful and thoughtful in their choice of content and presentation because of our growing belief that a well-executed panel communicates a respect for children as competent and valued people. Hoping that documentation would teach these lessons, we developed the following list and shared it with our students:

### Essential Elements of a Panel

❏ Focus on children's engagement and intentionality in meaningful experiences (i.e., a problem they are solving, question they are pursuing, or theory they are building).

❏ Determine who your audience will be (e.g., are the parents literate?).

❏ Describe the context of your observation.

❏ Include a verbatim dialogue and/or a very detailed observation in the present tense of what children are doing.

❏ Describe children's affect (quality of gestures, facial expressions, etc.).

❏ Be selective with visual components. (Photos should relate to what is being described.)

❏ Include enough information to be able to plan a follow-up experience.

❏ Consider the aesthetic presentation of the panel.


We feel that many of our students learned, if not all, then at least some of these lessons. But the process of learning is a complicated and, of course, developmental one. For example, our second-year students were initially challenged to draw on their prior knowledge but primarily experienced difficulty integrating their roles of documenter and "teacher," while the seniors' panels reflected an emerging ability to reflect *and* act on the meaning and significance of their observations in panels that engaged both adults and children.

The nature of the experience being documented as well as the documentation technique were also significant factors. Children's drawing and writing were particularly "documentable" through the use of audio recording and samples, while their dramatic play was best captured with video prints and transcripts. Polaroid photographs and written observations could reflect children's thinking and problem solving during simple play interactions or as they used materials that undergo relatively slow transformations such as play dough, Legos, and blocks. In general, the degree of attention and skill required to simultaneously document and facilitate the children's experience clearly affected the students' comfort level and success in the role of teacher/documenter.

# FINAL THOUGHTS

Reflecting on our accomplishments, we feel alternately gratified and humbled. We were heartened by the clear gains made in our students' skills as observers and interpreters of children's knowledge construction. We were also pleased by the seniors' success in using panels as a means of communicating the value of children's play and exploration to the children themselves, their parents, and other teachers. We were less successful in our efforts to use the panels to teach students how to engage children in revisiting their experiences to develop more child-sensitive practices. Falling short of these goals will demand considerable attention, since we consider them essential components of a constructivist perspective.

In response to both our successes and shortcomings, we have developed several recommendations to guide our future efforts and support other teacher-training programs interested in pursuing documentation as a vehicle for professional development.

*(1) Remember, it takes time—find it.* Documentation is time-intensive. Clearly, our expectation that students could construct a panel in 30 minutes was, at the very least, naive. Students need time to get comfortable in a new setting; to observe, reflect, discuss; and, of course, to translate these activities into meaningful panels. However, we also feel committed to exploring ways of making the documentation process a realistic practice (not only for our students but also for practitioners in the field) in terms of the amount of time it requires. We are particularly interested in exploring the practice of "instant" documentation at a point in the students' experience when their knowledge base, skills, and comfort level are high, rather than as a beginning strategy when they are their most vulnerable.

*(2) The role of observation cannot be overemphasized.* Considerable effort must be dedicated to teaching students how to observe, with additional review and practice provided as students enter new settings. Discussion of how their observations relate to theory and practice must also be ongoing and prioritized. The skill of sharing observations recorded on documentation panels with children, parents, and other teachers must also be taught: it does not happen without skillful facilitation.

*(3) Be mindful of the relationships between students' knowledge base and skills, the context, and documentation technique.* Thought and care must be given when assigning a documentation panel. Questions to address include these: What are students' skills and knowledge base? Which documentation technique is most appropriate given the students' backgrounds and the experiences being observed? Is it feasible for students to plan follow-up experiences given the amount of time they are actually in the classroom?

*(4)  Just do it!*    As one of our faculty observed about documentation, "You just have to do it." As constructivists, we sincerely believe in the necessity of taking risks to learn and construct knowledge. So it has been for us in our decision to explore the use of documentation in our teacher-training program. We trust that as our own knowledge base increases and documentation experiences are more appropriately embedded throughout the program, our students will be more effective in using documentation to support and challenge children's thinking and problem solving. Finally, we look forward to continuing this journey together, appreciating the role that documentation can play in our students' professional development as well as in our own. As one of our students concluded:

> This, then, is the greatest "discovery" I've made thus far: there are no easy answers. . . . They really do come from the interactions and observations we make. This shouldn't sound so revealing, since it is what we study, but somehow I never really connected the philosophy to myself. It really is a process. You said this all along and I nodded and agreed and said "Yes, yes, it is," and I thought I knew what you meant. But I didn't. And I don't know if I do now, either (but I think I do). And I am on the road, finally, and that is what I wanted.

That is what we want, too—to be on the road together. And perhaps to look back occasionally and reflect on and celebrate the distance we have covered, and look forward to the challenges that await us.

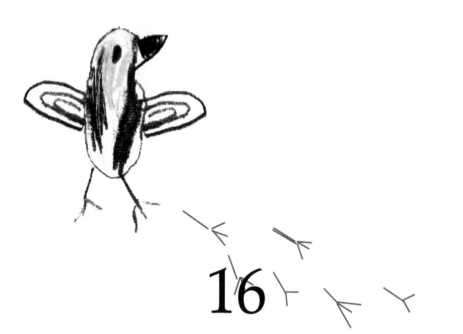

# 16

# *Reconceptualizing Early Childhood Teacher Education*

## Preservice Teachers as Ethnographers

*Mary Jane Moran*

Instructor, Department of Family Studies, and Assistant Director, Child Study and Development Center, University of New Hampshire

Three years ago, I could not remember whether it was Reggio Emilia or Emilia Reggio. My story is about a transformation in my beliefs and practice about how to teach preservice teachers more effectively by using the project approach in training undergraduate teachers at the University of New Hampshire enrolled in the Department of Family Studies Young Child or Nursery School–Kindergarten certification option. My personal interpretation of the project approach, which I first witnessed in Reggio Emilia, Italy, during the fall of 1992, has been incorporated into a beginning methods class. My primary goal there is to provide opportunities for preservice teachers to develop thoughtful and improvisational practice as they gain pedagogical competency.

Before my exposure to the Reggio Emilia Approach, my teaching was compartmentalized, broken down into pieces of information related to children's development, curriculum planning, and strategies for implementing activities with 3-, 4- and 5-year-old children. I was spoon-feeding my young, inexperienced students because I believed that was all they could handle. My teaching was technical and prescriptive. I expected students to integrate separate pieces of methodology and development without providing them with contexts for integrating their knowledge and skills—contexts in which to merge theory and practice by behaving as learners, researchers, and collaborators and by participating in owning decisions about their professional development.

My conflict was not about the content I was teaching but about the way in which my students experienced and came to know about such content as emergent curricula, child-initiated activities, developmentally appropriate practice, and teaching strategies such as higher-order questioning, selecting appropriate materials, and managing challenging behavior.

Before incorporating projects into the methods class, I faced many dilemmas, including the facts that:

❑ preservice teachers were in the classroom for a limited portion of children's time in school;

❑ they often implemented close-ended yet theme-related activities;

❑ they had limited time and need to revisit, discuss, and reflect on their teaching with one another;

❑ their observations were typically documentation of developmental milestones for child study rather than documentation to inform practice; and

❑ they lacked a passion and energy for teaching.

As a result, preservice teachers developed plans in isolation from one another and were more wedded to their plans than to children's processes of learning. Children were rarely consulted about what interested them, and their previous days' work and play were not connected to subsequent days. Materials were typically "prepared" by preservice teachers so that children put materials together to complete a predetermined product, while evidence of these activities went home each day to be put up on refrigerator doors with little left behind as a visual reminder of children's and teacher's work together. Preservice teachers looked to cooperating teachers or their teacher educator more often than to themselves for feedback, even after considerable time and effort were spent in the classroom.

Although I felt dissatisfied, I lacked a satisfactory vehicle for responding to these dilemmas until I observed Reggio teachers and children together. They were frequently engaged in fervent conversation, close observations of representational work, and negotiations about next steps. Teachers listened carefully and respectfully and responded to children's ideas and questions thoughtfully. They took time to confer with one another to determine the best response to children's efforts.

As I witnessed this approach at Reggio Emilia, I began to think carefully about these important teacher characteristics and the value of project work not only for children *but for teachers.* I surmised that projects were an important reason for such a responsive, passionate learning environment—an environment I wanted my own students to experience.

## *TEACHERS AS ETHNOGRAPHERS*

When I returned from Reggio Emilia, I resolved to make some changes in my approach to teaching to see whether I might possibly construct such an environment. After modifying the course, I now teach preservice teachers how to implement projects, use documentation to guide steps within a project, and analyze change in children's knowing and in their developing image of self as educator. My primary objectives include the development of the preservice teachers' capacity to view themselves three-dimensionally: as learner, as researcher, and as collaborator. Practically speaking, this means at least three things: they must consider their professional development to be a life-long process in which they use strategies to guide, investigate, and analyze children's learning as well as their own; they must develop practices and an attitude that expect and support collaboration with colleagues, parents, and children; and they must take time and seek opportunities to think about the impact of their teaching on children's meaning making. In short, they must develop skills including those typically associated with the role of ethnographer (New, 1994).

Thus, the focus of this chapter is on describing the processes of teaching students how to *use* data for professional development rather than how to gather it. Data in this context include children's words, behaviors, and representations of knowing during the evolution of a project. As a result of preservice teachers *using* data, continuity of programming directed by children's interests is embedded in the developing attitudes, actions, and activities of preservice teachers. Therefore, teaching in isolation from one another or being more wedded to one's lesson plan than to children's questions and interests becomes as foreign a practice as reading *Dick and Jane*.

One of the most vivid lessons I learned at Reggio Emilia about using data effectively was that collaboration among staff members was an essential part of reflecting on and using the data they had collected. Following that lead, I concluded that it would be necessary for my students also to engage in collaborative teaching and learning as *they* reflected on the children's words and behaviors and their own responses to those words and behaviors.

The problem was how to make this possible in a situation where each student only worked with children once a week. How could we maintain continuity of projects for those students and, even more importantly, the children under these circumstances?

## OVERVIEW OF THE REVISED INTRODUCTORY COURSE

The first step I took was to revise the structure of the course into three phases: orientation (weeks 1 through 5), application (weeks 6 through 11), and interpretation (weeks 12 through 14). Effort and time during the orientation phase are placed on learning basic content, while during the second phase, more effort is placed on applying knowledge and technique within the context of analyses of projects. During the final, interpretation phase, teachers reflect on the evolution of their projects to interpret how children's and teachers' knowledge and skills changed. Within each phase, the role of the teacher educator changes in response to shifts made by the preservice teacher because her emphasis varies at different times.

As the two graphs in Figure 16–1 indicate, during these phases the roles of the teacher educator and preservice teachers are fluid and dynamic. The teacher educator progresses from a prescriptive, directive role, toward a mediational, participant-observer role, toward, ultimately, a mentor, nondirective role (Bredekamp & Rosegrant, 1992). In concert with those changes, the abilities and skills of the preservice teachers also undergo change as they develop an increasing dependence on one another and their children and rely less on the teacher educator for ideas and feedback.

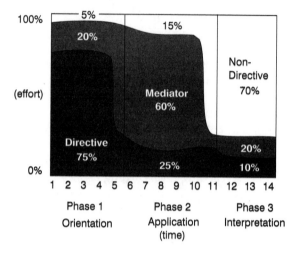

**Graph 1**

**Teacher Educator Time and Effort**

Phase 1
Orientation

Phase 2
Application
(time)

Phase 3
Interpretation

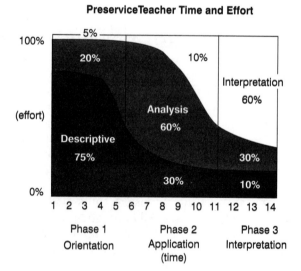

**Graph 2**

**PreserviceTeacher Time and Effort**

Phase 1
Orientation

Phase 2
Application
(time)

Phase 3
Interpretation

**FIGURE 16–1**

Approximate time devoted to various roles during the course

Preservice teachers attend two 80-minute lectures and a 4-hour practicum with either 3-, 4-, or 5-year-old children each week in the practicum. They are assigned to a particular program and a group of five or six children for the semester. Texts for the course include *The Hundred Languages of Children* (Edwards et al., 1993), *Engaging Children's Mind: The Project Approach* (Katz & Chard, 1989), and *Enquiring Teachers Enquiring Learners: A Constructivist Approach for Teaching* (Fosnot, 1989), along with selected articles on the Reggio Emilia Approach to early education.

## THE ORIENTATION PHASE

### Common Concerns and Questions
*Who will be on my teaching team? How do my children learn best? What is a project?*

The role of "learner" dominates the orientation phase as key concepts and guidelines associated with projects are described, defined, and explored. Preservice teachers are in their classrooms beginning the first week of the semester and learn basic routines, schedules, and procedures as they familiarize themselves with the physical environment and spend time with the children in their program. Approximately 1 hour each week is spent with their cooperating teacher who has the primary responsibility for orienting students to their program, introducing students to families, and coordinating activities for students to implement with children.

A part of each day includes small-group time. Each preservice teacher is assigned a group of six children and is responsible for leading a small-group activity that is initially developed by the cooperating teacher and later replaced by project-related activities developed by the preservice teachers. The earlier activities may be part of a project or may be developed to help children and preservice teachers get to know one another and frequently reflect the current classroom theme.

### Classroom Themes and Projects Run Side by Side

The implementation of projects is not an either-or proposition in which either a thematic approach or a project approach is used. Instead, teachers have continued to choose themes and develop activities, morning meetings, book and music selections, and free-choice activities reflective of those themes. In addition, during a 15- to 30-minute part of each 3-hour day, children meet in their small group and engage in activities led by their preservice teacher. This is the time of day allotted to projects, although, as projects develop, children often choose to continue project work during their free-choice time. A project teaching team is made up of three or four preservice teachers, and each team member teaches 1 day a week.

Information related to social constructivist theory, strategies for implementing small-group activities, and managing challenging behavior are provided through lecture and group tasks. Group tasks are a way in which the teacher educator begins to "script" a sense of community among teams. Without this initial "community scripting," preservice teachers are reluctant and even fearful to take the initial steps of implementing a project. These tasks include performing guided reviews of videotapes, working on webbing, preparing a project topic, experimenting with materials, and transcribing children's conversations from audiotape.

During class, basic concepts such as *guided participation* (Rogoff, 1990), *zones of proximal development,* and *collaborative learning* are discussed, and project benchmarks are identified that provide direction for the design of provocations for children while not dictating setting, materials, or particular time frames. These include (a) recognizing the current stage of a project in the sequence of *exploration followed by representation,* which repeats throughout the life of a project; (b) envisioning a topic *three-dimensionally;* and (c) considering children's *developmental capabilities, skills* to be strengthened, and whether the *focus* will be primarily an investigation, dramatization, or construction (Katz & Chard, 1989).

Preservice teachers from previous semesters present guest lectures and discuss both the evolution of their project and the impact of their project on their own professional development. Presentations include a review of documentation panels and selected videotape clips. The intention is to inform new preservice teachers of the diversity of subject matter as well as the variability among teams' pursuit of their topics. Emphasis is placed on how previous preservice teachers used perceived errors as an opportunity for professional growth as well as freedom and flexibility about ways to implement a project.

I make it clear there are no expectations of a particular product that must be generated. Instead, I anticipate the creation of a string of connected learning experiences directed and shared by a group of children and a teaching team that emerge from previous days' work and play. The goal is continuity of learning as well as content, for both preservice teachers and children, with desired outcomes not limited to "academic" ones. Therefore, teams are encouraged to generate both academic and social goals and to review those goals periodically throughout the project.

An overriding principle of this framework is that adults and children learn in similar ways by coconstructing knowledge and that what is valuable for adults to work on is likewise valuable for children. Therefore, all teams are encouraged to recommend a collaborative task to their children (the collaborative task for the team is the implementation of their project). These tasks have ranged from constructing tents, to creating a horse show, to building castles.

## THE IMPLEMENTATION PHASE

### Common Concerns and Questions

*How do we get started? I'm afraid we'll run out of things to do—they'll get bored. How will we know what to do next? What do we document?*

## The Learning Process

During this phase, the context and process for learning move from lecture to the practicum and team meetings. Time and effort of preservice teachers shift from simply absorbing and exploring basic techniques and language associated with constructivist teaching toward the application and integration of that knowledge and technique. I continue to discuss ways to use basic teaching techniques effectively, but now daily teaching episodes of projects provide a rich source of relevant dilemmas, questions, and issues for analysis and integration of conceptual understanding within classroom practice.

During this phase, the roles of collaborator and researcher emerge and begin to merge as preservice teachers take on the work of "classroom ethnographers" (New, 1994, p. 75) through the gathering of data and reflection on and analysis of that data in order to plan subsequent steps in a project.

## Logistics of Team Management

The class is divided, with half the teams beginning week 6 and the second half beginning week 7. They continue to alternate; thus, each project lasts only 3 weeks. In this way, I am responsible for videotaping, providing written feedback, and meeting with half the teams at one time. Their off weeks offer them additional time to meet and bring to the class concerns and questions, gather additional materials, transcribe important dialogue, and develop photographs.

Teams are not required to audiotape every session because they can rely on the audio portion of their video. However, they soon learn the clarity of the audiotape is superior to the video. They bring their own cameras and are responsible for taking photographs. Typically, one teammate will come in and photograph for another as well as help out when an activity is particularly complicated, such as painting a large mural or putting finishing touches on horse show jumps. The preservice teachers assist one another but do not formally critique one another. Following the teaching day, the preservice teacher must reflect on the teaching immediately because of the responsibility for contacting the teacher for the next day. Together they identify possible directions the project may be taking as the preservice teacher conveys children's questions and comments believed to be important to pursue. Together they decide on what should happen next. If they are unsure, they contact the rest of the team and/or talk to me.

The preservice teacher's analysis of the day is aided by the videotape, which is reviewed at home, either alone or with the team. The tape returns to the classroom with the next team member. During weekly lectures, clips of these videotapes are often shared with the entire class by teams so they can receive advice on how to proceed. I meet regularly with teaching teams and serve as both a guide and participant-observer of each team. The processes used to analyze each step of the project include both collaboration and reflective practice; thus, the role of "collaborator" dominates. These processes of collaboration and reflection are modeled by the teacher educator during lecture but are practiced primarily during teaching team conferences.

During team conferences, documentation of data covers the conference table, while the VCR is available for the preview of particular videotape clips. There are seven important questions I continually ask as I mediate a team's analysis:

1. Which stage are you in, an exploratory one or a representational one?
2. What representation of knowledge has spiraled?
3. What do you think is the next step?
4. What examples of documentation do you have? What do you need?
5. How has the children's knowledge changed?
6. What information do you still need to provide? Revisit?
7. Do you plan to have a collaborative task? If so, what suggestions can you offer the children?

In addition to the weekly verbal feedback during team meetings, I provide immediate written feedback and meet periodically with individual preservice teachers. The written feedback is recorded on a "project critique sheet" that lists skills and techniques categorized into child management skills, teaching techniques, and group guidance skills. Students are rated on as many as 40 different skills and techniques ranging from "facial affect and body language" to "acknowledges when child responds to limit setting." A narrative portion is added along with the rating sheet that addresses the preservice teacher's role, how a cycle of symbolization was used, or whether opportunities were missed to scaffold further learning, for example. The feedback is focused on both teacher technique and whether the activity is a meaningful reflection of the particular stage of the project. For example, preservice teachers are encouraged to follow an exploratory stage with a representational one, as happened in the Tide Pool Project.

The Tide Pool Project scheduled a visit to a local nature center so that children could see large tide pools and handle ocean animals. They went to the edge of the water and looked at actual tide pools, took photographs, and videotaped their trip. Following the trip, children were invited to revisit the trip with the photographs and videotapes used as provocations for conversation. After this exploration phase, children decided they would like to construct their own tide pool, so containers, ocean water, seaweed, shells, and styrofoam animals were created. A second exploration phase was prompted when the team projected a photo of a tide pool onto a wall, turned on recorded sounds of the ocean, and invited children to act out their favorite tide pool animal. A representational stage followed as teachers offered a variety of media for children to construct tide pool animals. Thus, the teachers planned and spent time choosing materials that encouraged children to represent what they knew. They did not dictate that children build tide pools or construct animals, but they did offer suggestions and ask children whether they were interested. Had the children not been interested in constructing tide pool animals, teachers had to be willing to listen to their suggestions and respond by moving in a different direction.

## INTERPRETATION PHASE

### Common Concerns and Questions

*What will we choose to include in our panels? What were some of the most significant changes we made? The children made? If we could do it over, what would we change?*

As the implementation phase nears completion, effort and time by both teacher educator and preservice teacher shift once again. I continue to move away from a mediational role toward a more nondirective role; thus the amount of time working with teaching teams decreases. I am available for consultation, but the teams must increase their out-of-classroom time and behave more as researchers as they interpret their data, create documentation panels, and prepare their oral presentation for their peers.

Teams have freedom to determine how to present their documentation. Some teams edit videotapes that capture significant moments of a project such as collaboration, particular discoveries, and dramatizations. If the project ended with a collaborative product such as a mural, a book, a tent, or a train, then these artifacts become part of the documentation.

Among the most challenging work by preservice teachers are their decisions about which data to focus their attention on and how to organize their documentation so it is clear and compelling. Criteria for decisions vary from simply describing the evolution of a project to calling attention to the change in meaning making of a particular child or entire group of children. Such change among children is often demonstrated by (a) comparing and contrasting early and later dialogue; (b) early and later graphics, constructions, and dramatic representations; and (c) examples of changes in the social and collaborative behaviors of a group as revealed by exclamations that a child's idea is a good one, increased helping and sharing behaviors, and/or seeking advice from one another.

Additionally, preservice teachers discuss their perceived errors and ways they learned from them as exemplified in the Canoe Project that was implemented with 3-year-olds. In the following excerpts from one of the team's panels, they describe how they learned to more appropriately scaffold children's learning through the choice of materials and the use of a more realistic experience.

> On our first day of representation, we chose to use a material called craypas (a thick black crayon). We felt it would be exciting for the children to use. Contrary to our thoughts, we learned the materials did not afford the children ease of representation of a canoe. We also discovered drawing a canoe was too developmentally advanced at this point in the project. Our next step was to try to scaffold the children's knowledge by exploring the shape of a canoe. We did this by using the shape of a banana. The association of the shape of a canoe and shape of a banana was too abstract. This is where we decided the children needed some real hands-on with a canoe. A canoe was brought to school, trips were taken, paddles were used, and life jackets were buckled. Children made miniature canoes that floated out of styrofoam blocks that were hollowed out. Children's final graphic representations were surprisingly sophisticated. They included detail and form and were a representation of a meaningful experience.

A critical perspective is gained when preservice teachers reflect on the entire project together as they construct their presentation. They pore over data and engage in lengthy conversations about its meaning and importance. They are pushed to be very selective because they are given only 30 minutes to present their interpretation to the class.

By trying to decide what we were going to do as our panels, we were able to reflect on what had occurred during the duration of our project. We were able to see changes in the children (working together, their shift in knowledge, and especially their collaborative behavior) and ourselves (our abilities to communicate with each other and the children and our teaching styles). We needed to make a lot of decisions. The things the children learned and their processes of learning jumped out when we looked at all their dialogue, drawings, and photographs.

The passion for their work is most evident as students begin to piece together vignettes of their project. Preservice teachers own this work and value their relationships with one another and the ways in which they responded with respect and care to children's interests. This attitude generates both a confidence that they are capable of continuing to go into classrooms and take the lead from children as well as an anticipation that what will follow will be fun, provocative, and have far more potential for learning than any curriculum a teacher could create on her own.

The panels really make you reflect on the project as a whole. It made us pick out the most important things that occurred, which was very helpful. This was excellent for the growing social cohesion of our team because we all helped each other so much. The whole process was an incredible amount of work but well worth it. It was so rewarding and inspiring and it is something that has changed my life and now will always stay with me.

## CONCLUSION

Implementation of projects offers a promising context for teaching preservice teachers both the "craft" of teaching along with strategies for collaborative teaching and reflective practice. As a result, preservice teachers enter and leave the classroom more thoughtfully and work to ensure that their responses to children are improvisational yet purposeful. They document their work with children as a way to continue their own professional development and to communicate to others how children are learning in their classroom.

They no longer consider themselves the "expert" as they realize and accept that their perspective is limited, thus requiring collaboration with other teachers, children, and parents. They are motivated by the ownership of their work and are impassioned by their anticipation of what is to come. They are inquisitive and pause to look a second time at the meaning of a child's word or the representation of his or her knowledge. Best of all, they listen more carefully as they become convinced that "going back" is a way of "going forward."

# VI

## Where Do We Go from Here?

Many of the educators in *First Steps* conclude their chapters by outlining future plans—the next steps they intend to take—but it remains to Rebecca New to point out that our role as educators must go beyond that. As educators, we must think beyond the individual steps we are contemplating and do our best to advocate more broadly for the children in our care. She reminds us of the example our Reggio friends have set for use in this regard and urges us to follow their lead as we advance the Reggio Approach.

Finally, in the closing chapter entitled "Why Not?," Joanne Hendrick singles out a variety of objections she categorizes as the "yes buts" and "if onlys." By identifying these objections and replying to them, she provides practical encouragement for overcoming a variety of obstacles as we accept Becky New's challenge.

# 17

# Next Steps in Teaching "The Reggio Way"

## Advocating for a New Image of Children

*Rebecca S. New*

Associate Professor, Early Childhood Education, University of
New Hampshire

What does it mean when a community decides to create a world-class traveling exhibition featuring its work and accomplishments in early child care and education? How might historians explain the widespread interest among American early childhood professionals in the educational approach featured in such an exhibition? This chapter begins by considering these two phenomena as a means of responding to yet another question implied by the title of this volume: What are reasonable "next steps" to take in our efforts to best utilize what we are learning from our Reggio Emilia colleagues on behalf of young children in the United States?

The underlying postulate of this chapter is that the Reggio Emilia Approach—including the display and dissemination of information about its early childhood program with such unabashed fervor—is based on core values that increasingly resonate with the personal ethics and professional concerns of many American early childhood educators. Reggio Emilia's decision to translate the exhibition ("The Hundred Languages of Children") so that it might travel to other nations and continents, and its willingness to welcome foreign delegations to the small northern Italian city, have less to do with the aim of promoting Reggio Emilia practices per se than the desire to challenge individual and collective views of children and their interdependent relationship with society. Together, these decisions and their related goals reveal much about the philosophical and political bases of the work being done in Reggio Emilia. They also provide a window for contemplating the current American enthusiasm for any and all Reggio Emilia–related topics and determining our next steps in making sense of and putting to good use those aspects of Reggio Emilia that are transportable to the United States.

It is now well established that America's keen interest in the work of Reggio Emilia reflects our delight in discovering what it means to see some of our traditions' most cherished ideas put into practice. Reggio Emilia shows us what it looks like when a community takes child care seriously, when children's questions are as vital to the curriculum as those generated by teachers, and when social relationships (among children *and* adults) are nurtured in substantive and emotionally supportive ways. Many American early childhood educators have been inspired anew by Reggio Emilia's success at achieving some of our field's long-standing goals. In numerous ways, Reggio Emilia reminds us of what we believe in and demonstrates the feasibility of our common goals. Yet our motivation to grapple with what Reggio Emilia has to offer also draws support from something less apparent but perhaps more important in the long run, and that is the growing conviction that there is something genuine to be gained in more clearly defining our roles and goals as educators and citizens. The relevance of Reggio Emilia to the field of early childhood education in the United States corresponds to our growing understanding of the linkages between educational practice and the larger sociopolitical context, between our personal ethics and our professional responsibilities. To that end, the most critical next step in learning to "teach the Reggio way" is to move to an expanded role of early childhood educators as advocates for a new image of young children.

## PAST AND PRESENT CONCEPTIONS OF ADVOCACY

Interpretations of early education—its mission and its methods—have varied tremendously within the field's history, fluctuating in response to sociohistorical conditions as well as political climates. As such, images of American early childhood leaders and advocates have also been diverse, ranging from Elizabeth Palmer Peabody's radical and romantic campaign for kindergarten in the mid-19th century to the quiet but persistent press for more comprehensive programs for children and families by such scholars as Sharon Lynn Kagan, Bettye Caldwell, and Edward Zigler (Beatty, 1995). Collectively, such individuals combine traditional interpretations of *leaders* (those who provide direction, guidance, or instruction in an area of expertise) and *advocates* (those who defend, endorse, or promote particular ideas, individuals, or principles). Many early childhood classroom teachers and child care providers in the United States identify with these roles as they describe their work with young children. Yet these same early childhood professionals have often been less willing to embrace leadership roles that convey a sense of authority, a hesitancy that is not surprising given the field's characteristic low status in this country. Nor have many in our field comfortably acknowledged the political ramifications of their advocacy roles, an interpretation that entails going beyond personal support for a worthy cause to include a willingness to make public proclamations regarding controversial issues and contested values.

As the 20th century comes to a close, these expanded definitions of leadership and advocacy have increased relevance for the field of early childhood education and contemporary American society. Leadership skills are now considered essential elements of professional development and teacher education (Rodd, 1994). Many have come to view advocacy as a means not only of improving circumstances for individual children and the field itself but for the lives and well-being of *all* young children. In response to this heightened sense of need, there is a growing body of literature on the ways in which early childhood professionals might work on behalf of young children (see Fennimore, 1989; Goffin & Lombardi, 1988), with most current discussions directed at two levels of advocacy: within and outside the classroom (Dimidjian, 1989).

Reggio Emilia's interpretation of quality child care and early education expands on current presumptions of leadership and advocacy. It also provides key insights into both the challenges and opportunities available for professionals who see their responsibilities as moving beyond working *with* young children to include working *for* them. Of all the many possible contributions Reggio Emilia has to offer American early childhood educators, none surpasses their example of how to advocate more effectively on behalf of young children in our society.

## LEADERSHIP AND ADVOCACY REGGIO EMILIA STYLE

There are multiple causes and occasions within and outside early childhood classrooms that elicit advocacy on the part of early childhood professionals. Reggio Emilia teachers have taken advantage of existing opportunities for advocacy and created additional ones as well within the actual early educational settings as well as within the larger community. The cumulative result of their efforts supports a new conceptualization of the role of adults, policies, and programs in promoting and defending the rights, abilities, and needs of young children. Reggio Emilia examples of advocacy may be found in key *organizational features* of the infant-toddler centers and preprimary schools, common characteristics of the *physical environment,* and curricular decisions regarding *pedagogical content and practices.* Although the features themselves are likely to be familiar to most Reggio Emilia enthusiasts in the United States, their advocacy potentials—for children, their families, and the field of early education—warrant further illumination and discussion.

### Taking a Stand: Advocacy Through Organizational Priorities

Numerous organizational features of the preprimary schools and child care centers[*] proclaim and promote the philosophical bases of "the Reggio Emilia Approach." For example, the philosophy of schooling as a "system of relationships" (Malaguzzi, 1993b, p. 63) is put into practice in a manner that not only *endorses* but also *makes possible* high-quality and enduring social relationships in the lives of young children. An emphasis on relationships serves as both a primary rationale *and* a consequence of numerous organizational decisions, such as having children remain with the same peers and

---

[*] Here and throughout the chapter, all references to Reggio Emilia schools, preprimary schools, child care centers, and so forth, are referring solely to the municipally funded preprimary schools and infant-toddler centers that have been the focus of American interest. This reference does *not* include the many private, public, and church-operated programs for young children that are also available in Reggio Emilia.

teachers for 3 years. The congruence between the declared philosophy and implemented school organization serves to support related educational goals. Thus, the concept of classrooms as communities of learners stands a good chance of becoming a reality—much more so than would be the case when children's and adults' relationships are disrupted on a yearly basis. In reflecting this philosophical stance, school organization decisions serve an advocacy role by prioritizing children's social lives and highlighting teachers' abilities to respond best to children and families they know well.

Reggio Emilia's premise of the value of social relations also respects the interdependent relationship between family functioning and children's well-being. The organizational response to this cultural value is expressed in a variety of forms of support for parents and families of young children. When children first enroll in the infant-toddler or preprimary program, teachers and parents work out a daily routine that meets the child's needs and complements the family's particular circumstances, including work schedules and the availability of extended family members. Such exchanges serve as a form of family support as well as child advocacy; they set the stage for a high-quality and enduring home-school relationship that develops over the next 3 years as parents, teachers, and children share a wealth of experiences. The subsequent level of trust that develops contributes to a partnership that enables teachers and parents to maximize their respective contributions to the child's early educational experiences, including the shared responsibility of evaluation and assessment through jointly created notebooks or portfolios. Parent education programs in the United States rarely acknowledge the benefits to be gained when mothers and fathers are provided with support *and* treated as experts regarding their own child's development.

The highly personalized and respectful exchanges that characterize parent-teacher relations are one means by which Reggio Emilia has expanded on the Italian principle of community involvement—*gestione sociale*—in early child care and education. Large- and small-group parent meetings reflect similar goals, achieved through discussions of selected child development topics; the articulation of a "bill of rights" for parents, teachers, and children; and planning sessions to develop strategies to promote school agenda to the larger community. Such meetings, held late in the evening, are often attended by other citizens of the community as well as parents of enrolled children. These practices diverge significantly from American parent-teacher organizations in which parents' role is limited to fund-raising and school enrichment projects. These examples of organizational features that draw on Reggio Emilia's interpretation of schooling as a "system of relationships" illustrate some of the many ways in which schools can directly support and advocate for young children's development, as well as involve and empower parents as advocates for their own children.

## Caregiving Environments That Advocate for Quality Child Care

The physical environments of Reggio Emilia preprimary schools and infant-toddler centers convey many messages about children and the quality of care appropriate for them that are difficult to ignore. In fact, the contrasts between Reggio Emilia environments and many preschool settings in the United States are dramatic and, in some cases, unsettling. After visiting Reggio Emilia schools, American educators may find it increasingly difficult to rationalize placing public preschool programs in windowless church basements or decorating classrooms with manufactured alphabets and cartoon figures. Such indifference to the environmental conditions of child care and early education programs stands in stark juxtaposition to the care with which classrooms, hallways, and even the bathrooms of Reggio Emilia schools have been designed to stimulate children's intellect, respond to their sense of wonder, and promote a sense of belonging. As adults experience and marvel at the qualitative dimensions of the Reggio Emilia caregiving environments, their conceptions of children's need for and right to such nurturing also expand. Indeed, the *care* with which Reggio Emilia environments have been conceptualized and implemented brings new meaning to the concept of high-quality child *care*.

In addition to conveying important messages about children and their worth, Reggio Emilia environments actively promote children's development through means often neglected or denied, including the critical role of social relations and sociocognitive conflict. Dress-up areas are typically shared by all of the children within a single school, thereby acknowledging the abilities and interests of children of various ages to assist one another in putting on costumes and to negotiate roles in mixed-age play scenarios. Talking tubes, functional telephones, windows between classrooms, and an expansive central *piazza* are among the many features of the environment that loudly proclaim that young children have the need, ability, and *right* to connect, engage, argue with, and enjoy one another in school settings. American early childhood educators talk often about the value of play and other social exchanges, including conflicts, to young children's development; yet some teachers seem to spend much of their time admonishing children to leave one another alone, stop arguing, and listen to the teacher rather than to one another.

The physical environment also promotes parent involvement, welcoming parents from the time they walk into the door and inviting them to stay, observe, and contribute. All visitors have easy access to compelling displays of information about the events and the people in the school. Central piazzas and classrooms are enhanced with adult-sized furniture and educational equipment that parents have designed and created. Parents are also well informed of their child's experiences within the school setting through formal documentation as well as the daily descriptions of children's activities posted on the classroom door. These features of the physical environment promote genuine, focused conversations between parents and children as well as between parents and teachers. They also reinforce the advocacy message that schools are places for adults as well as children.

## Pedagogy as Endorsement of Children's Rights

Certainly, the most obvious means by which Reggio Emilia teachers advocate for young children is through the reciprocally linked documentation and *progetazzione,* each of which emphasizes the processes and products of children's emotional concerns, social relations, and creative and intellectual pursuits as they occur within the context of collaborative problem solving. Reggio Emilia projects do more, however, than just applaud and defend children's cognitive abilities, emotional needs, and social rights; they actively nurture children's capacities to work hard and learn from and with one another. This pedagogical principle is manifest in the design of activities and projects that require children to collaborate in the attainment of common goals as well as the determination of processes to achieve those goals. Reggio Emilia children have spent many hours over the course of many days determining how best to measure a table, plan a school athletic event, design a water wheel, or build a bridge out of clay. Through such projects, teachers promote children's knowledge of meaningful content. They also support children's abilities to advocate for themselves, even as teachers encourage and model a respect for diversity and multiple points of view.

The extensive documentation associated with the Reggio Emilia Approach contributes to the development as well as the dissemination of project work. Projects often evolve out of teacher documentation of children's interests, fears, abilities, and needs—intellectual as well as emotional. The resulting topics selected for investigation—aging, gender identity, shadows, war—convey both the exploratory nature and the seriousness with which Reggio Emilia teachers regard children's ways of responding to the world around them. Projects also often involve children's families, in both the planning and evaluation stages.

For example, when teachers determined that children were discussing the Persian Gulf War during free-play activities, they shared their observations and concerns with parents. As a result of the ensuing discussion, the adults agreed that opportunities should be provided by which young children could draw and talk about their fears and anxieties in a supportive environment. In this example, teachers used documentation to advocate for children's emotional lives to be acknowledged and respected. As a result of that (documented) activity, teachers and parents gained insights into children's ways of thinking about and responding to the larger global society.

Because of the entire experience, they were also reminded of children's reliance on adults to make the world a safer place.

Through Reggio Emilia's particular interpretation of an emergent curriculum and documentation, teachers promote a conception of children's needs, rights, and capabilities that expands on the beliefs of many parents and teachers (in Italy and around the world). They also demonstrate the possibilities of a school system that is alert and responsive to those capabilities. Advocacy outcomes of Reggio Emilia's pedagogical approach to working with young children are therefore directed at both children and adults. All are encouraged to appreciate diverse points of view. All are reminded of the benefits of in-depth investigation of problems that are authentic and personally meaningful. And all are provided with ample evidence that school can and should be a place where the "basics" of early education include the development of nurturing and collaborative relationships and the fostering of creative problem-solving skills.

## *Advocacy as a Way of Thinking About Young Children*

Reggio Emilia has challenged the distinction between two separate forms of advocacy—within and outside the classroom—that are typically ascribed to the early childhood profession. The organizational principles, physical characteristics, and pedagogical strategies of the Reggio Emilia Approach combine to play a strong and overt advocacy role for young children that belies the traditional distinctions between home and school, classroom and community. The examples shared, along with many other features of the Reggio Emilia Approach, also serve as a more subtle form of advocacy by provoking, informing, empowering, and inspiring adults—parents, teachers, and other community members—who are themselves in positions to advocate for and make a difference in the lives of young children.

The cumulative effects of what children, parents, teachers, and community members experience in Reggio Emilia validates the rich complexities of children's lives, serves as a compelling endorsement of parental rights and involvement in early care and education, and highlights the broader community's responsibility to assure young children a high quality of early care and education. These experiences also combine to serve as a highly visible form of advocacy for the profession of early childhood. As they have grown in their shared understanding of what it is that children, families, and schools are capable of, it is no wonder, then, that the citizens of Reggio Emilia have been able to work together to ensure optimal funding, negotiate school policy, and collaborate in the maintenance of an early childhood program that has been proclaimed as "the best in the world" (*Newsweek*, 1991). There is much to aspire to as we consider advocacy needs of young children in the United States.

## WANTED: ADVOCATES FOR YOUNG
## CHILDREN IN THE UNITED STATES

The heightened emphasis on leadership and advocacy among American early childhood professionals reflects a sense of heightened need—not for resources, but for resolve. The contrast between our nation's ability and its will to care for its youngest citizens has never been so clear. The United States now boasts *both* the highest standard of living *and* the highest rate of childhood poverty among all industrialized nations. The human consequences of this national indifference are poignantly detailed in a growing number of accounts of children and families whose lives are "on the edge" (Polakow, 1993). The legacy of our nation's racist past continues to influence life in and out of the classroom, where—especially for children of racial minorities—the quality of the educational experience remains problematic (Miller, 1995; New & Mallory, in press). As the social conditions and economic circumstances of many families worsen, a conservative political climate threatens to undo three decades of programs designed to address the educational, health, and developmental needs of young children. In spite of considerable evidence in support of such programs, sufficient changes have taken place in our nation's political climate so that we can no longer be optimistic that all "Americans and their elected officials are . . . convinced that investments in programs for young children are monies well spent" (Zigler & Styfco, 1993, p. 132).

The marginal status of children in our society is not limited to those who are impoverished or discriminated against because of their racial or cultural heritage. Rather, the rights of children as a whole are systematically denied and infringed on. At the time of this writing, the United States has yet to ratify the United Nations Convention on the Rights of the Child,* thereby keeping company with such nations as Iraq and Somalia (Cohen & Bitensky, 1994). This denial of children's equality under American law is underscored by the fact that 24 of our 50 states continue to endorse corporal punishment as reasonable school practice, including "teacher immunity" laws in such states as Alabama and Virginia (Harp & Miller, 1995).

---

* The convention proclaims children's rights, for example, to a "standard of living adequate for the child's physical, mental, spiritual, moral, and social development" (Cohen & Bitensky, 1994).

## CONCLUSION: A NEW IMAGE OF CHILDREN, SCHOOLS, AND SOCIETY

The exhibition "The Hundred Languages of Children" serves as a metaphor for three decades of hard work by parents, teachers, and citizens of Reggio Emilia and a model for a new vision of advocacy in our field. It portrays the benefits of commitment, collaboration, and respect for children and the adults who care for and about them. It profiles a community that not only embraces the *concept* of high-quality early child care and education but makes it an actual reality. In its traveling mission around the world, the exhibition conveys an image of the child that is strong, powerful, and competent, and "most of all, connected to adults and other children" (Malaguzzi, 1993a, p. 10). And, finally, the exhibition serves to remind us that children have rights as well as potentials and that educators have a responsibility to convey that complex message. As such, Reggio Emilia's purposely portrayed image of the child also contributes to a *new image of society* as well, an image in which the responsibility for children's well-being entails a commitment of support and collaboration on the part of *all* citizens.

The power of these images lies not only in their ability to help us imagine the previously unimaginable; this recognition also entails tremendous responsibility once we admit to what we have seen (Bredekamp, 1993). In other words, these images—of children *and* a more civil society—will remain amorphous, at least outside Reggio Emilia, until we define them on our own terms and commit ourselves to a new form of advocacy.

Thus, the gift of Reggio Emilia's illustrious example comes in the form of a challenge to American educators—a challenge not only to improve our practices and to align them more closely with our beliefs, but also to learn how to draw public attention to our work and to the children for whom we are working. It behooves us, if we truly wish to take advantage of what Reggio Emilia has to offer, to turn often to the mirror our Italian friends hold up so that we might better know ourselves, discover children's capabilities, and acknowledge our responsibilities. Surely these are the most critical "next steps" that we can take on behalf of young children in our society. Reggio Emilia can point the way. But we must decide if we wish to follow.

# 18

# Why Not?

*Joanne Hendrick*
Professor, Emerita, University of Oklahoma

In my earlier chapter comparing Reggian and American approaches, I posed the question "Telling them apart and putting them together—can we do it?" Then evidence was presented in a number of chapters that some schools and universities are already answering yes to that query. They *can* do it—or, at least, they have taken a first step toward doing it.

It is fortunate indeed that we have these examples of successful change to encourage us because most of us have not come that far and we need the encouragement. In my talks around the country, I find that the majority of my listeners are at a much earlier stage of development where integrating Reggio principles is concerned. I see them as teetering on the brink of these new ideas—half tempted to plunge in, and half filled with indecision and misgivings about what the contemplated "water" will be like and whether they can stay afloat amid all these new ideas.

It seems to me these misgivings can be grouped into two categories. I call them the "yes buts" and the "if onlys." Because they represent such sticking points for so many people, it is useful not only to identify some of the most frequently stated concerns but also to provide encouragement for overcoming them.

## THINKING ABOUT THE "YES BUTS"

*Yes, but—is it really developmentally appropriate? Isn't it awfully teacher dominated?*

It is only natural that these objections come to mind when viewing the extraordinary children's work that abounds in "The Hundred Languages" exhibit and adorns the schools as well. There is no doubt this work is more advanced than what American children of the same age are typically producing at the preschool level—and this is true both graphically and intellectually speaking.

It is also true that the relationship between the Reggio teachers and children is more intense and that the teachers offer more concrete help than we Americans do when children are confronted with problems and/or difficulties. Teachers may "lend" a child a skill or knowledge in order to facilitate his accomplishing a desired goal by showing him how to do something, but they do not seem to tell him *what* to do. This restraint by the teacher is what keeps the child's work at *his* level rather than at a too advanced adult level.

If teachers offer so much "help," how can we tell whether the children are not being pushed beyond their abilities? In my opinion, the thing that prevents the help from becoming intrusive or dominating is the fact that the teachers' response is based on paying careful attention to what the children are thinking and telling them and then subjecting these observations about the children's responses to intense scrutiny and analysis by the adults working together. This collaborative analysis not only stimulates a wealth of fertile possibilities to explore further with the children but also protects teachers from generating overblown expectations and goals.

The other evidence of developmental appropriateness, while less amenable to concrete documentation but nonetheless apparent to school visitors, is the general air of ease and happiness one feels during such visits. No one, neither children nor adults, seems harried or under strain. Instead, there is a sense of harmony and a kind of energetic calm that testifies to the value of what is transpiring for the children there.

*Yes, but—you just don't understand how hard it is!*

Of course, it is hard! Without exception, the venturesome authors of the previous chapters make no secret of their difficulties and anxieties. As Katz points out in Chapter 8, change is always fraught with uncertainty and anxiety. These are certainly not comfortable feelings to live with. On the other hand, also without exception, those same authors assure us the satisfaction experienced by themselves, their students, and staff resulting from these changes has more than compensated them for the discomfort they are experiencing along the way.

*Yes, but—there's only me.*

This is a toughy. We have seen that collaboration at all levels is the essence of the Reggio Approach. The stimulation, support, and continuing revisiting and reevaluation of experience such collaboration provides are regarded as being essential for effecting change. Yet many of us Reggio enthusiasts feel we are voices crying alone in the wilderness.

The remedy for such isolation, of course, is to locate some like-minded spirits and arrange to have continued, regular contact with them as you struggle along together. (And, on a practical note, one of those people had better be your director or principal!)

*Yes, but—you don't know what the rest of the teachers are like!*

Yes, I do! I know they are tired, harassed, have personal problems, and, despite these difficulties, want to do the best they can. I know they are threatened by the thought of change and the possibility of foreswearing some of their most cherished principles. It is only to be expected they will be quick to defend themselves by using ridicule, expressing doubts, or citing their superior years of experience.

My advice about this is, don't waste your time trying to convince them. The truth is that in the long run the only person you can ever really change is yourself, so that is the best place to concentrate your energies. Perhaps your lighted candle will eventually illuminate their darkness; perhaps it won't.

*Yes, but—the parents won't like it!*

You won't know whether the parents will like it or not unless you try it! Of course, communication is the key here. Parents are entitled to explanations, and it is vital to take time to clearly communicate your purposes and reasons for making whatever changes you have in mind.

A good point to stress with families is that besides fostering joy in learning, the Reggio Approach also elicits the use of higher-order thinking skills by the children. For example, cite the consistent emphasis on uncovering what children know, problem solving, and expecting that children will be able to shift from using one symbolic system to another to express and communicate their ideas. Speak of this as being *metacognitive* learning.

Another point: If you remember that in Reggio parents are regarded as indispensable partners in learning and you regard them that way too, their cooperation and positive attitudes are bound to increase.

## DEALING WITH THE "IF ONLYS"

*If only—I had more time.*

There's no denying that this is a genuine problem—and one frequently cited throughout this book. In particular, the time required for collaboration and also for documentation is difficult to find. Unlike our Reggio peers, we do not have five paid hours to work without the children being present. Indeed, many of us are not even paid for attending staff meetings.

The answer to the time problem boils down to a question of priorities. If we decide the Reggio concepts are valuable enough, we will *find* the time—perhaps by jettisoning something we decide is less important or perhaps by simply disciplining ourselves to waste less time on more trivial occupations during the day.

*If only—I had the money.*

It would be wonderful to have the budget for film, xeroxing, and some kinds of materials used so commonly in the Reggio Emilia schools—but this need not be beyond our reach if we put our minds to it. For example, families could be asked to contribute a roll of film once a semester, or a materials charge could be part of the admission costs just as many schools now charge a small fee for annual insurance, or some kind of fund-raiser such as a yard sale could be sponsored. Happily, many of the self-expressive materials used by the children at Reggio are "found" items donated from home and so cost nothing at all.

*If only—I understood the philosophy better.*

My Reggio friends will hate me for saying this, but who's to know whether you have done something the exactly perfect Reggio way? After all, we are not attempting to duplicate what happens there. The staff in the Reggio schools would be the first to emphasize they wish their schools to be an inspiration to us, not a model for us to duplicate. As a matter of fact, *we must always be meticulously careful to make this fact clear to everyone: none of us is attempting a replication.* What we *are* doing is interpreting various principles that underlie the Reggio philosophy to the best of our ability and incorporating some of those principles into our own schools as best we can.

Learning about the Reggio Approach is not a finite body of knowledge that can be acquired, anyway. No matter how much you know about Reggio, something is always left to learn. I have heard Lilian Katz say she has been there eight times and is still deepening her knowledge at every visit.

*If only—I could visit Reggio.*

There are, of course, ways to accomplish this. Several delegations from the United States visit Reggio Emilia every year for special seminars. The easiest way to find out about how to join one of these groups is to subscribe to the quarterly newsletter *Innovations.*

Lacking that opportunity, the interest in the Reggio Approach that is burgeoning in the United States also means that seminars and workshops are increasing. It is always possible to attend those as well as to read articles and books about the Reggio Approach.

---

* Subscription information may be obtained from *Innovations in Early Education: The International Reggio Exchange,* Wayne State University, The Merrill-Palmer Institute, 71-A E. Ferry Ave., Detroit, MI 48202.

## *A WORD OF ENCOURAGEMENT*

Some of these wistful-sounding "if onlys" involve facing reality—thinking of solutions when possible and doing the best you can about dealing with the rest. Some of them, however, are really just ways to stall, just as some of the "yes buts" are. If we really want to change, these objections must be recognized for what they are and brushed aside.

Fortunately, there is a cheerful counterpoint to bear in mind when we feel dismayed by some of the more real obstacles in our way. For one thing, those of us who decide to take our first steps toward teaching the Reggio way are not stepping onto uncharted ground. We have many encouraging examples of others who are venturing in the same direction.

For another, *we need to realize that we have more freedom to act than we are generally willing to recognize or admit to ourselves.* If we choose to recognize and use this freedom, we will have all the power we need to transform the "yes buts" and "if onlys" into the "what ifs" and "how tos."

The reward for taking these steps will be knowing in our hearts we are doing what is best for children.

# References

Anselmo, S. (1987). *Early childhood development: Prenatal through age eight.* Upper Saddle River, NJ: Merrill/Prentice Hall.

Ayers, W. (1994). *Teachers and learning.* Paper presented at National-Louis University, Evanston, IL.

Beatty, B. (1995). *Preschool education in America: The culture of young children from the colonial era to the present.* New Haven, CT: Yale University Press.

Berk, L. E., & Winsler, A. (1995). *Scaffolding children's learning: Vygotsky and early childhood education.* Washington, DC: National Association for the Education of Young Children.

Bredekamp, S. (1987). *Developmentally appropriate practice in early childhood programs serving children from birth through age 8.* Washington, DC: National Association for the Education of Young Children.

Bredekamp, S. (1993). Reflections on Reggio Emilia. *Young Children, 49(1),* 13–17.

Bredekamp, S., & Rosegrant, T. (Eds.). (1992). *Reaching potentials: Appropriate curriculum and assessment for young children.* Washington, DC: National Association for the Education of Young Children.

City of Reggio Emilia. (1987). *The hundred languages of children: Catalog of the exhibit.* Reggio Emilia, Italy: Assessorato Scuole Infanzia e Asili Nido.

Cohen, C. P., & Bitensky, S. H. (1994). *United Nations Convention on the Rights of the Child: Answers to 30 questions.* New York: Child Rights International Research Institute.

Dewey, J. (1936). The theory of the Chicago experiment. In K. C. Mayhew & A. C. Edwards (Eds.), *The Dewey school.* New York: Appleton-Century.

Dewey, J. (1938). *Experience and education.* New York: Macmillan.

Dewey, J. (1959a). The child and the curriculum. In M. S. Dworkin (Ed.), *Dewey on education.* New York: Teachers College Press.

Dewey, J. (1959b). My pedagogic creed. In M. S. Dworkin (Ed.), *Dewey on education.* New York: Teachers College Press.

Dewey, J. (1959c). The school and society. In M. S. Dworkin (Ed.), *Dewey on education.* New York: Teachers College Press.

Dewey, J. (1966). *Democracy and education.* New York: Free Press.

Dimidjian, V. J. (1989). *Early childhood at risk: Actions and advocacy for young children.* Washington, DC: National Education Association.

Doyle, W., & Ponder, G. (1977–78). The practicality ethic in teacher decision-making. *Interchange, 8*(3), 1–12.

Edwards, C. (1993). Partner, nurturer and guide: The roles of the Reggio teacher in action. In C. Edwards, L. Gandini, & G. Forman (Eds.), *The hundred languages of children: The Reggio Emilia approach to early childhood education.* Norwood, NJ: Ablex.

Edwards, C., & Springate, K. (1993). Inviting children into project work. *Dimensions of Early Childhood, 22*(1), 9–12, +40.

Edwards, C., Gandini, L., & Forman, G. (Eds.). (1993). *The hundred languages of children: The Reggio Emilia approach to early childhood education.* Norwood, NJ: Ablex.

Erikson, E. (1950). *Childhood and society.* New York: Norton.

Fennimore, B. S. (1989). *Child advocacy for early childhood educators.* New York: Teachers College Press.

Filippini, T. (1990). *The Reggio Approach.* Paper presented at the National Association for the Education of Young Children Conference, November, Washington, DC.

Flavell, J. H. (1963). *The developmental psychology of Jean Piaget.* Princeton, NJ: Van Nostrand.

Forman, E. A., Minick, N., & Stone, C. A. (Eds.). (1993). *Contexts for learning: Sociocultural dynamics in children's development.* New York: Oxford University Press.

Forman, G. (1992a). The constructivist perspective to early education. In J. Roopnarine & J. Johnson (Eds.), *Approaches to early childhood education* (2nd ed.). Upper Saddle River, NJ: Merrill/Prentice Hall.

Forman, G. (1992b). Helping children ask good questions. In B. Neugebauer (Ed.), *The wonder of it: Exploring how the world works.* Redmond, WA: Exchange Press.

Forman, G. (1995). The amusement park for birds and the fountains. In G. Piazza (Ed.), *The fountains.* Reggio Emilia: Reggio Children S.rl.

Forman, G., & Gandini, L. (1994). *An amusement park for birds.* [Video]. Amherst, MA: Performanetics.

Forman, G. E., & Kuschner, D. S. (1983). *The child's construction of knowledge: Piaget for teaching children.* Washington, DC: National Association for the Education of Young Children.

Fosnot, C. T. (1989). *Enquiring teachers enquiring learners: A constructivist approach to teaching.* New York: Teachers College Press.

Fullan, M. G., & Miles, M. B. (1992, June). Getting reform right: What works and what doesn't. *Phi Delta Kappan,* pp. 745–752.

Fyfe, B. (1994). Images from the United States: Using ideas from the Reggio Emilia experience with American educators. In L. G. Katz & B. Cesarone (Eds.), *Reflections on the Reggio Emilia Approach.* Urbana, IL: ERIC Clearinghouse on Elementary & Early Childhood Education.

Fyfe, B., & Cadwell, L. (1993). Bringing Reggio Emilia home. *Growing Times, 10*(3).

Gandini, L. (1984, Summer). Not just anywhere: Making child care centers into "particular" places. *Beginnings,* pp. 17–20.

Gandini, L. (1991). Not just anywhere: Making child care centers into "particular" places. *Child Care Information Exchange, 78,* 5–9.

Gandini, L. (1993a). Educational and caring spaces. In D. Edwards, L. Gandini, & G. Forman (Eds.), *The hundred languages of children: The Reggio Emilia Approach to early childhood education.* Norwood, NJ: Ablex.

Gandini, L. (1993b). Fundamentals of the Reggio Emilia Approach to early childhood education. *Young Children, 49*(1), 4–8.

Gandini, L. (1994a). Not just anywhere: Making child care centers into "particular" places. *Child Care Information Exchange, 96,* 50.

Gandini, L. (1994b). What we can learn from Reggio Emilia: An Italian-American collaboration. *Child Care Information Exchange, 96,* 62–66.

Gandini, L., & Edwards, C. (1988). Early childhood integration of the visual arts. *Gifted International, 5*(2), 14–18.

Goffin, S., & Lombardi, J. (1988). *Speaking out: Early childhood advocacy.* Washington, DC: National Association for the Education of Young Children.

Goldhaber, J., & Smith, D. (1993). Infants and toddlers at play: Looking for meaning. *Day Care and Early Education, 20*(3), 9–12.

Harp, L., & Miller, L. (1995, September 6). States turn up heat in debate over paddlings. *Education Week, 15*(1).

Hayes, L. F. (1990). From scribbling to writing: Smoothing the way. *Young Children, 46*(3), 62–68.

Isaacs, S. (1930). *Intellectual growth in young children.* London: Routledge.

Kagan, S. (1991). *United we stand: Collaboration for child care and early education services.* New York: Teachers College Press.

Katz, L. (1993). What can we learn from Reggio Emilia. In C. Edwards, L. Gandini, & G. Forman (Eds.). *The hundred languages of children: The Reggio Emilia Approach to early childhood education.* Norwood, NJ: Ablex.

Katz, L., & Chard, S. (1989). *Engaging children's minds: The project approach.* Norwood, NJ: Ablex.

Katz, L. G., Evangelou, D., & Hartman, J. (1990). *The case for mixed-age grouping in the early years.* Washington, DC: National Association for the Education of Young Children.

Kotlowitz, A. (1991). *There are no children here.* New York: Doubleday.

Lowenfeld, V. (1975). *Creative and mental growth.* New York: Macmillan.

Malaguzzi, L. (1990). Poem. (Written as an introduction to the European exhibition "The Hundred Languages of Children.")

Malaguzzi, L. (1992, May). *Introduction to the educational philosophy of Reggio Emilia.* Address to delegation, Reggio Emilia, Italy.

Malaguzzi, L. (1993a). For an education based on relationships. *Young Children, 49*(1), 9–12.

Malaguzzi, L. (1993b). History, ideas, and basic philosophy. In C. Edwards, L. Gandini, & G. Forman (Eds.), *The hundred languages of children: The Reggio Emilia Approach to early childhood education.* Norwood, NJ: Ablex.

Malaguzzi, L. (1993c). A bill of three rights. *Innovations in Early Education: The International Reggio Exchange, 2*(1), 9.

Malaguzzi, L. (1994). Your image of the child: Where teaching begins. *Child Care Information Exchange, 61.*

Mayhew, K. C., & Edwards, A. (1936). *The Dewey school.* New York: Appleton-Century.

McLaughlin, M. (1995, May). Will Reggio Emilia change your child's preschool? *Working Mother,* pp. 62–68.

Miller, L. (1995, Summer). Tracking the progress of *Brown. Teachers College Record, 96*(4), 609–613.

Missouri Department of Elementary and Secondary Education. (1992). *Project Construct: A framework for curriculum and assessment.* Jefferson City: Author.

Municipality of Reggio Emilia. (1994). *Historical notes and general information.* Reggio Emilia, Italy: Department of Education, Municipal Infant-Toddler Centers and Preschools, the Municipality.

New, R. (1990). Excellent early education: A city in Italy has it! *Young Children, 45*(6), 4–6.

New, R. (1991, Winter). Preschool curriculum ideas from Reggio Emilia. *Montessori Life,* pp. 26–28.

New, R. (1993). Cultural variations on developmentally appropriate practice. In C. Edwards, L. Gandini, & G. Forman (Eds.), *The hundred languages of children: The Reggio Emilia Approach to early childhood education.* Norwood, NJ: Ablex.

New, R. S. (1994). Culture, child development, and developmentally appropriate practices: Teachers as collaborative researchers. In B. L. Mallory & R. S. New (Eds.), *Diversity & developmentally appropriate practices: Challenges for early childhood education.* New York: Teachers College Press.

New, R. S., & Mallory, B. (in press). The paradox of diversity in early care and education. In E. Erwin (Ed.), *Critical issues in the lives of young children and their families.* Baltimore, MD: Brookes.

*Newsweek.* (1991, December 2). The best schools in the world. Pp. 60–64.

Paley, V. (1995). Lessons of room 284. *Chicago Tribune Magazine*, pp. 112–119, +28–29.

Piaget, J. (1965). *The child's conception of number*. New York: Norton.

Piaget, J. (1973). *To understand is to invent: The future of education*. New York: Grossman.

Piaget, J., & Inhelder, B. (1969). *The psychology of the child*. New York: Basic Books.

Piazza, G. (Ed.). (1995). *The fountains*. Reggio Emilia, Italy: Reggio Children S.rl.

Polakow, V. (1993). *Lives on the edge: Single mothers and their children in the other America*. Chicago: University of Chicago Press.

Rankin, B. M. (1993). Curriculum development in Reggio Emilia: A long-term curriculum project about dinosaurs. In C. Edwards, L. Gandini, & G. Forman (Eds.), *The hundred languages of children: The Reggio Emilia Approach to early childhood education*. Norwood, NJ: Ablex.

Rankin, B. M. (1995). *Collaboration as the basis of early childhood curriculum development: A case study from Reggio Emilia, Italy*. Unpublished doctoral dissertation, Boston University, Boston.

Rawcliffe, F. W. (1924). *Practical problem projects*. Chicago: Compton.

Rinaldi, C. (1992, May). *Social constructivism in Reggio Emilia, Italy*. Paper presented at the Summer Institute, "Images of the Child: An International Exchange with Leading Educators from Reggio Emilia, Italy," Newton, MA.

Rinaldi, C. (1993a). The emergent curriculum and social constructivism. In C. Edwards, L. Gandini, & G. Forman (Eds.), *The hundred languages of children: The Reggio Emilia Approach to early childhood education*. Norwood, NJ: Ablex.

Rinaldi, C. (1993b, May). *Short and long term projects*. Paper presented at the Reggio Emilia Symposium: Practices of the Schools for Young Children in Reggio Emilia and Their Implications for Schools in the United States, Washington, DC.

Rinaldi, C. (1994a, June). *The philosophy of Reggio Emilia*. Paper presented at the Study Seminar on the Experience of the Municipal Infant-Toddler Centers and Pre-primary Schools of Reggio Emilia, Reggio Emilia, Italy.

Rinaldi, C. (1994b, June). *The significance of observation and documentation in the Reggio Emilia experience*. Paper presented at the Study Seminar on the Experience of the Municipal Infant-Toddler Centers and Pre-primary Schools of Reggio Emilia, Reggio Emilia, Italy.

Rodd, J. (1994). *Leadership in early childhood: The pathway to professionalism*. New York: Teachers College press.

Rogoff, B. (1990). *Apprenticeship in thinking: Cognitive development in social context*. New York: Oxford University Press.

Rogoff, B., & Wertsch, J. V. (Eds.). (1984). *Children's learning in the "zone of proximal development."* San Francisco: Jossey-Bass.

Sheldon-Harsh, L., with Gandini, L. (1995a). The model early learning center: An interview with teachers inspired by the Reggio Approach. *Innovations in Early Education: The International Reggio Exchange, 2*(4), 3.

Sheldon-Harsh, L., with Gandini, L. (1995b). The model early learning center: An interview with teachers inspired by the Reggio Approach. *Innovations in Early Education: The International Reggio Exchange, 3*(1), 3.

Tarini, E. (1993). Reflections. *Innovations in Early Childhood Education: The International Reggio Exchange, 1*(2), 4–5.

Van Hoorn, J., Nourot, P. M., Scales, B., & Alward, A. (1993). *Play at the center of the curriculum.* Upper Saddle River, NJ: Prentice Hall.

Vygotsky, L. S. (1978). *Mind in society: The development of higher psychological processes.* Cambridge, MA: Harvard University Press.

Vygotsky, L. S. (1987). *Thinking and speech.* In R. W. Rieber & A. S. Carton (Eds.), *The collected works of L. S. Vygotsky* (N. Minick, trans.). New York: Plenum.

Weber, E. (1970). *Early childhood education: Perspectives on change.* Worthington, OH: Jones.

Wertsch, J. (1985). *Vygotsky and the social formation of mind.* Cambridge, MA: Harvard University Press.

Wertsch, J., & Tulviste, P. (1992). L. S. Vygotsky and contemporary developmental psychology. *Developmental Psychology, 28*(4), 548–557.

Zigler, E., & Styfco, S. J. (Eds.). (1993). *Head Start and beyond: A national plan for extended childhood intervention.* New Haven, CT: Yale University Press.

# Index

## DATE DUE

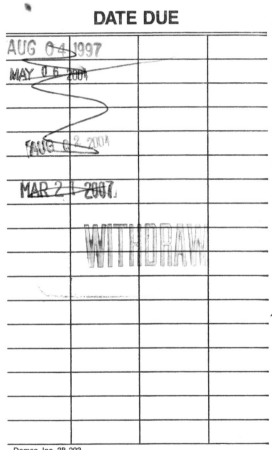

| | | |
|---|---|---|
| AUG 04 1997 | | |
| MAY 0 6 2004 | | |
| | | |
| | | |
| AUG 0 2 2004 | | |
| | | |
| MAR 2 1 2007 | | |
| WITHDRAW | | |
| | | |
| | | |
| | | |
| | | |
| | | |

Demco, Inc. 38-293